Commando
Medics
in the
Falkland War

MALCOLM HAZELL

Design, typesetting and publishing by UK Book Publishing

www.ukbookpublishing.com

ISBN: 978-1-915338-57-0

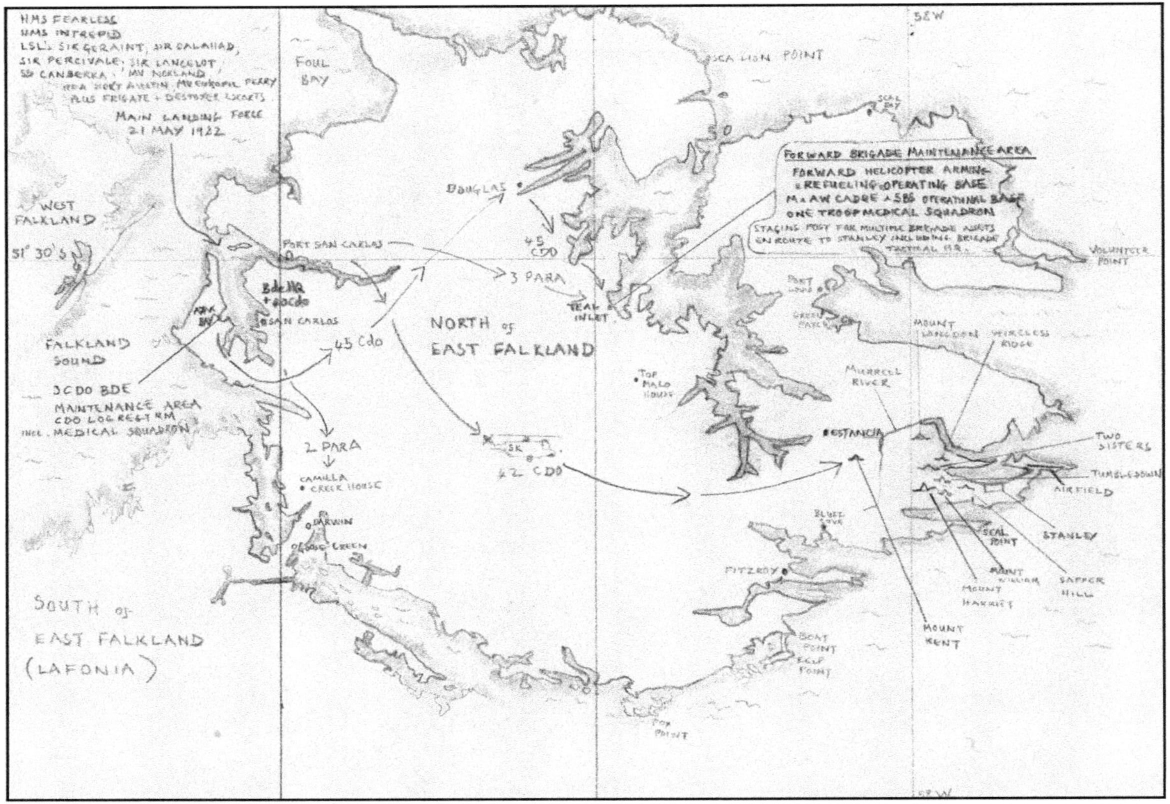
HMS FEARLESS
HMS INTREPID
LSL's SIR GERAINT, SIR GALAHAD,
SIR PERCIVALE, SIR LANCELOT
SS CANBERRA, MV NORLAND
MAIN LANDING FORCE
21 MAY 1982
FOUL BAY
SEA LION POINT
SEAL BAY
58W
WEST FALKLAND
51° 30'S
FALKLAND SOUND
3 CDO BDE
MAINTENANCE AREA
CDO LOG REGT RM
MEDICAL SQUADRON
PORT SAN CARLOS
Bde HQ
SAN CARLOS
45 Cdo
2 PARA
CAMILLA CREEK HOUSE
DARWIN
GOOSE GREEN
DOUGLAS
45 CDO
3 PARA
TEAL INLET
NORTH of
EAST FALKLAND
42 CDO
SK
TOP MALO HOUSE
FORWARD BRIGADE MAINTENANCE AREA
FORWARD HELICOPTER ARMING
& REFUELING OPERATING BASE
ONE TROOP MEDICAL SQUADRON
VOLUNTEER POINT
PORT LOUIS
GREEN PATCH
MOUNT LONGDON
WIRELESS RIDGE
MURRELL RIVER
ESTANCIA
TWO SISTERS
TUMBLEDOWN
AIRFIELD
STANLEY
SEAL POINT
MOUNT WILLIAM
SAPPER HILL
MOUNT HARRIET
MOUNT KENT
BLUFF COVE
FITZROY
BOAT POINT
FOX POINT
SOUTH of
EAST FALKLAND
(LAFONIA)

Foreword

This is the story of the Falkland War, its land battles and their amphibious naval support, as seen through the Commando Forces forward medical facility, One Troop Medical Squadron, radio call sign Starlight One Zero. It gives unique insight into our six week long voyage South, from sailing with our parent Unit, the Commando Logistic Regiment Royal Marines, to landing at Ajax Bay from the ill-fated landing ship Sir Galahad, to moving forward to Teal Inlet, and finally into Stanley. The well documented land battles are re-told to emphasise the reality of the war and to highlight the importance of the casualty evacuation chain, and the vital role that many individuals, and particularly helicopters and their aircrews, played in this respect.

Ajax Bay was the Logistic Maintenance Area for the entire landing force, and following One Troop Medical Squadron's initial time at the medical facility, which is recorded herein, their subsequent move to Teal Inlet gives a graphic and important account of the role that Teal Inlet played in the successful Operations conducted by 3 Commando Brigade Royal Marines, including the Parachute Battalions that were attached to the Brigade, and Special Forces. Much of this aspect of the Falkland War, including the forward medical support provided by One troop Medical Squadron at Teal Inlet, has never been told. Indeed, as a result of writing this account, it became apparent that anomalies exist regarding the fatalities we received and buried at Teal Inlet; anomalies which are problematic for all concerned.

This account is written as a tribute to all the Commando and Parachute medical personnel, who took part in Operation Sutton, the land phase of Operation Corporate, and to the helicopter aircrews who also risked their lives ensuring a viable casualty evacuation chain which was rarely found wanting. Above all it is also written to remember those who paid the ultimate sacrifice.

Acknowledgments:

Much of the material depicting battles, skirmishes, and such like is produced in abundance on the internet, but it is often not validated. Moreover, some of it reinforces and some of it contradicts my own understanding and recollections of what happened. As a result, throughout this account I have often used the book Nine Battles of Stanley, written by 3 Commando Brigade's Operation Corporate Intelligence Officer, Nick Van Der Bijl, as the authoritative account to determine the accuracy of such events. It is important that in retelling accounts after so long that we strive to be as historically accurate as possible. Nick's book has certainly helped me produce my account, and the new insights I have been able to write alongside a much distilled precis of his very detailed account of the various land battles, and I would be remiss if I did not thank Nick Van Der Bijl for his exceptionally detailed study of the various battles which I have been able to refer to.

Secondly, amateur historian Falkland War specialist and avid medal collector Andre Chissel motivated and inspired me to produce this account, particularly of Teal Inlet, having himself produced a very detailed collection of individual recollections of events at Ajax Bay, with abundant photographic depictions. Andre has taken the trouble to proof-read what has been written, and provided support to me whenever I sought it and I am indebted to him.

Thirdly, Neil Rowlands, who was just 16 and was living in the Bunk House at Teal Inlet when One Troop Medical Squadron deployed there. He also took several photographs of the build-up of 3 Commando Brigade at Teal, and as such he has unique pictures of some of what occurred at Teal Inlet. I would be remiss if I did not thank him for the photograph of my Troop which was taken shortly before we moved to Stanley; and for any help he extended to British military forces in 1982 including One Troop Medical Squadron; and for his help in checking this written account.

Finally, I would like to thank Jon Clare. A Royal Marine Corporal in our Troop in 1982, Jon went on to attain the Rank of Major. He has contributed some of his own recollections and pictures herein that help to emphasise the important role General Duty Royal Marine Commandos played in ensuring the success of the Medical Squadron in our quest to save lives in the Falkland War. These men were our 'honorary medics' for whom no task proved too daunting. They were never found wanting.

Commando Medics in the Falkland War

The Service Background of the Author, a former Royal Navy Commando Medical Service Officer, Commanding One Troop, Medical Squadron.

When Argentina invaded the Falkland Islands on 2 April 1982, I was a young Sub Lieutenant with a Commando specialist background, in the Royal Navy Medical Service. I had gained my commission at BRNC Dartmouth at the end of 1980, having spent over 10 years in the RN Medical Branch, and risen to Acting Chief Petty Officer Medical Assistant (CPOMA) before joining Dartmouth in August that year.

I had joined the Navy as a boy of 15, at HMS Ganges in October 1970, and started clinical training at Ganges in the spring of 1971. This training included a secondment to the Clyde Submarine Base at Faslane, for familiarity with the Submarine Service medical specialism, and to the Junior Marines at RM Deal and onward to Loch Ewe, NW Scotland, for training alongside those recruits, similarly for familiarity with the Commando Service medical specialism. I also was sent to the Mortar Troop of 42 Commando who were doing live firing at Sennybridge, in the Brecon Beacons,

Wales, and for me the Commando Service was an exhilarating experience that would later lead me to volunteer and pass the All Arms Commando Course in 1974.

I left Ganges in the summer of 1971 but being too young by some margin to start formal clinical training at RN Hospital Haslar in Gosport, I was sent to sea for 7 months aboard the Commando Helicopter Carrier HMS Bulwark, which I joined in Malta in October, aged 16 years 2 months. I was accommodated in the Naval Air Squadron mess deck 2 alpha, with well over 100 other sailors, but worked in the Sick Bay, and also assisted the Dental Officer once a week. There was a serious fire in the engine boiler room in mid-December, which was situated below the Sick Bay, and it resulted in the ship returning to the UK for repairs over Christmas, but we redeployed immediately in the New Year as this was meant to be the UK withdrawal from Malta and Bulwark was being used as a floating removal wagon. Ultimately the then PM of Malta accepted a settlement of £6m for the UK's continued use of bases, and Bulwark returned home in time for Easter 1972.

I started my four month theory based clinical training at the Training Division of RNH Haslar in the Summer of 1972, and subsequently joined RN Hospital Stonehouse, Plymouth, to commence my 9 months practical training in October 1972, whilst I was still a Junior Medical Assistant. This training involved working on Medical and Surgical wards, and in Accident and Emergency, and in the Operating Theatres. Its conclusion was exam based, and I was fortunate to qualify for Leading Medical Assistant at that stage in June 1973, but it was to be another 2 years before I gained promotion to Acting Leading Medical Assistant.

I left RN Hospital Plymouth in in July 1973, just before my 18th birthday, and joined the Sick Bay at Portland Naval Base and Air Station, HMS Osprey, for the final stage of my formal supervised clinical training. This phase involved a great deal of one-to-one mentoring alongside the medical team, and particularly with the doctors, but we were very much working and watch keeping at this very busy establishment, and on three occasions I had to winch down to passing foreign vessels to assess and winch up casualties.

I left Portland on 14 August 1974, having volunteered for the All Arms Commando Course, and started the 'Beat-Up' for the course at Stonehouse Barracks, Plymouth the following day. The Beat Up was followed by the actual course at the Commando Training Centre Lympstone. For me, it was a good challenge and largely enjoyable, and organised in a very professional manner. Importantly, my secondments from HMS Ganges had provided me with a good insight into what was required, and I was fit.

I went on to join 40 Commando RM at Seaton Barracks in Plymouth on 18 November 1974. I served over two years with the Unit, including two full tours in West Belfast in 1975 and South Armagh in 1976, and two embarked force voyages on my former ship, the Commando Carrier HMS Bulwark. This was a full-on demanding period by any measure.

In December 1976 I joined RM Poole as a member of the Commando detachment known as Naval Party 8901. We underwent 3 months training to relieve the detachment at Moody Brook, Stanley, East Falkland, on 25 March 1977, for our tour which was to last until 14 April the following year. We flew to Montevideo in Uruguay, sharing the flight with a nuclear submarine crew, who were also set to relieve their alternate crew and remain on station in the South Atlantic. It was somewhat surreal that both the 8901 detachment, and the submarine crew, boarded fishing vessels, and as the submarine crew headed out to transfer to their Nuclear Boat, we headed out to board the Ice Patrol Ship HMS Endurance, and faced a week long passage to Stanley, living and sleeping on the deck of the ship's helicopter hanger.

During my 13 months on the Islands, I provided the detachment's primary care, and otherwise was part of the OC's patrol group, which managed to visit just about every inhabited outpost of these remote Islands, sometimes on foot, sometimes on an aging BSA

B40 motorcycle, and sometimes in a Land Rover. We crossed to west Falkland and to other smaller islands, using the small ship MV (Motor Vessel) Forrest which could take two Land Rovers and 3 motorcycles on its deck. When at Moody Brook camp I was able to also work in the local King Edward Memorial Hospital, including assisting in the operating theatre, where the team uniquely routinely practiced surgery using spinal anaesthesia, because of the difficulty in obtaining medical gases. I was also fortunate to escort the diplomatic bag to the British Embassy in Buenos Aries, Argentina, on one occasion. During our deployment the only landing facility for aircraft was a temporary metal strip, rolled out on the beach to the East of Stanley, and we relied on an Argentine Airforce Fokker 28 aircraft to make the crossing, and provide mail once a fortnight, weather permitting – which sometimes it didn't. The threat that Argentina posed was real and recognised, and we knew if the nuclear submarine was withdrawn, we were the main deterrent to an invasion. We had no leave until we returned to the UK nearly 13 months later, using the same means as we came.

Argentine Airforce Fokker 28 on metal strip beach runway, just East of Stanley 1977/78.

The base at Moody Brook, for the Commando detachment designated Naval Party 8901, situated at the end of the bay, just West of Stanley.

The Motor Vessel Forrest loading a Land Rover as the Commando detachment OC's Patrol Group prepare to cross from Port San Carlos East Falkland, to West Falkland in 1977/78.

*Aging B40 BSA motor bikes were used by the Commando detachment
to patrol the Islands and proved remarkably tough and reliable, if
somewhat heavy to handle given the absence of roads beyond Stanley.
Corporal Pete Worgan (mechanic), Marine Jimmy Moffatt, and the
author, then Leading Medic, Malcolm Hazell, 1977/78, backpack 'urgent
medical supplies' for remote settlements – mostly whisky I recall!*

*Another view towards Moody Brook (in the far distance)
during the Falkland winter of 1977.*

Upon returning to the UK I was sent to the Commando Training Centre (CTC) and worked in the Sick Bay for 2 years. During this time my clinical skills were tested daily. I also passed the Medical Service Officer entry exam which I sat at RNH Haslar, and the Admiralty Interview Board 2 day selection process at HMS Sultan. I was promoted to Petty Officer just before my 24th birthday, and sent to the RN Hospital Stonehouse, in February 1980 to get used to wearing an RN uniform again, and to hone my administrative skills, prior to joining the Royal Naval College Britannia (BRNC) in September 1980 in the acting rate of CPOMA. I then attended RNC Greenwich in January as an Acting Sub Lieutenant, and on conclusion of that hurdle, spent a brief period back at RNH Plymouth, prior to joining the Commando Logistic Regiment Royal Marines as OC of One Troop Medical Squadron.

A key point is that with the exception of gaining a Commission, all the RN Commando Medical Assistants in One and Three Troops Medical Squadron, as well as those providing direct medical support to the fighting Units, had a very similar background to that outlined above. They were embedded within the Commando Forces Royal Marines, and the Royal Marine Commandos serving with the Squadron worked alongside these RN Commando MA's in a support role, to help us set up and strike the respective 50 bed surgical facilities (that we still referred to as 'dressing stations') and to care for their wounded and sick comrades when operational.

This is our story, and of the Surgical teams that served with us, during the brief but brutal Falkland war in 1982. As well as adding new detail to the events at Ajax Bay, it gives unique insight into the significant role that **Teal Inlet** played in the 'teeth arms' Operational, Logistic and Medical aspects of winning the Falkland War, much of which has never been documented.

The Argentine Claim to the Falkland Islands

The origin to the Argentine claim to the Falkland Islands can be traced back to 1494 when Spain claimed all the world to the West of Cape Verde and went on to colonise much of South America, with terrible consequences for the indigenous South American people. By the late 1600's the Spanish claim was frankly fatuous as Britain had largely secured the whole of North America and much of the Caribbean, as the Royal Navy became the predominant world force.

The Falkland Islands may have been sighted by Spanish seafarers in the 1500's but the English sea captain John Davies makes the first recorded sighting in 1592, and 98 years later Captain John Strong RN made the first recorded landing in 1690.The Islands remained totally uninhabited until the French established a small settlement at Port Louis on East Falkland, to the North of present day Stanley, in 1764, which they abandoned following pressure from Spain.

Britain then established a settlement of about 100 people, called Port Egmont, on Saunders Island, off West Falkland, just 2 years later in 1766, which Spain forcibly removed in 1770, using 1,400 troops landed by 5 frigates. Faced with the threat of war, Spain backed down and the British settlement was re-established, but vacated in 1774 leaving a plaque to assert Britain's claim, which was removed by the Spanish authorities in Buenos Aires.

It is important to emphasise at this point that the nation we now call Argentina did not exist, and the Spanish authorities in Buenos Aires presided over an area known as the Viceroyalty of the River Plate (Rio de la Plata) which spanned the banks of the Plate to include what is now Montevideo and the upper part of Argentina. Native Americans were all but extinct in this Viceroy, which was now mostly inhabited by the Spanish, along with some Italian and other Europeans.

In 1810 these Spanish and other European inhabitants rebelled against their founders and in 1816 declared independence, as the United Provinces of the River Plate (Rio de la Plata), but they assumed this also applied to the inheritance of the Falkland Islands, which is an assumption that has no legal basis. They raised the United Provinces flag at Port Louis in 1820 (which had been re-named Puerto Soldad) and a small colony was established later that decade until the Americans took exception to the seizure of three of its vessels over a fishing rights dispute, and the USS Lexington sent the post-colonial Rio de la Plata Spanish packing.

This is the basis of the Argentine claim. Argentina, as it extends today, was not fully established until the 1850's. Their claim to the Falkland Islands is essentially that they maintain they inherited the Islands when they secured independence from their Spanish ancestors. This is what they teach children in their schools and colleges and thus the belief prevails to this day. The Falkland Islands were never inhabited by these European people except for the brief period before they were expelled by the USS Lexington, but this is the basis of which they asserted it was quite in order to invade an archipelago that lies some 300 miles off mainland Argentina, and to place a curfew on the 2,000 men women and children who have made this remote archipelago their home, for several generations. Even more tenuously, this was also the basis to forcibly capture South Georgia 600 miles further South East.

It was right that we went to re-capture the Falkland Islands, and to liberate its inhabitants. We should never apologise for doing so and should strive to ensure our children know the truth of the Argentine occupation; that a former Spanish colony tried to reverse what had already long been achieved before Admiral Nelson defeated the Spanish at Trafalgar in 1805. That defeat was the last nail in the coffin that marked the end of Spain's colonial history.

How ironic that Nelson, and the wider actions of the Royal Navy, made a major contribution to the formation of an independent, free Argentine people, the sons and daughters of Spanish and other European ancestors, that Britain quickly recognised, but who have subsequently sought to maintain a fatuous claim over its fellow former Anglo European neighbours 300 miles away, who have lived a peaceful existence for over 180 years on the remote Falkland Islands. Moreover, that Argentina has consistently sought to depict the Falkland Islanders as the colonialists, is surely the height of hypocrisy and the definition of the 'pot calling the kettle black'.

Argentine Actions in South Georgia and the Antarctica

Argentina had occupied the remote island of South Thule in 1976. That Island is part of the overall Falkland Islands, South Georgia, and South Sandwich group of islands that fall within the UK sphere of the Falkland Island dependencies, and it remained occupied beyond the Argentine invasion of the Falkland Islands in 1982. The Argentine authorities, having noted the somewhat muted response from the UK to that occupation, subsequently allowed their aspirations to capture the entire dependencies to grow.

Doctor Paul Griffiths was employed by the British Antarctic Survey as a medical officer, and he picks up the story below.

'I was initially based at Grytviken, South Georgia from October 1980 to March 1981 to cover diving operations whilst the Royal Engineers were installing new dolphins for the quayside. Mostly the divers seem to spend their time recovering an endless number of tools that fell in the water. The Engineers' quayside site meetings would slowly and imperceptibly enlarge as passing king penguins sidled into the margins: if it's vertical and moves, it's another penguin and must be stood next to.'

'I over-wintered at Rothera Station on Adelaide Island, western Antarctic Peninsula where we had two fatalities in a crevasse

accident. The rescue of the two survivors of the four man skidoo party benefitted greatly from the presence of an Ex Royal Marine with Arctic training as one of our complement.'

'Shortly before I left Rothera we had a totally unexpected visit from two large Argentinian naval ships, the Irizar and Q5. They suddenly appeared in the bay and they radioed to say they were sending a party ashore for a visit. They were a group of ten high ranking officers, quite senior with lots of scrambled egg on their hats and metal bling on their chests, and some scientists. They were given a tour of the base, posing for photographs wherever they went, then sat in our bar for a very pleasant couple of hours drinking and chatting, departing at midnight with enthusiastic handshakes and hearty farewells. Shortly before the ships left next morning, a helicopter came over from the ship with a cargo net containing a crate of fine Argentinian red wine. We were blissfully ignorant of what was going on but later realised that this was probably a photo-reconnaissance. Under the terms of the Antarctic Treaty, participating nations are permitted to visit each other's bases but I believe they are normally obliged to give 24 hours notice. I later suggested that my decision to give them Welsh whisky (yes, it does exist) may have been what precipitated the Falklands War.'

'I left Rothera in April 1982 on the Royal Research Ship Bransfield. As we disembarked at Punta Arenas a small group of military personnel dressed in combat gear were getting on the ship. I was told they were paras, but with no explanation of what they were doing.' *

This insight from Dr Paul Griffiths demonstrates the depths of the duplicity that Argentina stooped in its meticulous pre-invasion planning.

Another example is that the then Governor of the Falkland Islands, Rex Hunt, was also to express his regret that he had been similarly duped, as he gave a copy of the plans of his residence to a visiting Argentinian, who had expressed an interest in the building's architecture, shortly before the invasion. For the

Falkland Islanders, and those of us who know the very modest and unremarkable Governor's residence, this tale is incredulous but sadly true.

Argentina enacted its preparations to capture the Falkland Islands with the same convivial charm used by gangsters stealing life savings from the elderly.

* The Paras that Dr Paul Griffiths refers to above may actually have been SAS and the date was on or shortly after 18 May 1982. Launched from the aircraft carrier HMS Invincible, a team of eight SAS men had been inserted by a Sea King helicopter of 846 Naval Air Squadron, into Argentina, to establish an observation post at the Rio Grande airfield. Poor visibility forced the helicopter to land early, and the SAS team attempted to insert themselves covertly on foot. They believed they were seen by an Argentine patrol and decided to abort the mission, codenamed Plum Duff, and headed for Punta Arenas Chile instead, where the Sea King crew of 3 had also flown to and destroyed their helicopter. The aim of Operation Plum Duff had been to gather intelligence that would have enabled a larger SAS team to conduct an Air Landed raid on the target airfield, codenamed Operation Mikado, but this was also cancelled.

Immediately before the main Argentine Invasion of East and West Falkland

I was appointed as the Officer Commanding One Troop, Medical Squadron, Commando Logistic Regiment (CLR), Royal Marines, in the late spring of 1981. Based at Coypool in Plympton, Plymouth. It was quite a run-down World War Two site that was comprised of massive steel hangars. These buildings were very suitable for the Regiment's Workshop, Transport, and Ordnance Squadrons, and similarly for Medical Squadron's tentage and general (G1098) stores, but only just adequate for its Medical (11248) Stores. Fortunately, the hangars were watertight, but in winter they were quite cold, and in summer they could be quite hot, which was not ideal for the storage and regular maintenance of medicines. There was no living accommodation at Coypool whatsoever, and all 'inliers' had to use RM Barracks Stonehouse, which was several miles away.

My only other experience with Medical Squadron had been a brief secondment with it on completion of the All Arms Commando Course in 1974, for a 10 day Brigade deployment on Salisbury Plain, which included the full participation of the Commando Naval Air Squadrons from the Naval Air Station at Yeovilton, together with the 3 Brigade Air Squadron (3 BAS), and Mobile Air Operations Teams (MAOTs), and was a significant deployment. In 1974 Medical Squadron had only recently been formed. It relied on vintage tentage, and all its military and medical equipment was housed in old stone-built sheds by the former Royal William Yard in Stonehouse, Plymouth. Coypool was an improvement on this. The Salisbury Plain exercise was a static deployment for Medical Squadron, of what was then effectively configured as a light field hospital. I was a lowly Medical Assistant (Able Rating) at that time, and it was the first time I served with Petty Officer Medical Assistant Graham Edwards, with whom I went on to serve in Northern Ireland; The Falkland war; The First Gulf War; and Northern Iraq for Operation Haven, as well as several winters in Norway.

So aside from a couple of weeks in 1974, and despite 11 years' experience in the RN Medical Branch, 1981 was my first draft (appointment) to the Squadron. By this time the Squadron had evolved into two manoeuvre dressing stations, each with a 27 man Surgical Support Team, both equipped and trained to enable either two operating tables to function concurrently for as long as they could keep going, or a single table on an 8 or 12 hour rotational basis. The Surgical Teams were based at the two RN Hospitals. SST1 was Haslar based, and SST2 Plymouth based. The teams would normally undertake one or two exercises in the UK each year, and if possible, the final exercise at the end of each winter deployment in Norway, to which the Brigade was committed as part of the then deterrent to the former USSR. Selected SST Arctic novices could also undertake arctic training alongside regular Squadron personnel. Some SST members were Commando trained, but the majority were not. They relied on the training provided by the Squadron, and its parent Commando Logistic Regiment Royal Marines.

In addition, the Royal Marine Band at the Commando Training Centre (CTCRM) were trained to act as stretcher bearers, and to provide casualty chemical decontamination. They too would train with the Squadron in this role, about as frequently as the SST's, and they represented a significant increase to the Squadron's establishment numbers. Like the SST's they were not Commando trained.

In essence, One Troop and Three Troop provided the regular cadre of Commando personnel to staff two Field Dressing Stations. Of these personnel only a quarter were RN Commando Medical Branch specialists, and the remainder were Royal Marine Commandos with limited in house first aid training. This underlines the importance of the Surgical Support Teams to provide not just surgery, but essential additional medical experience and expertise. With Surgical Support Teams integrated with the Field Dressing Stations they were effectively mobile Light Field Hospitals, similar in their concept to that of the Parachute Clearing Troop (PCT) and its 9 man Field Surgical Teams (FST's), but larger. Both had evolved to meet different concepts of Operation, but had developed similar effective clinical structures, albeit the Medical Squadron was designed and scaled to support the entire 3 Commando Brigade, whilst the Parachute Clearing Troop and its Field Surgical Teams were designed to support Parachute Battalions and their equipment and re-supply scales were significantly less than the Medical Squadron's.

Additionally, the Squadron had wheeled ambulances, and in the summer of 1981 it took delivery of several of the then new one tonne V8 ambulances. In Norway the Squadron relied much more on BV202's tracked vehicles for casualty collection, but these were stockpiled in Norway. In all theatres of Operation the Squadron was used to working routinely with helicopters for casualty evacuation (casevac). All the tentage and medical equipment and stores were normally transported in 4 ton military trucks. Each troop was allocated six such trucks, and a further 8 Land Rover and trailers for personnel lift. Only the ambulances were to go to the Falklands because of the absence of roads beyond Stanley and the very harsh North East Falkland terrain.

The Squadron HQ role in the field was essentially that of a standard command post function, as you might expect of any military squadron, but it differed from RAMC Field Ambulances because the Standard Operating Procedures for Medical Squadron, reflected it was an amphibious asset. Before landings take place, beaches have to first be identified and reconnoitred (usually by the Special Boat Squadron, SBS), and they are then designated to the respective Units for landings, and the landings co-ordinated by the Amphibious Warfare Staff on the Assault Ships, Landing Platform Docks (LPDs), which at that time were HMS Fearless, and HMS Intrepid. It would be fanciful to think that a medical facility could be designated its own beach, requiring as it would all the amphibious assets to support such landings, such as the Beach Recovery Vehicle (a converted tank), and metal landing tracks, and requiring additional defensive cover. Thus, the medical facilities were integral with logistic assets, such as the Brigade Maintenance Area. With regard to communication, they operated on the Landing Force Administrative net, and all assets on that net would be aware of air, land, and sea movements, events and intensions, within their area of responsibility. Similarly, any movement of forward Units, that required forward logistic and medical support, would be planned and co-ordinated with the Commanding Officer of the Commando Logistic Regiment as well as with the Brigade.

Personnel staff (designated G1 in the Armed Forces) could be directly attached to the Squadron Command Post and forward asset Command Posts, to speed casualty and fatality reporting. The signallers on the Squadron strength were, in Coypool, normally administered within a central HQ Signal Troop, to ensure their skills were current and their equipment centrally maintained. They deployed with the Squadron for all exercises and operations, and helped ensure that the Squadron could confidently rely on its ability to communicate with all other assets on the Landing Force Administration Net (known as LF Admin), and beyond, as required.

In the summer of 1981 One Troop Medical Squadron, together with elements of HQ and the other Squadrons, headed to Browndown Beach near Gosport on the Solent, where, under the leadership of the Commando Logistic Regiment 2ic, Major Terry Knot RM, we conducted repeated amphibious landings as a Land Rover trailer borne Field Dressing Station, to demonstrate the effectiveness of such operations, watched by the Secretary of Defence and his entourage, in an effort to prevent the Government from scrapping the two vital amphibious LPD's (Landing Platform Docking). We had limited success insofar as the Government went on to announce that HMS Intrepid was to be mothballed at the end of the year. Moreover, it was also announced that the Ice Patrol Ship HMS Endurance was to be withdrawn from service in late spring 1982.

By December 1981 One Troop had participated in several exercises during my tenure as OC and I was fully satisfied that we were all capable of delivering on our responsibilities if we were called upon to do so, which at that time seemed a very remote possibility.

My Troop deployed to Norway in January 1982, with the remainder of Medical Squadron, but I had already been sent to Elverum in Norway to attend the Norwegian Winter Warfare Course, where I found myself alongside US Marines, Royal Marine Commandos from all Units, and UK Army personnel, notably members of

G Squadron SAS. I had no experience on skis, but expected I should be quite adept, due to my fitness and reasonable ability as a cross country runner, but that proved an ill-founded expectation, and only my fitness ensured I could survive the 30km biathlon. Moreover, the Norwegian rifles we were issued with, made my UK SLR seem like a sniper's rifle, as I found it difficult to hit a proverbial barn door with the Norwegian weapon. To compound this the temperature dropped to minus 40c that winter, and to the credit of the Norwegian Instructors and all the participants, we just 'soldiered on'.

When the course finished in early March 1982, I flew back to the UK to join the Medical Squadron Rear Party until the main Norway deployment finished and everyone had returned. This time was profitable and fortuitous, as it had enabled me to further familiarise myself with my Troop's medical scale of equipment, and ensure it was properly stocked and in-date. I noted the scale in my Troop notebook, which I have kept to this day.

Medical Squadron main body returned towards the end of March 1982, and by 1 April the BBC News was announcing the impending invasion of the Falkland Islands by an Argentine Invasion Force. Suddenly the potential for the Medical Squadron to be deployed not just operationally, but in its amphibious mode that we had trained so remorselessly for, became very real.

At this point it is worth mentioning that HMS Endurance, which was due to be scrapped later that spring, was the UK's only warship South of the equator! She was an unarmed vessel that was already engaged in defending the British territory of South Georgia, with a small detachment of Royal Marines.

The Argentine Invasion of East and West Falkland 2 April 1982

Argentina did indeed invade on 2 April 1982 and the remote island of South Georgia was captured the following day. We were immediately issued with a warning order to move. None of our 4 ton trucks or general service Land Rovers were to deploy. Only the one tonne Ambulances were to go and would tow our generators, water bowsers, cook-sets, and such like. All other equipment, tentage, and medical stores, was packed into Logistic Chatham Containers (Chacons). These containers normally were used for our Arctic Equipment, such as skis, and therefore needed emptying before they could be re-packed and dispatched on 4 ton trucks to Marchwood Military Port on 3 and 4 April. One troop, together with around 175 other members of the Commando Logistic Regiment (HQ, Ordnance, Workshops, and Transport Squadrons), departed Plymouth late in the evening of 4 April, and joined the Landing Ship Logistic (LSL) Sir Lancelot, which sailed on the early tide the next morning, with no ceremony, and nobody waving us off, we quietly made our way into the Solent, and headed out sea.

I had tried to phone home from a coin operated call box in Marchwood Military Port before we sailed that morning, but my wife Bev was engaged, no doubt talking to friends and family and saying that she had not heard from me. From here on, letters would be our only form of contact with home, and, right up to our landings, we were sending ordinary letters and having to pay for stamps, which soon ran out, and so I wrote home on 8 April 1982 and advised my wife I couldn't get a stamp so could she send me some. Thankfully my unstamped letter arrived in the UK on 21 April 1982 and my wife paid the delivery fee, and some stamps were dispatched. I also advised my wife that the voyage South would take at least three weeks. That was to prove very optimistic.

Lancelot was not quite the first to sail. Three nuclear submarines (SSN's) were already underway, as HMS Spartan headed south from Gibraltar on 1 April along with several surface warships, followed by SSN HMS Splendid from Faslane the same day, and SSN HMS Conqueror on 4 April. Of course, an SSBN was already at sea, providing the UK's continuous nuclear deterrent. The main warship Task Force sailed after us later that same day, with a huge send off and with much media attention, led by the aircraft carriers HMS Hermes and HMS Invincible, this was the vanguard of what rapidly morphed into a 73 warship and auxiliary vessel fleet, plus nuclear submarines, and a further 54 merchant ships taken up from the trade. Over 170 aircraft (rotary and fixed wing) were deployed with this fleet by the Fleet Air Arm, and innovations such as Night Vision Goggles, were to prove decisive to the Logistic and Medical efforts of the war, as well as to the operational success of the fighting elements.

The Recapture of South Georgia

South Georgia offered the British Task Force the only realistic alternative harbours and potential repair and recovery locations within reasonable sailing distance of the main Falkland Island archipelago, and it was decided that it should be recaptured as quickly as possible. D Squadron SAS; 2 Troop SBS; 2 Naval Gunfire Forward Observation parties from RM Poole; and M Company 42 Commando RM with Recce Troop and Support Company enhancements, supported by an RN Commando medical team, were all moved to join HMS Antrim and HMS Plymouth and the Royal Fleet Auxiliary tanker Tidespring, which were already sailing South from Gibraltar.

6 Troop SBS had similarly joined the submarine HMS Conqueror and conducted a reconnaissance of key areas around South Georgia on 18 April 1982. On 21 April two Wessex Mk 5 from RFA Tidespring were lost attempting to recover an SAS insertion which had to be aborted due to extreme gales of up to 100mph and a 'white out' zero visibility snowstorm in freezing conditions.

Fortunately, there were no serious casualties and HMS Antrim's Wessex Mk 3 eventually recovered all the men.

HMS Endurance at Rothera British Antarctic Survey Station. On 3 April 1982 her detachment of 22 Royal Marines opposed the capture of South Georgia by 60 Argentine troops, killing 3 and wounding 9, they shot down a helicopter and severely damaged an Argentine Corvette, before surrendering when their ammunition was all but expended. (Photo provided by Dr Paul Griffiths)

The following day another tanker, the RFA Brambleleaf arrived in the area, but she had sustained structural storm damage and it was decided that RFA Tidespring should be dispatched to rendezvous with her and transfer all the fuel, which was vital to the entire fleet. Unfortunately, most of the M Company group were still aboard Tidespring and this evolution took them hundreds of miles from their assault station. Nonetheless it was decided to press on, and SAS Boat Troop succeeded in establishing an Observation Post ashore on 22/23 April 1982. They established that there was no sign of Argentine activity in the South Georgia Stromness area.

However, HMS Antrim's Wessex helicopter detected the Argentine submarine Santa Fe on 25 April. The submarine had dropped off resupplies and additional personnel and was heading out to sea when Antrim's Wessex attacked the vessel with depth charges.

HMS Brilliant had joined the fray with her Lynx helicopter to help ease the earlier loss of the two Wessex Mk 5's, and the Lynx attacked the submarine with a Mk 46 torpedo but missed and resorted to strafing the submarine with machine gun fire which proved effective. Wasp Helicopters from HMS Plymouth and HMS Endurance fired AS12 air to surface missiles which both struck home. The Santa Fe limped back to Grytviken Harbour South Georgia, and HMS Antrim and HMS Plymouth moved within range and bombarded the harbour. The Argentine forces at Grytviken subsequently surrendered to elements of M Company 42 Commando RM and the main Argentine force at Leith Harbour surrendered the following day. Britain had restored a potential safe haven for its ships and troops should the need arise, albeit at an inhospitable location that made the main Falkland archipelago seem positively tropical.

The Long Voyage South

Most of the embarked force on our Landing Ship Logistic were familiar with life afloat on a grey ship, but the mess decks for the junior ranks and ratings were cramped and austere, and never intended to be used for such a prolonged voyage. The Royal Fleet Auxiliary Officers aboard the LSL Sir Lancelot were very professional and eager to make the voyage as reasonable and comfortable as they could, but potable water was always going to be in short supply, as these flat bottomed, shallow draft vessels, were originally conceived to support British forces in Europe. As a result, water was rationed, and showers could only be used for 5 seconds to get wet, turn off, soap up as required, and turn on for another 5 second rinse. One Troop Medical Squadron exercised daily, and the Port and Starboard forward covered outer gangways alongside the Tank Deck, were frequently used for jogging, whilst the flight deck was also used for PT as well as weapon training, first aid training and such like.

We learnt from the BBC World Service News on 7 April, that the UK had declared a 200 mile exclusion zone around the Falkland Islands, effective from 12 April.

I managed to borrow a stamp on 9 April from Surgeon Lieutenant Graham Briars, with whom I was sharing a cabin, along with two other officers from other Squadrons, and so I wrote a longer letter home, confident that at some stage it would be delivered. I commented how lucky I was to have sheets and blankets for my bunk, and share a cabin with just three other chaps, whereas the men were in very cramped mess deck accommodation and having to use their sleeping bags. I commented that we were in company with other ships, but not the two Carrier Groups. This letter was actually received together with my earlier unstamped note on 23 April when my wife paid the 15.5p fee. The requirement to pay for stamps for our letters remained until we finally moved ashore on 21 May 1982, when Forces Air Mail letters were issued and the need to use stamps was finally waived. No other concessions were forthcoming. In fact, throughout my Service career which spanned well over two decades, we all paid full UK taxes, regardless of operational deployments.

On 10 April 1982 it was announced that the liner SS Uganda, which was used as an education vessel for school children, had been requisitioned for use as a hospital ship. She had been cruising the Mediterranean and put in to Gibraltar on 16 April, where the children left the ship and work immediately started to equip her with a helicopter landing pad, and convert her into the Hospital Ship Uganda. Remarkably, Uganda sailed from Gibraltar just 60 hours later, when on 19 April, her structural transformation having been completed, and with a strong consultant led clinical team on board, she too headed South. Ultimately 3 additional Survey Ships were also to follow in the role of Hospital Ship and would evacuate all the casualties off Uganda to Montevideo.

Our journey on the LSL Sir Lancelot slowly progressed, often with no sign of other vessels that would form the landing Force, the weather got hotter, and the sea calmer, and after about two weeks we transited the Doldrums, with the sea dead flat calm, and huge sea weed growing right up from the bottom of the ocean. The humidity and temperature was extreme, and again, the vessel was not designed for such a climate! Bizarrely, because seven of us aboard had intended to run in the Inter-Service Marathon Championship at RAF Swinderby, we actually staged our own marathon on 17 April, on the forward gangways, devising a 45 metre 'track' with lines which had to be crossed fore and aft, to ensure a minimum 90 metres, out and back, 513 times, with judges at either end to ensure the lines were crossed and to count each out and back lap. The event started at 0500, but the temperature was already close to 30 degrees C and rising. Those running on the Port side had the benefit of a very slight breeze, but for three of us on the starboard side the humidity was unbelievably intense. Marine Paul Brindley from Workshop Squadron finished first on the Port side, followed four minutes later by myself on the Starboard side, followed by Marines Neil Blain, and Paul Gibson. Because of the water shortage, we celebrated the event that evening with a few cans of beer! Most importantly we had raised around £400 for Falkland charities, and our Landing Ship had moved within 260 miles of the equator as the last man crossed the line for the final time. The feat was later reported quite widely, including in the book by newspaper journalist Bob McGowan 'Don't cry for me Sergeant Major' who was on the ship, and in the Athletics Weekly publication of 21 August 1982, and Running Magazine of September 1982.

Cpl Jon Clare was one of One Troop Medical Squadron's JNCO's, and here he sets out his brief recollections of life for those in the Troop Mess: *'At this stage monotony was the enemy. Food became a focus, and the meals were the highlight of the day, but we were not spoilt for choice. A typical dinner for example would be a slice of spam, some tinned potatoes, and some broad beans, and pudding might be angel delight. Conversations at the dining tables would often revolve around food fantasies of what we would eat if we had an endless choice. Physical training (PT) in the form of short circuits and static exercises was another daily event, and endless weapon training helped to plug the gaps between meals. On a brighter note, beer was available but usually restricted to a couple of cans per man each day. With a bit of ingenuity and creative accounting we sometimes managed to exceed this level for special occasions such as birthdays. Simple games, such as charades and storytelling wee mess-deck favourites to while away the evenings…we knew we were in for a long haul!'*

We crossed the Equator on or around 20 April, which happened to be the halfway point on our voyage South, as London is the same distance North of the equator, as the Falkland Islands are South of the equator. Later the following day, 21 April, we sighted the tiny atoll of Ascension Island, an arid volcanic pimple, about 300 miles further south of the equator, that has no natural water source! We entered a bay that in the era of flying boats, was used as an international landing stage for such aircraft heading from Europe and America to Africa and beyond; but the day we entered these waters, we were confronted with a very different sight as the bay was packed with RN warships and Royal Fleet Auxiliary (RFA) Landing Ships (LSL) and resupply vessels.

The P&O liner Canberra had been requisitioned and had sailed four days after us on 9 April, with 40 and 42 Commando Units, and the 3rd Parachute Battalion embarked, together with HQ and 3 Troop Medical Squadron, and 2 Surgical Support Team (RN Hospital Plymouth), and the RM Band from the Commando Training Centre. Canberra also anchored in the Bay. Meanwhile 45 Commando Unit had embarked on the supply ship RFA Stromness, together with some Ordnance Squadron personnel of the Commando Logistic Regiment. Special Forces were on various warships, including the aircraft carrier HMS Hermes.

Ascension Island

We subsequently learnt that the P&O Ferry Norland had been requisitioned on 15 April for the operation, and had sailed on 26 April, some 3 weeks after our departure, with the 2nd Parachute Battalion embarked, together with the Parachute Clearing Troop (PCT) and 2 Field Surgical Teams (FST's) on board; and that all the Parachute Regiment assets would be integral with an expanded 3 Commando Brigade.

We were still anchored at Ascension Island when the MV Norland left the UK, and here Cpl Jon Clare describes what life was like for him at Ascension Island: *'We had hoped to get ashore often for advanced training and physical exercise, but thoughts of plenty of time ashore were quickly dashed because of the very limited facilities to cope with the huge Task Force, not to mention limited assets to move people ashore, as the landing craft and mexi floats were constantly ferrying supplies and equipment from shore to ship, and ship to ship. Nobody in One Troop Medical Squadron had any truck with giving the fighting Units priority use at the ranges and other limited training areas however, and we did get to conduct basic weapon tests enabling us to zero our weapons. We also had a single visit to the village of Two*

Boats, population 120, at the foot of Green Mountain. Royal Marines have a long and interesting historic association on the Island, but sadly we had no opportunity to explore it, as for the most part we remained afloat where we worked on honing our medical skills, often practicing inserting intravenous drip needles on each other, before the focus shifted to cross decking all our stores and equipment to the ill-fated LSL Sir Galahad, which was to become our new home'.

So, any idea that Ascension Island was some sort of tropical paradise for us to rest up on, was wide off the mark. Not just because the waters were infested with sharks, and much smaller fish that would seemingly consume anything, like a sort of saltwater piranha, but also, as Jon Clare has alluded to, because we were told that all the logistic and medical assets and kit on the Lancelot, had to cross deck via mexi floats, to Galahad. Such a feat would take a full day if we were alongside a jetty with cranes and vehicles to facilitate the cross-deck, but in the middle of this Bay, it would take several days. Ironically the Galahad had been in Devonport when we loaded aboard the Lancelot in Marchwood. We were not alone in this evolution however, as all the Landing Ship loading plans were juggled whilst afloat, perhaps to some extent reflecting that LSL Sir Bedivere had joined the Task Force from Vancouver, and LSL Sir Tristram from Belize.

US resupply vessels also entered the Bay and provided fuel and water to the growing number of ships. I was sent ashore to the Airbase, which was accustomed to seeing two, perhaps three aircraft a week. I cannot recall why I was sent to the airfield, which was my only opportunity to experience terra firma at Ascension, but vividly remember the awe-inspiring view of all the available aircraft parking spots being filled with former V bomber Victor Tankers. Clearly something was afoot!

Finally, the Commando Logistic Regiment assets and personnel, including One Troop Medical Squadron that had been aboard the LSL Lancelot, were reloaded with all equipment and personal kit, in the Galahad. We did not have just a new ships company to get to know, but also members of C Flight of 3 Brigade Air Squadron, together with their 3 Gazelle Helicopters on the rear flight deck – putting it largely out of bounds for physical and military training. The mood of the ship's officers was rather more sombre than had existed on Lancelot, as the enormity of the task that lay ahead for them was hitting home, and we finally weighed anchor on 1 May, and restarted our journey South, water still rationed, and the seas rolling more with each mile covered.

I cannot remember the exact date, but at some stage, possibly whilst we were still at Ascension, or perhaps shortly after we set sail, the ship's crew started to set-up anti-aircraft guns. Out at sea, and alone once more, these were test fired by the ship's crew ratings, who were Hong Kong Chinese seamen, but there was no real opportunity for proper target practice.

Our own weapons were similarly tested, and some limited opportunity to again zero the weapons was afforded. One Troop Medical Squadron was mainly equipped with 7.62 high velocity Self Loading Rifles (SLR's), one of which I carried. We had a single 9ml pistol which was issued to Dr Graham Briars, and several RN Medical Assistants carried 9ml Sub Machine Guns, because they were lighter and less cumbersome than SLR's. My Troop also carried lightweight disposable 66mm rocket launchers, and since I had discovered just before sailing that I really needed spectacles for distant vision, I also carried one of these, to improve our chances should we need to ward off unfriendly forces!

I wrote home at the beginning of May and remarked that mail had just caught up with us for the first time. Because of security I had not mentioned that we had been at anchor off Ascension, just that we were continuing our slow relentless journey South. I commented that we were not in a good position to receive any further mail for 'some weeks', and I remarked how the sea was gradually gathering a swell again with the ship rolling in 'monotonous sequence'. I also remarked 'Everything seems to be going very well for the fleet. Let's hope that this situation continues; as it will, providing none of the other South American countries gives military support to Argentina'. Our postal address was Name and Unit followed by BFPO 666. I'm not sure how they arrived at that BFPO number, but it didn't seem too comforting.

The ship would broadcast the BBC World Service news each day, and Jon Clare picks up the story of our voyage again: *'The information age was still 20 years away and we relied upon the BBC World Service for snippets of information. We looked forward to the Boss's daily briefings, which usually consisted of the World Service news plus any non-secret information from daily signal traffic. Sometimes the briefings would be in the dining area of the galley, but more often than not it was held in our mess-deck. As soon as his shoes appeared on the steps we reverted to sensible marine mode and listened attentively. Often there wasn't much to say but from a leadership and man management point of view Malcolm Hazell used these briefings to good effect, keeping in touch and gleaning information from us whilst checking on our well-being and morale, which was normally high. On my birthday, the Boss (as we knew him), and all the lads, had managed to keep a Dundee cake, sent to me from my home, a complete surprise until my 21st birthday on 12 May, making a special occasion out of it, for which I was very grateful! I was a section commander but in reality, I was the youngest and least operationally experienced man in my team, and after my short birthday celebration I refocussed my mind on the potential job that lay ahead of us'.*

To this juncture much of the BBC World Service news covered the diplomatic efforts to resolve the situation, but there was never anything promising in that regard, and Argentina was reportedly reinforcing its invading force as each day passed. Shortly after sailing from Ascension on 1 May, we heard the news that the RAF had struck the runway at Stanley using Vulcan bombers and inflight refuelling – thus why the Victors were at Wide Awake on Ascension. This was at the time the longest bombing raid in history. Much more recently I read that this was the first such raid, when a single Vulcan had dropped 21 bombs in an effort to destroy the runway, and Sea Harriers from our Carriers had also dropped 1000 pound bombs to destroy fuel and ammunition dumps.

The next day, 2 May, the nuclear submarine (SSN – Submersible Ship Nuclear) HMS Conqueror sank the Argentine cruiser Belgrano. The gloves were off! All of us afloat were saddened to learn of the inevitable loss of life, but we were quietly relieved that this action had been taken. The Belgrano may have been an aging ship, but she was a formidable weapon platform, with 15 six inch guns that could have wreaked havoc with the landing force and posed a very real risk to all of us. This single action sent a message to the Argentine Navy that our SSN's were in position and able to blockade all their vessels, or sink any who tried to run the gauntlet, which none did, and we were all at less risk as a result. It was just in the nick of time, as their aircraft carrier, Veintinco de Mayo, (which had earlier been used to convey 1,500 Argentine troops to Stanley) had, the same day that Belgrano was sunk, aborted a launch of its Sky Hawks against our own carriers, due to unfavourably light winds providing insufficient lift for their bomb laden aircraft to take off. Three Argentine Exocet armed Corvettes, two guided missile Type 42 Destroyers, and two other Destroyers, were also kept out of the fray by the threat posed by our SSN's.

The collective sigh of relief by all of us in the Task Force, was shattered two days later on 4 May, when we learnt, courtesy of the BBC World Service, that the Destroyer, HMS Sheffield, had been hit by an air launched Exocet missile fired from a Super Etendard Fighter Bomber, and the Argentines had acquired 5 of these lethal aircraft with such deadly weapon systems. 20 sailors died in this single incident, and another 26 were wounded. The survivors were safely evacuated off the stricken vessel by two Frigates that had come to its aid. The Sheffield was subsequently taken in tow, by HMS Yarmouth, which attempted to tow the vessel to South Georgia, but she shipped too much water whilst being towed, and finally sank on 10 May 1982.

Whilst the sea state permitted, we focussed on the task ahead, holding Command Post exercises between our Squadrons; receiving briefings about what we should and should not take ashore; what to do if we were captured; aircraft recognition; more first aid and broader clinical training and equipment familiarity, and so on.

But soon the sea state got worse, much worse. The ship was corkscrewing endlessly from one massive wave to the next. It was unremitting, and whilst most of us had adapted enough to avoid sea sickness, the instability of the ship was such that it was impossible to continue with routine training and tasks, and instead the challenge was to focus on not being thrown against a bulkhead and ensuring that all the heavy equipment remained properly secured. Our only source of news was the BBC World Service, but the reception was deteriorating and often inaudible, as our ship, Galahad, battled with the vast expanse of the South Atlantic Ocean seemingly raging against it. At this stage the sea was the enemy!

There were no press or other journalists on the Galahad, and at some stage we were briefed about the intention to land the entire Landing Force in San Carlos Waters – a large natural harbour to the North West side of East Falkland. Just to the North West of San Carlos Water, across from Falkland Sound that separates the main East and West Islands, lies Pebble Island, which I had visited whilst with NP8901 in 1977/78. Although it was only four years earlier, I could not immediately recollect its exact position, when Colonel Ivar Hellberg asked me if I could point it out on the map and he spotted its position before I did. He had posed this question 'out of the blue', when we were discussing the geography and topography of the Islands, as Colonel Ivar was aware of my NP8901 service. This conversation must have been around 11 May 1982, but the significance of his enquiry regarding the location of Pebble Island was not to become clear until a few days later, when on 15 May, struggling with others on the LSL to listen to the BBC World Service News on one of the ships tannoy address speakers, the lead news story was the SAS raid on Pebble Island, during the night of 14 and 15 May, destroying 11 Pucara ground attack aircraft and T34 Mentor Aircraft. It later emerged that the operation had been launched from HMS Hermes, utilizing two Sea King helicopters from 846 Naval Air Squadron, (one of two Commando Helicopter Squadrons based at RNAS Yeovilton when not deployed) for their insertion. 45 members of D Squadron SAS had set explosive charges against all the aircraft, and only engaged the 150 enemy forces after drawing attention to their presence having raked the aircraft with live rounds. One member of the raid was injured from an Improvised Explosive Device (IED), and it is understood that the Argentine OC was killed, but there were no other casualties. Concurrent with this raid, the destroyer HMS Glamorgan had fired its 4.5 inch guns into Argentine positions on West Falkland.

The news of the Pebble Island raid had provided further reassurance to all of us aboard Galahad that the SBS and SAS were doing what they had to do, to help ensure we would all get ashore safely. It came as something of a hammer blow 3 days later to hear, again courtesy of the BBC World Service, that 18 members of the SAS drowned as an 846 Naval Air Squadron helicopter had a bird strike whilst flying between the carrier HMS Hermes and the assault ship HMS Intrepid. An aircrewman also died, as did an RAF Signals specialist, who was the only RAF member to be killed as result of the war. As someone who started their career as an RN Junior Medical Assistant (MA), I was reminded and grateful that our training had included compulsory helicopter ditching and underwater escape drills, known as Dunker Training.

San Carlos Waters – the Landings

*Landing ships with vessels of the Task Force approaching
the Falklands on 20 May 1982*

As we neared the Islands the sea state settled down considerably.
We were briefed that 'D-day' was scheduled to be on 21 May 1982.
I received my orders, namely, to go ashore at Ajax Bay, at the
earliest opportunity, with the CLR advance party, with the aim of
establishing a Field Dressing Station. The equipment and men of
my Troop would then follow me ashore as soon as the situation
permitted. Everyone was issued with ammunition, and my Troop
issued Morphine to all the embarked force on Galahad, which they
signed for in my Troop notebook, which I have retained to this day.

I wrote a very brief letter home on 20 May, reminding my wife
Bev that I was a member of the Royal Navy Dependants Fund and
she would receive around £2,000 if 'something happened to me'.
I also reminded her that my life insurance was linked to the house
mortgage, but I subsequently realised it excluded acts of war.

As from the outset, the ship was fully darkened i.e. showing no external lights whatsoever as, on the evening of 20 May, we headed towards San Carlos Waters, under cover of darkness. We had little inclination of the air power that would be unleashed upon us the following morning, having largely accepted the established wisdom that the Argentine Airforce would find it difficult, if not impossible, to strike us, given that the airfield had been hit by bombing raids, and most of their aircraft surely lacked the range to conduct bombing runs against us and return to mainland Argentina. I just tried to make the most of the ship not rolling violently for a change, to get some 'shut eye' sleep. We apparently entered San Carlos Waters at around 0100 local on 21 May. This was 0400 Z Greenwich Mean Time, which is the time we maintained to mount the landings, and we had an early breakfast shortly after anchoring, probably around 0500Z which was 0200 local time, in the middle of the night.

The sun did not begin to rise until around 1100Z, (0800 local), and we were all very much still firmly in the ship. C Flight 3 Brigade Air Squadron had launched all 3 Gazelle helicopters off the flight deck. Only one was to return, flown by Captain Robin Makeig-Jones who himself had been shot at by small arms fire in the area of Port San Carlos, where a group of Argentinians were lurking. The other two helicopters were both shot down. Lt Ken Francis and his crewman L/Cpl Giffin were brought down by heavy machine gun fire and died instantly. Sgt Andy Evans RM and his crewman Sgt Eddy Candlish RM had ditched in San Carlos Water. Sgt Evans died but Sgt Candlish survived this brief but brutal encounter. Captain Rob Makeig-Jones RA made it back to Galahad and I chatted with him as he drank a cup of tea or coffee and shared his grim experience with me. He was clearly shaken by the incident and the loss of his friends - who wouldn't have been? His aircraft was patched up and, like many of his comrades from 3 Brigade Air Squadron and the Naval Air Squadrons had to do, he got on with the war. Time and time again 3 Brigade Air Squadron would subsequently be used to fly to forward positions, sometimes in tactical mode, and sometimes to collect casualties, both friend and foe. They were never found wanting, but these losses were sadly not to be the last that 'Teeny Weeny airlines' (as they were affectionately known by my team), would suffer.

News of the progress of the landings was hard to come by despite being in the thick of it, and certainly none of One Troop Medical Squadron new anything about the fact that Argentina had 2 tanker aircraft each capable of simultaneously refuelling two aircraft, thus enabling 4 of their aircraft to conduct bombing runs against us at any one time. We were about to find out, as the first wave of Argentine aircraft swept along barely above the waves, each carrying two 500lb bombs. They flew so fast and low that I found it impossible to discern whether they were Mirage or Skyhawk in the split- second sighting I had of them. I was confident however that they were not Harriers, and that became the 'gold standard' required thereafter to ensure we did not engage our own aircraft. Everything else was trying to kill us! Our ships antiaircraft guns opened up. I was in the main dining area and it must have been around 1200Z (0900 local), and the noise of our own guns firing, and the aircraft roaring past, was quite intimidating. There had been an Air Raid Warning Red, but it was literally a few seconds before the aircraft were on top of us. This pattern of events was to become a regular occurrence over the coming days. We had men deployed around the ship as first aid parties and firefighting parties, but fortunately at this stage none were tested. There was also a significant danger posed by firing at enemy aircraft flying so low, however, insofar as we risked hitting our own ships and troops, as tracer and shells was fired from all our vessels from all directions! Fortunately, again, we all survived our own barrage. Over the following two days however, three LSL's, Bedivere, Lancelot, and our ship Galahad, were to suffer bomb damage, as was the destroyer Antrim, and the frigate Ardent was lost, whilst Antelope, Argonaut, Brilliant, and Broadsword were all hit. In fact, of the escorts defending the landings, only the frigates Yarmouth and Plymouth were unscathed, and Broadsword was able to fully function despite being hit.

It was becoming clear that the Argentine pilots were flying so low when they dropped their bombs that the tails of the bombs, which needed to spin sufficiently to arm the bomb (like connecting a fuse) had insufficient height to do so. This was indeed fortunate, because otherwise 9 ships might have been lost in the first 3 days of the landings.

It was not until 1930Z (1630 local) on D Day 21 May, that the Commando Logistic Regiment advance party finally boarded a landing craft from one of the Assault Ships, Fearless or Intrepid, to move ashore. I had One Troop Medical Squadron's signaller, Marine Steve Gosling, with me, and Lt Richard Gaze RM of Workshop Squadron was standing next to me as we approached the designated landing beach at Ajax Bay. Such was the information black-out that we had no idea who might be ashore, and Richard Gaze made it clear that everybody in the craft should be prepared if necessary to engage the enemy. Fortunately, the beach had no enemy forces in close proximity, and Marine Steve Gosling and I were able to make our way up to the front entrance of the disused refrigeration plant, and enter the building, as the sun was going down over the horizon. We didn't even get wet feet, and it was a perfect evening, despite the approaching winter.

We had barely an hour of daylight left to ensure there were no surprises, such as explosive devices, hidden in the building. It was full of debris, dead birds and such like, and certainly gave the impression of nobody else having been in the building for many years. It was one of the few places I had not visited whilst patrolling the Islands with NP8901 during my 13 month deployment in 1977/8, and had apparently been abandoned for at least 28 years, but I would have said far longer, judging by the state it was in. It had been built to enable the export of frozen mutton, but the choice of Ajax Bay for such a site was bewildering. The lack of any road infrastructure on the Islands, and no natural water source at the site, led to its inevitable demise. Ajax Bay was one of the least accessible, uninhabited locations on East Falkland. Its two closest settlements of Port San Carlos to the far North of San Carlos Water, and San Carlos on the East of side of this large natural harbour, could only be easily reached by crossing in a boat, and in terms of expanse, it was like looking across to the Isle of Wight, from Brown Down Beach on the Solent. Aside from no fresh water, it obviously had no electric or any other services, but it did have this really well insulated building however, that was divided into some very large spaces, and Steve Gosling and I were far from cold as we set about clearing the site of debris and ensuring it was safe, and free of booby traps. We found a broom with a broken handle, and we had an entrenching tool (a shovel) and we set about clearing all the muck out. We continued in torchlight until the whole sound area of the building that was usable as a medical facility, was cleared. I then worked out how the facility might best be established within the building; planning where Reception for the triage and holding of new arrivals would take place; where Treatments (major and minor) could be conducted; where surgical tables could be set up; and where the holding and evacuation ward could be set up. These tasks took us beyond 2359Z and into D+1.

Meanwhile the remainder of One Troop Medical Squadron were still stuck on the Galahad, and Jon Clare picks up his story, whilst waiting to get ashore: *'At the forefront of a marine's mind when aboard a ship is HOW SOON CAN I GET OFF THIS TUB! The landings were continuing all around us and we had to wait our turn. The Boss had gone ashore with Steve Gosling and we wanted to join them. The marines in the Troop had many conversations during our long voyage down about being called upon to defend our medical facility ashore, come what may, but whilst we remained afloat on Galahad we felt like sardines in a tin can, being bombed and strafed. We endured some pretty close calls during the increasing air raids and the roar of Argentine Skyhawk jets and the exploding thumps of their 500lb bombs left us in no doubt we were currently on the receiving end of Argentina's air superiority. When our time came to move ashore I would be lying if I did not say I was slightly disappointed that unlike other marines and paras, we did not embark on a landing craft or fly ashore in a helicopter, but instead made our way to the beach at Ajax Bay somewhat less dramatically on one of the large flat bottomed barges known as Mexi-floats, which had large generators on deck to power them ashore at an unspectacular 3 or 4 knots. Something of a damp squib in the early hours of D +1. What happened over the next few days at Ajax Bay made every one of us realise that our role in this war, as Royal Marines in Medical Squadron, was to be significantly more important than we had initially thought and was also to become a harrowing, life changing experience'.*

Consolidation and Disposition of Friendly Forces on D Day

Remarkably, the first 24 hours of the beach landings had seen all major forward elements of 3 Command Brigade land ashore and largely, though not entirely, without contact with enemy ground forces. The exception was with regard to the SBS reconnaissance of the beach landing area the day prior to the main landings and its immediate hinterland just to the West of Port San Carlos. The SBS had detected a number of Argentine troops in the area known as Fanning Head and engaged them. The operation had also involved the destroyer HMS Antrim firing its 4.5 inch guns to provide Naval Gunfire Support, directed from ashore by 148 Commando Forward Observation Battery Royal Artillery. Eight Argentine conscripts, including four wounded, were captured by the SBS, but 11 others escaped eastward and eventually were to make it back to Stanley. It subsequently emerged that a further 40 had been in the settlement of Port San Carlos as the Paras moved towards the beach, and had transmitted the disposition of ships and landings back to their superiors at Goose Green, before themselves withdrawing and being extracted further to the East. This group were responsible for shooting down the two Gazelle helicopters from C Flight that had taken off from Galahad, killing 3 of the 4 aircrew, and for nearly bringing down the third helicopter similarly from Galahad. Their radio transmission appears to have been responsible for the precision of the Argentine air raids that became a persistent and determined feature thrown against us. So much so I doubt any one of us could recount just how many air raids there were in the coming days, without recourse to an official written log.

The presence of the Argentine Fanning Head Mob (FHM) as they became known, was to prove problematic for 3 Para in the most ghastly way, during the coming hours. Nonetheless, as D Day came to a close on 21 May 1982, 45 Commando were all landed on Red Beach at Ajax Bay; 3 Para on Green 1 at Port San Carlos; 42 Commando on Green 2 Beach at Port San Carlos; 40 Commando and HQ 3 Commando on Blue 1 and 2 Beaches at San Carlos; and 2 Para and a host of other Units also ashore across these beaches. 29 Commando RA gunners, with 24 105mm light guns in 4 Batteries were also ashore and operational on D Day. This was a phenomenal achievement.

D+1_22 May 1982
The Build Up of Medical Squadron at Ajax Bay

The first medical team to join my signaller Marine Steve Gosling and I ashore, were the Parachute Clearing Troop (PCT) with numbers 5 and 6 Field Surgical Teams (FST's). This medical team had sailed from the UK on the MV Norland, which was requisitioned on 15 April, when the 2nd Parachute Battalion was added to 3 Commando Brigade's order of battle (ORBAT). The Norland had not departed the UK until 26 April, remarkably some 3 weeks after my own Troop. Each Field Surgical Team was 9 strong and configured to run a single operating table. Inclusive of the two Field Surgical Teams the Parachute Clearing Troop were a similar strength to my Troop without Surgical Support. My Troop was delayed coming ashore as the offload was proceeding in the reverse of what had been initially intended, when it was decided by the Amphibious Warfare Staff on the LPD's not to risk beaching the ship and offloading from the forward bow door, but instead to keep Galahad anchored and to offload onto mexi floats from its aft end. In my mind's eye I recall the PCT/FST's arriving in daylight the next morning, but my notebook recorded them arriving around

0200z on 22 May, and my own Troop joining us 2 hours later. Regardless of the exact time, I met the PCT/FST's in the entrance to the building, told them who I was, and how I proposed the facility might be laid out. They understandably spent a brief time exploring the options for laying out the site, and then agreed with my conclusions. Much of their medical kit was man portable and having dumped their personal kit in the building they began to carry their equipment up the slip road from the landing point and into the building. When my own troop followed a couple of hours later, they arrived with our water bowser trailer, generator trailer, 2 one tonne ambulances, full galley (kitchen) facilities, and several Chatham Containers full of kit, tentage, heating equipment, and medical supplies, to ensure that between ourselves and the PCT we had the capacity to treat and if necessary, hold and care for, at least 100 casualties, with crisis expansion beyond this. Moreover, if necessary, to do so under canvas. Normally all this equipment would have been vehicle borne, but the use of Chatham Containers did not inhibit us very much.

By the time HQ Medical Squadron arrived ashore, having started to board a landing craft utility LCU at 0230Z, it was nearly 0400Z (0100 local), and the establishment of the facility was virtually complete, but a number of us had to persuade a few of the newcomers not to fix what wasn't broken and leave the progress that had been made alone. The Squadron HQ had brought with them a vital addition, namely 2 Surgical Support Team (SST) from RN Hospital Plymouth. This was a 27 man team that like the two Field Surgical Teams, would provide two operating tables with full operating teams. Importantly the RN Surgical Support Team also provided some laboratory capability, and intensive care standard nursing capability. I learnt at this point that the arrival of the Parachute Clearing Troop and its Field Surgical Teams, and HQ Medical Squadron, had been accelerated because both the Canberra (HQ Medical Squadron and 2 Surgical Support Team) and the Norland (Parachute Clearing Troop and Field Surgical Teams 5&6) had been ordered to sail under cover of darkness. In fact, the Canberra was headed to South Georgia and had retained 3 Troop

Medical Squadron on board. Those of us that were ashore now, would provide the only care ashore beyond the Regimental Aid Posts (RAP's) that was available to the Brigade, for at least the next 10 days, before 3 Troop might return, or further reinforcements from the UK might arrive.

Following daybreak our Troop Quartermaster, Chief Petty Officer Medical Assistant (CPOMA) John Smith, and his assistant Marine Whittaker, and our Chef, Marine Neil Blain, had established the galley, and we were all able to benefit from the fruits of their hard work and enjoy a welcome mug of tea and cooked breakfast, before concentrating again on ensuring the viability of this Field Surgical Hospital.

The 'Field Hospital' at Ajax Bay

Whilst a lot of post Operation Corporate and Operation Sutton (the land phase of the Operation) papers have tended to focus on Surgery and operating tables, it would be remiss not to emphasise the importance of the other clinical functions of medical facilities, both ashore and afloat.

Reception: Without an effective Reception area, tagging patients and triaging them into Major or Minor treatments, and holding them in order of priority for treatment, the situation at Ajax Bay would have been a chaotic mess.

Minor Treatment Section: The Minor Treatment section enabled less seriously ill or injured patients to be seen and treated, and hopefully returned forward, but regardless, without clogging the facility in areas delivering life saving care. If someone had a medical condition, such as a tummy upset for example, they could be admitted to the Evacuation Ward and cared for whilst recovering, or in more serious circumstances evacuated to the Hospital Ship Uganda. Uganda was a declared medical facility within the Geneva Convention however, which meant that patients evacuated to it, could not be returned to their Units. Minor Treatments ashore, were a vital means of retaining troops on the ground.

Major Treatments: Major Treatments provided life saving care to patients, who either did not need surgery, or needed stabilizing prior to surgery, or might otherwise, following interventions, be able to wait until they were aboard the Hospital Ship Uganda before being put under the knife! Such interventions might include intubation to ensure an airway; infusions of Normal Saline, Haemacell blood substitute, Hartman's blood volume, or less frequently whole blood or plasma, to ensure a reasonable blood volume, oxygenation, and blood pressure. Or perhaps inserting a chest drain to ensure a casualty's lungs were not overwhelmed with blood fluids (i.e. literally to stop someone drowning in their own blood); or sometimes stemming a gushing artery using standard Spencer Wells forceps. These interventions might also be attempted at Regimental Aid Post Level or even at the point of wounding, as they were certainly all taught to every RN Commando trained Medical Assistant on the Advanced Casualty Care Course, and similarly attended by Dental Officers and Junior Medical Officers serving with Commando Units, albeit no doubt with expanded clinical content for these doctors and dentists. My own experience during tours of duty in West Belfast and South Armagh had shown me how difficult it could be to actually administer some of these life saving techniques in operational situations, often in poor light, and freezing cold adverse weather. Not surprisingly, significant numbers of patients were to arrive requiring the prompt intervention of a resuscitation medical officer, and the provision of such medical officers in addition to Surgeons should not be underestimated, nor the presence of male State Registered Nurses qualified and adept at using these techniques regularly.

Evacuation Ward: The Evacuation Ward holding facility, whereby patients were cared for whilst awaiting evacuation, or recovering to return forward, was simply comprised of patients lying on the same stretchers they were first treated on. There were no beds. But again, the receipt of appropriate care in the evacuation Ward was of course vital to the continued well-being of patients, and often necessitated continuous monitoring of vital signs, without the benefit modern electrical equipment to do this.

The care patients received in these sections, here at Ajax Bay, and later also at Teal Inlet and Fitzroy forward facilities which have thus far received far too little attention in any written work, would serve to shape their recovery, just as importantly as the Operating capability would prove decisive in the care of penetrating wounds, traumatic amputations, and such like. Forward surgery did however differentiate what we were able to achieve in terms of saving lives, when compared with, for example, the D day Landings of Normandy which took place 38 years before these landings, just 100 miles from the UK's shores, and when a Dressing Station was simply that. The provision of Forward Surgery and Advanced Resuscitation were fundamental to ensure that lives were saved that might otherwise have been lost, regardless of what side of the conflict a patient had originated from. But, just like a civil hospital, the service provided to patients is defined by all the staff and departments. All too often patients are lost because of a weak link in that whole system approach, including the prompt collection by an ambulance. We were fortunate in Medical Squadron that with our Surgical Support Team, and together with our newly adopted partners from the Parachute Clearing Troop and their Field Surgical Teams, (who were remarkably similar in their planned mode of medical operation to Medical Squadron but were more lightly scaled) to have no such weak links. Moreover, 3 Brigade Air Squadron together with 845 and 846 Naval Air Squadrons, provided the ambulance lift as promptly as the tactical situation and weather permitted.

The medical scale that was carried by One Troop Medical Squadron was designated I1248 and based on a standard RAMC Field Ambulance scale that we had adapted to reflect our integrated surgical support. In addition we had deployed with a much greater supply of items such as Haemacell, Hartmans, and Normal Saline Infusions and giving sets; and a much greater scale of intravenous antibiotics.

D+1 was a day of consolidation for the Field hospital at Ajax Bay. We only admitted three casualties, two of whom were from 2 Para and involved a gunshot wound to a foot, which must have been an accidental (negligent) discharge, and an eye injury. The third was from 40 Commando Unit, and the individual was suffering from hypothermia. This was otherwise a period when our stores could be sorted into more workable arrangements, our defences, such as they were - usually a few piles of low stonewall sangers – built to try to afford some protection from air raids, and the Squadron Command Post (CP) was fully set up, together with G1 (personnel) staff seconded to deal with casualty and fatality reporting. The Squadron utilized the Land Force Admin (LF Admin) HF radio net, but the proximity of our parent HQ Commando Logistic Regiment, less than a couple of hundred yards to our South, meant a land line was suitable for most communication matters – particularly since non- essential radio transmission was not allowed.

Jon Clare also expands on our defensive preparations: *'When not moving equipment and stores into the field hospital and setting up the facility under the watchful eyes of the professional medics, the marines were able to revert to type and began establishing defensive positions around the hospital and wider logistic area. There was a basic defensive plan that encompassed the entire Logistic Regiment, and we were given arcs of fire in the event of an enemy attack. However, with such widely dispersed stores, equipment, and ammunition, stacked wherever possible, we focussed on protecting the hospital and the immediate surrounding area. We had received no Intelligence to suggest this was a safer area than other beach landing sites, and we had to assume an attack might occur. Logistic areas are always prime targets in conflicts, not just for aircraft to pick off, but for ground troops and special forces too. I do not think at this stage, given some of their demeanours, the doctors, nor many of the non-commando/para trained other medics, had more than a passing inclination or interest in the vulnerability of this location, and perhaps nor should they, as that is in part what we were there for. Their views were to change within a few short days. As best we could, among the stockpiles of ammunition and stores, the marines of One Troop Medical Squadron began siting and preparing the mutually supporting trenches with interlocking arcs and good lines of communication and cover from ground and air attack. I remember one of my marines saying "It's not if we get air attacks, it's when and how often". We stockpiled our own ammunition within the trenches and kept a few emergency rations just in case, as if to be ready for a long and bloody fight should the need arise'.*

Jon Clare continues: *'Over the next few days One Troop's marines became conversant with the environment in the hospital and we knew instinctively when and where to appear and offer assistance. We had been well trained by the professional medics in the Squadron and we all had roles within the facility, whether assisting in the aftercare of patients, collecting casualties from incoming helicopters, or actually assisting the medics administering treatment. Marine Neil Blain, our young chef, was displaying a truly heroic attitude for hard work and played a pivotal wider role in many diverse aspects of the Medical Squadron'.*

Defence trenches just outside the medical facility at Ajax Bay. Jim Giles (nearest) with 7.62 machine gun. Ammunition pallets are ready to be airlifted as underslung helicopter loads over the other side of the track above them.

One Troop Medical Squadron's chef, Neil Blain, on D+1 at his galley, before it was relocated with a centralised Commando Logistic Regiment galley.

RN Surgical Support Teams. Medical Squadron had two Surgical Support Teams (the other was on the Carrier Hermes) and each were capable of providing two Operating Teams and nine additional resuscitation and technical staff. One and Three Troops (Three Troop was aboard Canberra at this time), were each tasked to provide, maintain, and staff the wider facilities of two Field Dressing Stations, which clinically were, in reality, so much more. Indeed, as previously mentioned, with their surgical support these were mobile light field hospitals, and at Ajax Bay, the Squadron benefitted from the further addition of the Parachute Field Surgical Teams who were similarly capable of providing 2 surgical tables between them, thus providing half of the surgical capability at Ajax Bay from 22 May to 3 June. Moreover, within their Parachute Clearing Troop, they provided a third of the non-surgical staff and as such we had a highly capable integrated team.

Significantly however, Medical Squadron were scaled with equipment and stores to support 6,000 men in general war in

Norway, and this was a forte that the Parachute Clearing Troop, which was smaller than either of Medical Squadron's two Troops, nor its Field Surgical Teams, could match. They were reliant on Medical Squadron to provide all sustained services and resupply; thus they were integrated into our organisation from the outset.

All One Troop Medical Squadron's medical stores (except the resupply boxes) were in fibreglass containers known as Lacon Bins, which were about one metre long by 60 cm high and 40 cm deep. When the lid was removed these were tightly packed like ready to use items on shelving. These Lacon Bins formed the boundaries of clinical areas, and once they were put in their respective areas we were virtually ready to go. Stretchers were simply placed on metal trestle legs in Major Treatments and Minor Treatments, and some patients were treated on their stretchers on the floor.

When the Parachute Clearing Troop came ashore early, instead of my troop arriving as planned off Galahad, because Norland needed to sail, I invited them to set up their kit, in the layout I proposed, and they agreed with - namely as you enter the building through the main entrance, patients were triaged and all minor patients went to the right side, where the evacuation ward and CP was also established, whilst all major patients went in the left side where resuscitation/major treatment and surgery were set out, and this was achieved to a level where we were able to receive and treat patients within a couple of hours of arriving. Both the PCT and Medical Squadron were fully used to achieving this, indeed we were used to moving very regularly, always under canvas on exercises, to support the fighting Units. Some sources have claimed it took 36 hours for the facility to be set up and operational, but this is not correct. There are three factors where the 36 hour claim might have come from though:

Firstly, as my post operation report stated, our Lacon bins were packed as scaled by the Defence Medical (DMed) establishment at Ludgershall, and these were comprised of ridiculous tiny amounts of multiple products in each bin, so we basically set about ensuring the bins were better sorted, so a bin might for example have only giving sets for intravenous infusions. This process went on for quite some time but did not impact on our ability to receive and treat casualties.

Secondly, on D+1 Rick Jolly directed the Parachute Clearing Troop to pack away all their kit, and One Troop Medical Squadron and the SST had to replace it with our own equipment. Rick had then gone off to a Brigade meeting or some other commitment, having told the PCT to just sit in the back room (that had become our accommodation area) of the main building, where I found them in a despondent state. I said to one of their senior officers that I was sure Rick had sound reasons to ask them to pack their stores away, but I was equally sure he had intended them to continue to contribute their skilled clinical services, and it made sense if the PCT provided one part of a two watch system alongside my Troop and the SST; and this is how we proceeded thereafter. This whole evolution of packing the PCT stores and equipment away did cause some disruption, but it never compromised our operational ability to receive casualties.

Finally, One Troop's 12 kva generator had not weathered the six week voyage well - and it was a time consuming liability until Workshop Squadron replaced it with a smaller 6 kva machine that thankfully proved reliable.

The layout of the facility, and patient flows and treatment areas were essentially unchanged whilst One Troop was at Ajax Bay, but we did have to adapt to some very limiting conditions as Argentine air attacks found their mark.

Red Cross or No Red Cross?

It was impossible not to notice that B Echelon of 45 Commando had stockpiled the Unit's ammunition just to the rear of our facility, but within the same former refrigeration block. Surgeon Commander

Rick Jolly recounts in his book, The Red and Green Life Machine, holding discussions with the CO Commando Logistic Regiment, Lt Col Ivar Hellberg, and the Brigade Commander, Brigadier Julian Thompson, about the merits of placing Red Crosses on the Field hospital. He said that this was decided against, because of the proximity of ammunition and various other elements, such as 45 Commando personnel and Commando Logistic Regiment personnel, which would make the legal display of Red Crosses impossible. This is certainly true, but more to the point, in the 12 months I had been OC of One Med Troop, I had never come across any red cross insignia, and it was not part of our Standard Operating Procedure as previously outlined, as it would usually be very difficult, if not impossible, to dedicate a beach for sole use as a medical facility. Moreover, even with large red cross flags, Argentine Sky Hawks and Mirage jets would have only a split second to possibly spot them as they flew inches above the high ground before emerging a foot or two above the height of the former refrigeration plant, that was the newly created Field Hospital. I doubt we could have even found sufficient red paint from the entire Task Force to daub the roof with a red cross.

D+2 23 May 1982

Blue on Blue Incident. Whilst most of us with Medical Squadron had been able to get some sleep during the night, the fighting Units had patrols out ensuring the security of their respective areas. 3 Para was no different, and a patrol from A Company had been out longer than planned, looking for an ammunition dump that was thought to have been used by the Argentine Fanning Hill Mob. It was an extremely cold and dark night and the patrol found great difficulty in the freezing darkness to accurately pinpoint their position. They had a clansman radio but there was no Battalion Net to talk to patrols from other Companies, albeit they believed also that they were the only patrol out that night. It was decided they would lay low until it was possible at first light to determine their bearings, which they did, and they started to make their way back to their Company lines. Unfortunately at some point they spotted a larger patrol, about 1,000 metres away, which was from C Company 3 Para, and despite the best endeavours from both patrols to ascertain if the other patrol was 'friend or foe' i.e. more of the Fanning Hill Mob (FHM), by communicating back to their respective Company Command Posts, it was somehow determined by each patrol that the other was the FHM, and the C Company patrol brought in artillery fire, and their own machine gun fire against the A Company patrol. Ironically it later transpired that the 11 members of the FHM that had managed to slip away from the SBS on D minus 1, had been watching this initial standoff, and subsequent battle, thankful they were not the recipients of this onslaught.

The upshot was that eight men from A Company were injured, some severely. A Sea king helicopter from 846 Naval Air Squadron was flown to recover the wounded, but crashed on landing, as its tail rotor ploughed into peat soil and was ripped off. A second Sea king was then successfully dispatched, and the victims – who were convinced they had been attacked by the Argentine FHM – were initially flown to the nearest Resuscitation doctor and Surgeon, which was on the LPD HMS Intrepid, as Surgeon Lieutenant Commander Tim Douglas-Riley and Surgeon Lieutenant Nick Morgan had only the previous day been sent from Surgical Support Team 2 at Ajax Bay to provide some surgical capability afloat within the Amphibious Flotilla (possibly to support potential SF operations). They had the ships medical staff and some patrol medics from the SAS with them when the casualties were received, and after some effort were able to get all eight casualties into the ship and stabilised as best they could, but with the limited space, poor access, and small team available, Tim Douglas-Riley and Nick Morgan needed no persuading that the group would, having received initial resuscitative care, be more easily managed at Ajax Bay. These eight casualties were then evacuated to Ajax Bay and were the first multiple casualties received at our location.

Resuscitation Doctor Surgeon Lieutenant Commander Tim Douglas Riley recollects the situation:

"Once we knew we had significant casualties to deal with we knew we could not do that without space. So, we commandeered a part of the Junior Rates Dining Hall near to the door. Many JR's were eating lunch and we had to evict them from their tables and set up eight bays using a dining table as the Resus trollies. All the JRs stood around, mug of tea in one hand and sandwich in the other, watching. We used them as an available working party to go get things, stretcher bearers anything that needed doing that was not technical. They were brilliant. Also, there was a detachment of SAS troopers on board and they stepped forward and offered their medics, who were trained to a high standard and proved very capable and useful".

Surgeon Nick Morgan also recalls the events:

'Sunday May 23rd – Another day of almost continuous air attack. Surprisingly, I slept during some of the 'Take Covers' despite determined defence by the Seacat (anti-aircraft missile) crews above the Sick Bay. A reception area was set up in the Gun Room. At midday, news was received of two casualties. Seven arrived. Two unconscious patients with severe penetrating head injuries, (these would have been Danny Blair and David Poole) one penetrating chest injury subsequently shown to traverse the diaphragm, (probably Richard Etches) a penetrating buttock injury with rectal bleeding, (this is likely to have been John Hare, given the extent of the injuries that he had received) a compound fractured femur from a high velocity missile (clearly this was Michael Stanton from Brendan McWilliams's earlier comments) and two patients with minor shrapnel injuries (one was Christopher Smith and it is possible that Brendan McWilliams's injuries may have been mistaken for shrapnel wounds at this time)'

Nick Morgan continues:

'The medical team on board was overwhelmed. The Junior Rates dining hall was converted into a reception area and the young

paratroopers were resuscitated but definitive surgery could not be carried out. The three patients in need of early surgery were evacuated to Ajax Bay (presumably, Danny Blair, David Poole and John Hare) where Surgeon Lieutenant Commander Phil Shouler's RN Surgical Support Team and the Para Field Surgical Teams continued their management, those with head injuries having been treated with intravenous mannitol steroids and antibiotics, before being transferred to the refrigeration plant at Ajax Bay'

And Tim Douglas Riley summarises:

'We really provided an assessment and resus service, doing essential lifesaving fluid replacement, arrest of haemorrhage etc. but no definitive treatment. I think all the casualties had high velocity GSWs and a couple were certainly very severely injured. One (John Hare) had a penetrating buttock wound but no exit wound, so we imagined that the round had done great damage inside the pelvis without coming out. (It had). He was a major resus issue. I cannot recall the evacuation plans but we always seemed to get a Helicopter when needed and so when we felt we could evacuate the casualties to Ajax Bay, it all just happened. I think this medial resus incident was a great example of resourcefulness, flexibility and co-operation. A real team effort in a completely unplanned situation, but by using the basic principles of casualty management it did not matter whether this was on a dining table or in a fully equipped hospital casualty department. We did our best in the circumstances. I do not think we had any idea, nor was it of any relevance, that we were dealing with Blue-on-Blue. You deal with what is in front of you. I only heard rumours later that it was a Blue-on-Blue'.

By this stage our Command Post had been notified of the casualties and our Squadron OC, Surgeon Commander Rick Jolly, was concerned they had not arrived. We then learnt that they were on Intrepid. We had a Sea King helicopter seconded at this time and Rick Jolly flew across to Intrepid and subsequently ensured the unfortunate casualties were evacuated (casevaced) ashore to Ajax Bay. Four were initially flown, followed by the remaining four, including the two Gunshot Head Wound cases who had been deemed unlikely to survive (Priority 4) on board Intrepid. We always just loaded stretchers onto the deck of the support helicopters, as a dedicated stretcher fit took far too long to load and unload.

Our Helicopter 'landing site' (HLS) was a very rough piece of ground full of large stones, about 100 yards from the facility entrance, up towards the hill along our West side that often helped to shelter us from the typical Falkland wind, that averaged 19 mph but would frequently blow much more severely. Not a single day seemed to be free of the wind. The HLS was not in a great location, but it was the best area available to us.

I joined a number of individuals, of all ranks and specialty, and helped to carry one of the stretchers into our facility. I could see they were in a mess, but had received Resuscitative care, which I had always assumed had been provided in the field. It was not until years later that I learnt that the lifesaving interventions were the handy work of Nick Morgan, Tim Douglas- Riley, and their helpers on Intrepid. Despite going on to serve alongside Tim at Teal Inlet and later in Stanley, this was to become 'just another incident' and we never discussed it for 38 years!

The incident required a full surgical response in the Field Hospital. But for Argentine Air Raids making it all but impossible for helicopters to risk a longer journey, it might have been better if some had gone directly to the Hospital Ship Uganda.

It was clearly a brutal and tragic incident, as you would expect when two elite Sections of Paratroopers exchange fire, and I subsequently learnt they had also been on the receiving end of numerous 105mm shells from 29 Commando RA! We were fortunate that the cool Falkland climate helped to minimise bleeding, and thus helped prevent casualties from bleeding to death (exsanguination).

Even the two head injury victims had their wounds operated on, and one had a bullet removed, whilst the other had his broken mass of exposed skull and brain significantly tidied up. I believe that both went on to survive. That none of the victims of this incident died seemed like a miracle, and it was certainly a triumph for the whole team. The casualties were all later safely evacuated to the Hospital Ship Uganda on D+4 25 May.

Air Attacks and HMS Antelope

The 3 Para incident had been a significant incident that had been a major distraction from the air raids, which had continued that day, typically involving two Argentine aircraft each raid. To this juncture, the tally of Argentine Jets being shot down since D day was 27. The demise of these determined and capable Argentine airmen was due much less to the Rapier land-based Air Defence Systems than it was to the ship borne Air Defence Systems, such as Seacat missiles; and small arms fire from ship and shore; and last but not least our amazing Harrier aircraft with their lethal Sidewinder missiles. The Rapier systems had been placed on higher ground and all too often could not engage the Argentine jets flying at extremely low level beneath them. They might have had better success if they had been set-up around the shoreline. The Argentine Air Force still outnumbered our Harriers by five or six to one, and each raid tended to achieve hits with their bombs, only to be hampered by the bomb fuses often not fully engaging.

Nonetheless, despite looking quite unscathed, the Type 21 frigate HMS Antelope had been hit by at least two such bombs that had failed to explode, and she was moved into the North of Ajax Bay, a few hundred yards from our Field Hospital, later that afternoon on 23 May.

Antelope had sustained bomb hits on her port and her starboard sides, and these bombs were lodged deep within the ship, having both failed to explode. A crewman, Steward Mark Stephens had already died as a result of this attack. Stewards normally form up with First Aid Parties when RN Ships are at Action Stations, and he is likely to been deployed in such a capacity when he was killed. One of the aircraft that attacked was reported to have been shot down by the ships 20mm anti-aircraft cannon.

Two army bomb disposal men boarded the ship at Ajax Bay, S/Sgt Prescott and WO Phillips. They made 3 failed attempts to withdraw a fuse from one of the bombs, and then a 4th attempt was made to neutralise it with a small amount of explosive charge. This detonated the bomb, killing S/Sgt Prescott instantly, and severely wounding WO Phillips, who was evacuated to us at the Field Hospital by LMA Paul Youngman who was serving with 45 Commando, who were deployed around us. An arm was beyond saving and he underwent an emergency operation to surgically amputate it. I collected the arm from the small operating team and carried it outside in a black plastic bag, up to our makeshift oil drum incinerator, situated on the NW corner of the exterior of the building, and it was disposed of in the incinerator, in burning hot oil. These were the sort of tasks that had to be undertaken, and there was no time to waver. I carry the memory of such tasks to this day, but I am grateful it was not me being operated on.

Meanwhile, the Captain of HMS Antelope Cdr Nick Tobin, had ordered the ship to be immediately abandoned. It had a huge hole just above the waterline, there was no electric power, its firefighting equipment was not functioning, and the ship was burning before our eyes. There were occasional explosions, and she burnt all night, and I wondered how such a metal structure could burn like it was.

It had been a long, tiring grim day, but somehow the Medical Squadron team at Ajax Bay had to try and snatch some sleep during the night, in order to face whatever was to be thrown at us tomorrow.

D+3 24 May 1982

In the morning the hulk of what was HMS Antelope was still burning a little, but she was still afloat. I thought I was just really lucky to be able to get a mug of hot tea and a hot 'compo' ration breakfast from our galley, and was again grateful to our cheerful chef, Marine Neil Blain, and our quartermaster staff who had prepared it for us.

Within a few hours HMS Antelope slipped below the water.

It was to be another day of precision air attacks being inflicted upon us by the Argentine Air Force. They clearly were targeting warships and facilities, and were either doing so from information gathered from their earlier air raid missions, or being directed by an individual who had visual sight of us. The Landing Ship Galahad, which had conveyed One Troop Medical Squadron from Ascension to San Carlos Water, was hit with one 500lb bomb which failed to explode, and all non-essential members of the crew were put ashore at Ajax Bay. The Hong Kong Chinese seamen off the ship, congregated at the immediate beach area, and sometimes, when we were taking cover in our somewhat shallow trenches, they would come and look at us! There was nowhere for them to go, and for the most part they stood in a huddle on the stony beach! The Landing Ship Lancelot was also hit, with two bombs that had similarly failed to go off. A Fleet Clearance Diving Team (FCDT) designated Naval Party 1890 (a bomb disposal team in plain language), who were also working with an RAF Bomb Disposal Team 1531, and both accommodated on LSL Bedivere, were dispatched to neutralise the bombs.

Meanwhile one of the attacking aircraft had been hit during its bomb run, and the pilot had ejected into the icy cold sea of San Carlos Water. He was rescued by HMS Fearless, and casevaced over to Ajax Bay. 1st Lt Ricardo Lucero was our first Argentine casualty. He had clobbered his left knee against the side of the cockpit canopy bottom rim whilst being ejected, and severely dislocated the knee joint. This painful injury was resolved as best as the situation allowed, by surgical intervention.

Ricardo could apparently not speak English but was either an affable individual, or very well tutored on how best to behave if you get caught! Fortunately, such circumstances never arose for me, but I always remembered how his response to us brought out the most supportive and caring response from ourselves. There was little or no animosity between him and our team, which was remarkable considering that the Argentine pilots were doing their utmost to kill us all. They were however paying a heavy price themselves, losing a further 8 aircraft that day, bring the total lost since D Day to 35.

The Navy Clearance Diving (bomb disposal) team, who had crossed from LSL Bedivere to LSL Lancelot in a small inflatable dingy, found themselves marooned in their dingy on completion of their risky task, when the Bedivere had weighed anchor and put to sea without them. They made their way to Ajax Bay in the dingy, in pitch darkness, and were guided ashore by an observant sentry.

Meanwhile, apart from the Argentine Pilot 1st Lt Ricardo Lucero, Medical Squadron is relatively quiet, and the 3 Para casualties are very much still with us, albeit the two head injury victims are still in a critical condition.

D+4 25 May 1982

I am not sure if this is the exact day, but at one point, whilst we have an Argentine patient being treated, a delegation of the Red Cross arrives to assess whether we are adhering to the Geneva Convention. There are several of them – I have no idea how they got to us in this remote corner of East Falkland – but they are dressed as if they were going on a shopping spree down London's Oxford Street. I hover about 10 yards away, just close enough to listen in, in case there are questions I have at my fingertips, but not so close as to have to host them. The fact that an Argentine is a casualty and being well treated and cared for, must surely be a good thing, but they seem to spend an inordinate amount of time cross examining various clinicians – just as if they were the Care Quality Commission inspecting an NHS Hospital. They clearly had little grasp of the brutal nature of the conflict and the serious limitations we were working under. I believe they were then taken to the Hospital Ship Uganda. A similar visit subsequently took place at Ajax Bay after One Troop was relieved by Three Troop Medical Squadron, despite the facility never being declared to the International Red Cross.

Contrary to what some were muting however, Argentina was a signatory to the Geneva Convention, and whilst their invasion was clearly improper, their Armed Forces did mostly adhere to the principles espoused by the convention.

Casualty Evacuation to Uganda. The casualties from 3 Para's Blue on Blue incident, and casualties from the bombing incidents, are all flown out to The Hospital Ship Uganda at 1250Z or 0950 local time. Five stretcher cases are squeezed into the Sea king helicopter, simply placing the stretchers on the floor, and a further four cases are seated. They are accompanied by the senior, most experienced surgeon ashore, Lt Col Bill McGregor who is the surgeon with No. 6 Field Surgical Team, with the Parachute Clearing Troop. The Uganda is in a relatively safe, declared, Red Cross Box, but it is some 50 miles to our North, and the flight, the first of many, is far from risk free. The 846 Naval Air Squadron equipped with Sea King 4's comprised half of the Commando Helicopter Force. 845 Naval Air Squadron provided the remaining half, and were equipped with the much older Wessex 5 helicopters that had less lift capability, but were very dependable. All the commando helicopters are used for a huge range of tasks, and none is dedicated permanently as Casualty Evacuation aircraft, so like our facility ashore, none carry Red Cross markings. There are actually benefits to casualties with such a system however, as in my experience, no patient suffered a delay caused by non-availability of helicopter assets. If casualties needed a helicopter as an urgent priority, they were always forthcoming. Only the utmost immediate serious tactical threat of fixed wing Argentine aircraft, or the most appalling weather, would cause a delay. When a support helicopter, Wessex 5 or Sea king 4, was provided on 'stand by' at Ajax Bay, it tended to be a magnet for our OC Surgeon Commander Rick Jolly, who clearly revelled in the role of 'Flying Doctor', (something that is quite apparent in his book, Red and Green Life Machine that was subsequently published in 1983).

The loss of HMS Coventry. Two warships had been moved into the North of Falkland Sound, the Type 22 frigate HMS Broadsword, and the Type 42 destroyer HMS Coventry. They were intended to act in tandem to provide an air defence shield for the amphibious ships and assets ashore in and around San Carlos Water. This was a good plan if attacking aircraft were flying North – South along the Sound (or vice versa), but if Argentine Aircraft were flying West to East or East to West over the two main land masses of East and West Falkland, and flying low, then both ships would experience difficulty detecting such aircraft, and their weapon systems would struggle to lock on. Broadsword had the most modern Seawolf missile system, which was normally very effective, and could lock on to targets and fire in a split second; but Coventry's medium range Sea Dart system would prove unable to lock on to targets traversing within the confined area of the Falkland Sound.

The two ships successfully brought down two Skyhawks. Coventry hit one with its Seadart missile system, to the North of Pebble Island, which lies just at the Northern edge of West Falkland, at the top of Falkland Sound. The pilot did not eject. The second was similarly brought down to the North of Pebble Island, and the Pilot ejected. It had been intended to launch a helicopter to search for the pilot, but the situation was overtaken by events.

Two waves of two Skyhawk jets then attacked these two vessels. The first wave of two, each armed with 1000lb bombs, made a very low approach over West Falkland, and neither ship was able to lock on to them to engage them, before they had released their bombs. One bomb bounced on the waves and onto the flight deck of Broadsword, smashing into and destroying its helicopter, but failing to explode. The other bomb failed to hit either ship.

90 seconds later the second wave were headed towards Coventry, which again had been unable to lock on and, with the exception of small arms fire, was defenceless. Coventry manoeuvred evasively, to try to be end on to the attack, as opposed to side on, which presents a broader target for the aircraft to hit. This time Broadsword's weapon system had locked on successfully, but unfortunately Coventry had moved between Broadsword and the attacking aircraft, prohibiting the firing of Broadswords Sea Wolf missiles. Coventry was struck by three 250lb bombs. One did not explode, but another destroyed the ship's Operations Centre when it exploded. The third bomb ripped into the ship's Engine Room, and destroyed the main bulkhead when it exploded, causing the ship to immediately flood and list over.

Within 20 minutes of the air raid, the crew of Coventry had abandoned the ship, and she had keeled right over and capsized, before sinking. 19 men were dead, and a further 30 injured. Another of the injured was to die of his severe wounds in 1983.

Although we received a fatality and ten casualties later at Ajax Bay, I knew none of the details of this sinking, nor its close proximity to Ajax Bay, until later in life when I was Chief Executive of the Coventry and Warwickshire Ambulance Service NHS Trust and researched the incident. I was shocked to learn that in addition to the 20 men who had died as outlined above, more than that, in the intervening years, had gone on to take their own lives. This truly reflects the horror of such an incident that the crew endured. None of the crew received any special medal or honour, but a huge number clearly were mentally if not physically scarred for years to come. Post-Traumatic Stress Disorder (PTSD) was in this single incident as great a threat to the long-term well-being of the crew, as the bombs that exploded.

The only fatality to arrive at Ajax Bay from HMS Coventry was a drowned Hong Kong Chinese laundryman, B.K Kye. He was the first fatality we received during the conflict, and must surely have been whisked from the ocean and dropped off at our location within minutes of entering the water, but unfortunately, he was very dead. The sea temperature was probably around 5 degrees C. The man was only wearing his number 8 action working dress, and the sea temperature alone could have caused him to die, but we assumed the cause of death was drowning. His details and personal effects were given to the Field Records Office that had co-located with our own Command Post (CP), and he was placed in a body bag. He was later laid to rest in a shallow grave – the stony ground prohibiting anything deeper - with a few of us gathered to lend some dignity to his departure, and to record the debt our Country owes him.

We went on to receive ten of the casualties from Coventry. Presumably the remainder were less serious and able to be treated by the Medical Officer on Broadsword. Rick Jolly was to later note in his book Red and Green Life Machine, (as he had christened our facility, reflecting that it was a Commando Green Beret and Parachute Red Beret staffed entity) that these casualties were mainly suffering from burns and shock, and they were treated with

Flamazine cream, (which was rather like Nivea face cream in its consistency, but with excellent antibacterial and healing properties). For my part, I honestly cannot recollect these casualties – only the fatality. I do not dispute they came through out facility; I think it serves to demonstrate how memories can soon be blurred when dealing with repeatedly bad situations. In fact, two of the most senior British officers to be treated at Ajax Bay, were both from HMS Coventry, namely Commander Lang RN and Lieutenant Commander Young, together with eight others from the crew.

The Loss of Atlantic Conveyor. We were also to learn of the loss of the merchant ship Atlantic Conveyor, which was a large roll on roll off, logistic supply vessel, carrying four Chinook Helicopters, and six Wessex. Only one Chinook was to survive. Atlantic Conveyor was also carrying countless logistic supplies to meet the needs of our ever increasing military presence on the ground, and the impending arrival of 3 further battalions due to arrive in the coming days to form a second brigade. She had been about 90 miles NE of Stanley when 2 Super Etendard jets, which had used in-flight refuelling to achieve the necessary range, had both unleashed Exocet Missiles against the lumbering giant merchant vessel. 12 of the crew died, including the Captain, Ian North. The ship was a burning inferno, but did not sink until 28 May, when a tug attempted to bring her under tow.

The loss of 3 Chinook was a particularly bitter blow to the logisticians. Wrestling with the need to fly 105mm shells forward to keep 29 Commando gunners supplied for example, the Chinooks were capable of lifting five or six times as much forward in a single lift compared to the Wessex and Sea Kings, but they were not of course as flexible in their ability to land in the difficult terrain that covered most of the North of East Falkland. A dwindling helicopter force that was coping to support all the disparate logistic and medical tasks of an expanded 3 Command Brigade, would surely be stretched to its limit soon, in trying to support an additional Brigade – and potentially on a second axis.

However, the Argentine forces had initially thought that they had hit one of our two Aircraft Carriers, and some media were quick to report this with jubilation in Buenos Aires. The loss of Atlantic Conveyor was a blow, and it made finishing the war more difficult, but the loss of one of our Carriers would have been dire, and the loss of life considerable. That a carrier had not been hit was good news, and my men and I grasped this straw of comfort!

QE 2 rendezvous. HMS Antrim, RFA Stromness, the liner Canberra, and the Ferry Norland, rendezvous at South Georgia, and 5 Brigade begin to cross-deck from the QE2, which was not being risked to run the gauntlet of air raids around the Falkland Islands.

D+5 26 May 1982

Despite setbacks, things were moving forward. I was always personally convinced that our mission was just, and the fact that 3 Command Brigade were ashore en-masse, with 2 and 3 Para within our order of battle, surely would ultimately lead to the defeat of the invading Argentine forces.

Hospital Ship Uganda was temporarily moved right inshore to Middle Sound which lies just below Foul Bay off the far North West edge of East Falkland. This enables casualties being treated on various vessels afloat, to be flown to the Uganda without embarking on what still would otherwise be a dangerous 50 mile flight to the designated Red Cross Box for the vessel. It also means that this casevac evolution can largely be conducted by helicopter assets afloat, without recourse to the Landing Force assets. Uganda returns to her 'Box' on completion of this evolution.

The Military Disposition: 2 Para. It transpires that the previous day, Col H Jones, the Commanding Officer of 2nd Parachute Regiment (2 Para) had been given a warning order by the Brigade Commander, Brigadier Julian Thompson, that 2 Para were to launch an attack on Argentine Forces at Darwin and Goose Green. 2 Para is detailed for this mission on the simple basis that Darwin is around 18 miles march from their current position, and they are the closest Unit.

As a former member of Naval Party 8901, the Moody Brook based Commando detachment, (Moody Brook being the modest camp for 8901 before it was blown up by the invading Argentines), I had visited Darwin and Goose Green twice, and was struck by how open and relatively flat the surrounding area was. In fact, the whole of the South of East Falkland from Darwin and beyond was vastly different to the North of East Falkland, as it was much flatter, and exposed. The route East from Darwin to Fitzroy similarly had a well-established track that was far more exposed than the barely discernible trails to the North that amounted to little more than a few tyre tracks where aging Land Rovers and tractors had transited infrequently between the settlements to the North. Through its NP8901 veterans, 3 Commando possessed unique knowledge of the Falkland Islands, and I knew that any orders to attack Darwin and Goose Green must have reflected some pressure on the Brigade to pursue such an axis. If I had this insight, I was surely not alone?

I would not have minded the march that lay ahead for 2 Para, but I did not envy anybody who had to carry out an assault against a force that had the time to dig in and defend itself. 2 Para move from their position to a point taking them about halfway to Camilla Creek House.

L Company 42 Commando are flown by support helicopters from Port San Carlos to the Sussex Mountains. Presumably to protect our South and West sides around San Carlos Water, and bearing in mind that Argentine forces were known to be occupying Port Howard on West Falkland, from which they could have launched raids across the Falkland Sound.

SBS are operating in strength around the North East of the Island at Port Salvador and Teal Inlet. This is an indication of the Brigade's intention to exploit this area. Teal inlet is capable of Landing Ships being brought in right to the shore, and this settlement is only about 30 miles from Stanley, less as the crow flies. Is this an opportunity to demonstrate the use of guile?

Ajax Bay. Whilst some Units were moving forward, and others redeploying in defensive positions, as outlined above, it was a relatively quiet day for the medical facility. I realised that in 5 days since coming ashore at Ajax Bay, I had not ventured beyond our own Squadron lines. Our galley facility had been consolidated towards the rear of the complex in the North to South Tee part of the building, close to where 45 Commando B echelon ammunition was stored, and I cannot recall going beyond the galley within the building. On the East to West narrow road that ran up alongside the building I ventured further West to collect arriving casualties from mainly 3 Brigade Air Squadron helicopters, or to load treated casualties into support helicopters for casevac to Uganda. My only other reason to head in this area, was to bury the dead, which was a necessary infection control measure and spiritual obligation. We had both a Catholic Priest, Noel Mullins, and an Anglican Priest, David Leighton, to preside over these events.

Five days after moving ashore I managed to pen my first letter home:

'Dear Bev, I hope everything is well at home and you are managing alright. The situation here can only be described as 100% war. Argentine fighter planes attack our positions daily. Nearly all of them are eventually shot down, but they cause havoc. We have an Argentine pilot in the dressing station – he ejected when he was shot down yesterday. He is the only one to be picked up alive so far.'

'We have lost several ships and many casualties arrive at our location. I don't think I can really say where that is Bev – we are right in the middle of it all!'

'Erich (Bootland –LT RN OC 3 Troop Medical Squadron) is still not ashore, but although he is a lot more comfortable than us here I don't envy him – his ship is a very big target. Eddy (Middleton – Petty Officer HQ Medical Squadron) is here and OK.'

'The worst thing about it all is lack of sleep. I seem to be permanently tired. This is the first letter I have written since D day. Both of the LSL's I came down on were hit by bombs two days ago, but both ships seem o.k. A lot of my personal belongings were still onboard though, e.g. camera etc., and people who came off the ships say a lot of kit is ruined. It is the least of my concerns though.'

'Two days ago we all watched one of our ships explode and sink. Strangely it was an event that lacked any emotion, we just watched it happen and went back to our chores.'

'Everything is quiet for the moment. It is a bit chilly here but it is clear and sunny.'

'Hopefully I'll have some letters from you soon. All my love and kisses. Take care Bev.'

D+6 27 May 1982
The Military Disposition

SAS D Squadron carry out a reconnaissance of Mount Kent. Kent rises about 1100 feet from sea level and is about 10 miles from Stanley. It gives a full view of the neighbouring mountains, particularly the Two Sisters which are only 3 miles further East, towards Stanley. Two Sisters were a dominant feature to the West of the NP8901 former base at Moody Brook. This reconnaissance gives an early indication of Anti-Personnel Mines having been utilised by the Argentine forces, but the scale of that problem was only to be fully realised a long time after the Argentinians were defeated, and a number of individuals were to lose lower limbs below the knee, as a result of this Argentine defensive strategy.

45 Commando move out from Ajax Bay, around the South of San Carlos Water, and heading East towards Teal Inlet, about 35 miles away.

3 Para move from Port San Carlos, also heading towards Teal Inlet, about 30 miles to their East.

42 Commando remain at Port San Carlos minus **L Company** which is now to the South of Ajax Bay on the Sussex Mountains.

40 Commando remain at San Carlos. A patrol later captures an Argentine Marine Officer, Lieutenant Commander Dante Camilette, who has been caught in a concealed position above San Carlos Settlement, conducting surveillance of our operations and assets in and around San Carlos Water.

2 Para are en-route to their start point for the assault on Argentine positions at Darwin and Goose Green.

29 Commando RA fly three 105 mm howitzer light guns South to support 2 Para

Special Forces. The SBS continue reconnaissance operations around Teal Inlet, and the SAS continue their reconnaissance operations in the area of Mount Kent, with all of D Squadron now located at this forward area.

Ajax Bay. Medical Squadron is having a relatively quiet day. The weather is less favourable than it has been, but it is still quite clement for this late in May, albeit the notorious Falkland wind is blowing more typically at around 20mph at sea level, and no doubt a good deal more than that on high ground. A Sea King takes casualties from the sinking of HMS Coventry from our facility ashore here, to the Hospital Ship Uganda.

Jon Clare records his recollections: *'It had been a busy six days mainly as a result of enemy air attacks affecting our ground and naval assets, but also notably a couple of friendly fire incidents, all serving to provide a flow of casualties from both sides of the conflict into the hospital. We were experiencing what I describe as 'trauma inoculation', that is a sort of desensitisation to the traumatic situations we had to tackle, which can be a necessary but slippery slope to climb out of. I'm not sure when exactly it happened, but at some point, me and my three teammates (Marines Jock Ewing, John Thurlow and Jim Giles) were 'selected' to assist in the identification and preparation of the dead for burial. This involved collecting personal effects and witnessing the cause of death for certification. What qualification or qualities we possessed for this task is a mystery, but we were happy to help with whatever we were asked to do.'*

Marine Jock Ewing, Cpl Jon Clare, and Marines John Thurlow & Jim Giles – dependable stalwarts!

The grim reality of war, as Argentine bodies await burial at Ajax Bay.
These fatalities were never admitted into the medical complex but instead
examined and determined to be dead upon arrival. They thus do not appear
on the admission and discharge log of casualties received at Ajax Bay.

Our Squadron OC, Surgeon Commander Rick Jolly, is at Brigade HQ in the morning to discuss various options to support the move East towards Stanley which is already underway. One of the options considered was to use the LPD, HMS Intrepid, and to set up a medical facility on its tank deck. Rick rightly remarks that this is feasible but less than satisfactory i.e., it should ideally only be considered as an option of last resort. Rick later writes in his book, Red and Green Life Machine, that he discussed this as an option later in the afternoon, with the senior surgeon from our RN Surgical Support Team 2 (SST2), Surgeon Lieutenant Commander Phil Shouler, who was a Registrar from the RN Hospital Plymouth. What I can say is that he never shared any such discussions or considerations with me, his Troop Commander whom he will expect, with the rest of One Troop Medical Squadron, to set up and provide all the necessary facilities and including all other clinical, and non-clinical staff, who are equally essential (ranging for example from electrical generator maintenance and circuit provision, to catering for staff and patients, and defence of our location. I relied on gleaning 'intel' regarding our Brigade's disposition and intentions, from our parent Commando Logistic Regiment RM.

Two Argentine casualties with Gunshot Wounds (GSW) were flown in by 3 Brigade Air Squadron later in the afternoon at about 1700Z (1400 local) – probably from engagements with our Special Forces. Both individuals are initially admitted through reception, and the triage process determines they will require operative care for penetrating wounds. Major Treatments prepares them for surgery, invoking standard treatment regimes, and resuscitation protocols, whilst both Surgeons of the Field Surgical Teams, Lt Col Bill McGregor, and Maj Charles Batty, are again on shift and ready their teams. It is now about 1800Z (1500 local)

The Bombing of Ajax Bay and San Carlos

At 1900Z (1600 local) the galley is open. It is catering for well over 200 men of the Commando Logistic Regiment, including Medical Squadron, as well as other elements now operating within the increasingly tight confines of this Brigade Maintenance Area (BMA), such as the combined RN/RAF Bomb Disposal Unit, and support helicopter riggers for internal and external (underslung) loads, including a team to load/rig the sole UK Chinook to have survived the Exocet hit on Atlantic Conveyor, and a number of individuals from 45 Commando. The galley was staffed mainly by Command Logistic Regiment chefs but also some who had been allocated to 45 Commando's RAP.

There are no plates or cutlery provided; it is a field galley and everyone uses their own mess tins, and 'eating irons' (Forces slang for Knife, Fork, and Spoon). Washing up is done in a single soapy bucket and rinsed in a (supposedly) clear water bucket!

Most of this significant number of 'diners' have collected their compo meal, and, by the grace of good fortune, moved out of the galley area, including myself. I eat my meal, wash my mess tins and KFS, and am moving around our medical facility with a mug of tea in one hand, ensuring all the clinical areas are functioning OK and that patients are being properly provided for; that the generator is filled with fuel for the night ahead, and the temperature of the facility is adequate.

Whistles Blew! Air Raid Red came the shout. Across San Carlos Water, two aircraft are dropping bombs – trying to knock out our Brigade HQ. Two Argentine Casualties are both being operated on under anaesthetic, so both teams continue, as all teams have previously. There is no sense of panic. We have done this relentlessly over the past 6 days, and there is a sense that going outside to a shallow trench is probably little safer than staying inside. Having checked everything is OK and all required patient care was being attended to, tea mug still in hand, I walk out of the main front door, just as an Argentine jet is roaring just above the top of the building and over my head. I instinctively kneel down on one knee just across the trackway, still holding my mug of tea. A really loud explosion goes off behind me within the building I have just left, and a bomb comes through the top of the building, bouncing about 5 yards from me down me towards the beach. It bounces with such velocity that it goes a good 200 yards away towards the beach area that the ill-fated HMS Antelope had been anchored off before she sank.

Four frigates, HM Ships Argonaut, Arrow, Plymouth, and Yarmouth are anchored in San Carlos Water, helping to provide anti-aircraft defence cover to the Landing Force, and there are four amphibious ships also, the two LPD's HM Ships Fearless and Intrepid, and 2 LSL's, namely One Troop Medical Squadron's familiar ships, the RFA's Galahad and Lancelot. All their weapon systems retaliate against the aircraft creating an inimitable scene one normally only sees on a World War 2 film. Another Argentine

Jet follows the leading one over Ajax Bay, and a second loud explosion goes off.

45 Commando B echelon has significant quantities of ammunition piled high, including Milan missiles and 7.62 ammunition, around the immediate area of the bomb blast, and pallets of mortar bombs on the helicopter LZ 30 yards from the heart of the blast. The sole Chinook, Bravo November, had only just landed when the Air Raid Red alert came in, and it had taken off with riggers just having boarded, just in the nick of time! It managed to land safely close to San Carlos settlement.

Another helicopter, a Mk 5 Wessex, had been on a fuel resupply mission for the sole Rapier anti-aircraft missile system to the West above our position, and that too had managed to lift off and land further to the South i.e., towards the oncoming Skyhawks.

The Rapier system mentioned above, unfortunately was not the latest 'blind fire' variant, so it was no use at night and its team had just shut its generator down for the night when the attack came in. Had it not been shut down the situation that ensued might have been averted. Two hand held Blow Pipe missiles were fired by a Royal marine Blow Pipe detachment located at Ajax Bay, as the aircraft flew over, but unfortunately both narrowly missed their targets.

Yet a third helicopter, a Wasp from HMS Yarmouth, was at Ajax Bay, and it was caught hovering with an underslung load of sandbags, but managed to avoid damage.

The ammunition dump also immediately started to explode as a fire burnt through it – possibly caused by anti-aircraft fire from the ships! It was impossible to try to contain it – to do so would surely have cost more lives. And lives had been lost.

Across at San Carlos 2 men had died. Marine McAndrews and Sapper Gandhi were sadly killed outright. Marine Jeffreys was injured and flown direct to Uganda. Brigade HQ was not damaged however.

Between HMS Fearless and HMS Intrepid they certainly could claim to have hit one of the second wave of aircraft, as smoke started to trail from it. The aircraft managed to reach West Falkland before the Pilot ejected safely to the North West of Port Howard. The wreckage of the aircraft later showed its clock had stopped at 1950Z (1650 local) so this is the latest possible time the aircraft crashed, and just 5 minutes after the Air Raid Red warning was given. The pilot headed off on foot towards Fox Bay as he apparently feared Argentine forces at Port Howard may have surrendered. He took refuge in a shepherd's cabin until 31 May when 3 Falkland shepherds on horseback came across him and advised the Argentinians at Port Howard of his plight. A second of the attacking aircraft is reported to have been shot down by a Harrier on Combat Air Patrol.

Because of the situation with the exploding ammunition dump, with projectiles being hurled in all directions and at all angles for what seemed at least 2 hours, it was not at first possible to determine accurately what the casualty situation was. 5 men died, and another 17 were injured. So, with the sun long since set, and darkness having fallen, we got on with the task of treating our wounded, and clearing up a bloody mess. The two Field Surgical Teams had continued to operate on the Argentine wounded soldiers that had been brought in earlier in the day, and a number of other staff had stayed at their respective posts throughout. Now the RN Surgical Support Team also prepared their tables, to operate on the victims of this attack.

It was a scene of carnage, and it was tragic that 5 of our comrades had died, and 27 injured, 17 seriously. LMA Paul Youngman from 45 Commando, recently reminded me that 3 of the dead, and one of the wounded, comprised his First Aid Team. But the Hospital was largely undamaged, and whilst the loss of ammunition was a setback, all this was relatively minor compared to what might have happened had all the bombs gone off. It appears on this occasion that the bombs were fitted with parachutes to slow their drop and allow their tails to spin and arm the bombs. This requires the bombs to be dropped at least 100 feet above the ground however, and the fact that some bombs had, yet again, not exploded, indicates that the aircraft were not 100 feet above the sea, let alone the ground. As all observers were to comment, the aircraft were barely above the roof height of the buildings, and that is between 30 or 40 feet above the ground.

Jon Clare adds his personal recollection of the terrible events: *'My short walk to the rear of the evening meal queue was interrupted with whistle blasts signalling an impending air raid, followed shortly after by the screech of at least two Argentine Skyhawk jets hugging the opposite coastline near the Brigade HQ. I caught sight of the jets and immediately realised this could just be the first wave of an attack. I remember turning to the guys, we all had the same idea - get back to the trench and man the guns! We got back to the trench just in time as the first Skyhawk appeared over the top of a small hill 150 metres to our south at about 100 feet altitude flying directly towards us. All the details, rivets and bombs underneath the aircraft, clearly visible. Another Skyhawk was just behind the first but lower and at more of an angle to us. The next few seconds seemed to last an entire age as so many things happened concurrently; as grey bombs were released from both aircraft, parachutes retarding them...hitting the hospital, and one bouncing just the other side of the road but failing to explode, and friendly weapons firing from all over the BMA. There was a smaller explosion from the nearby hillside as shoulder mounted hand held Blowpipe anti-aircraft missiles engaged. Jock Ewing, incredible, firing the GPMG from the shoulder (OK when you're big enough), me and the rest unloading hundreds of rounds at the leading edges of the aircraft as they swept past. Tracer rounds criss-crossed the dimming evening sky. Absolute bedlam! Chances of blue on blue all over the area, including from and to the ships in the bay. I remember watching as one of the 500lb bombs fell from the bottom of the Skyhawk, its parachute oscillating weakly behind, and explode on its target, the rear of the hospital and 45 Commandos B Echelon area. Then, wallop!*

A second ear shattering explosion followed by another immense and reverberating shock wave. The ammunition stockpile had been hit and had started secondary explosions. Chaos, noise, confusion as darkness began to fall. We could see, remarkably, that the hospital had been largely spared but other areas were badly damaged. Unable to move initially, due to live ammunition popping all around us, we eventually climbed out to help where we could. We'd taken casualties, including the Regiment's Provost team whose bunker was behind the building that took the brunt of the blast. I said goodbye to one of my closest friends later that evening'.

Later that night the Hospital Ship Uganda is brought right into Grantham Sound, between San Carlos Water and Goose Green, to receive our casualties.

Men returning from a burial service at Ajax Bay. The bomb damage to the roof is clearly visible.

Argentine Fixed Wing Air Attack Assets

It is worth examining the Argentine Air assets, and their losses at this juncture. As previously mentioned, UK Forces claimed 40 Argentine aircraft had been shot down by the end of 25 May, and a further 2 aircraft today 27 May, but had some of these losses been double counted, for example by two ships claiming the same aircraft?

Skyhawks. The aircraft in the raid at Ajax Bay on the evening of 27 May 1982 were all A4B Skyhawks. Douglas Skyhawks first flew in 1952 and remained in production for 25 years. It is worth remembering that the English Electric Lightning was in service with the RAF until the late 1980's and had been developed during the same era. The USA sold Argentina its reconditioned Douglas Skyhawks between 1966 and 1970. At the outset of their invasion 35 type A4B and 15 A4C aircraft were in service with the Argentine Airforce, and 8 A4Q variants were operational with their Navy. 58 Skyhawks in total. They claim to have flown 231 missions and they all required mid-air refuelling to operate over the Falklands. The Argentines report 20 were lost in action, and two had been lost over the Jason Islands to the far West of West Falkland, during their invasion of the Islands (possibly a mid-air collision or Blue on Blue?). So, the Argentine summary is 58 originally in service; 22 lost.

Daggers. Argentina had 30 operational Israeli Nesher which it renamed as Daggers. These aircraft were Mirage 5's with Israeli avionics. Israel had built them from 1971 and they flew in the 1973 Yom Kipur war. They were not equipped for mid-air refuelling and had to fly using the shortest possible corridor to the Falkland Islands, to enable them to return to Argentina. This only gave the aircraft 10 minutes over the Archipelago to find and attack their targets. They claim to have flown 153 missions, and to having lost 11 such aircraft.

Dassault Mirage Mk 3. Argentina had 12 operational Mirage 3 at the start of the conflict, having purchased 10 new single seat and 2 new twin seat aircraft which started to be delivered from September 1972. During the Falkland war they were mainly kept on the mainland, in case Vulcan Bombers or Harriers attacked Argentina. However, they also reported them having flown 58 'decoy' missions (including on 8 June). Two of these aircraft were lost, on the day of their invasion, when one was brought down by a Harrier's Sidewinder missile, and the second was hit by Argentine forces at Stanley Airport, who mistook the aircraft for a UK asset.

They flew their last mission of the war escorting Canberra Bombers over Mount Kent on 12 June 1982.

Super Etendard. The Argentine Navy had just 5 of these aircraft, and one had been cannibalised for spares before the start of the invasion, thus 4 were operational. They were all capable of firing Air to Surface Exocet missiles, but they had just 5 of these deadly weapons. British Military Intelligence had worked tirelessly to prevent more falling into their hands. This was fortunate, given the lethality of the system. Argentina reported no losses of the 4 Super Etendard.

Pucara. Argentina had 25 of these aircraft at the start of the invasion, and all but one was deployed to the Falkland Islands. These were twin engine ground attack turbo prop aircraft capable of posing a significant threat to the UK Landing Force. 12 were lost, and the majority of these were destroyed during the SAS raid on Pebble Island. A further 11 were seized when the Argentine forces surrendered. Just one Pucara appears to have made its way back to Argentina.

C130. One of these was used to bomb the tanker British Wye on 29 May just North of South Georgia, where the QE2 had cross decked 5 Brigade to the Canberra, Stromness, and Norland. The aircraft was shot down 3 days later.

Aermacchi N-339 Six of these modern Italian jet trainers/attack aircraft, which first flew in 1976, were in service with the Argentine Navy, and deployed via Stanley Airport for re-fuelling. 2 were lost, one of them at Goose Green, brought down by 3 Commando Air Defence Troop.

Summary of Argentine Admitted Air Losses. Argentina therefore confirmed losing 22 Skyhawk; 11 Daggers; 2 Mirage; 12 Pucara; and one C130; 2 Aermacchi; with a further 11 Pucara seized on conclusion of the surrender. Total lost/seized: 61

D+7 28 May 1982

Aftermath of the Bombing of Ajax Bay. Unfortunately, with the exception of the bombs that had exploded, and the one that had bounced by my side and landed on the beach, there were a number unaccounted for, and the RN and RAF Bomb disposal teams who had only recently joined our growing numbers at Ajax Bay, were already on the case. Towards the rear of our complex, close to where we had all gathered earlier to get our evening meal, two 500lb bombs, with their parachutes still attached are found. One is lodged in the roof-work above, and another is lodged in what looks like old plant machinery. There is a discussion between the RAF Bomb disposal team leader, Flt Lt Alan Swann, our boss Surgeon Commander Rick Jolly, and Colonel Ivar Hellberg CO Command Logistic Regiment. Alan Swann points out that in normal circumstances the presence of UXB's dictated evacuating the area, but these were not usual circumstances; casualties were already being treated and operated on, and the BMA was about to swing into action to support the 2 Para attack at Goose Green. The Brigade Commander arrived, and the decision was confirmed that the BMA would hold fast.

Alternative Medical Facility Reconnaissance. I was immediately tasked with going to Port San Carlos to explore the feasibility of establishing a medical facility at that location. Two Rigid Raiding Craft from Raiding Squadron were made available. I briefed my signaller Marine Steve Gosling and one of my JNCO's Corporal Cy Worrall - I had three excellent RM JNCO's as the selection process for their promotion to Corporal was extremely rigorous, (the other two were Tim (aka Tom) Robinson, and Jon Claire) but Cpl Worrall was an Assault Engineer and therefore had a broader knowledge of explosives, and I had thought, whilst Steve Gosling and I had cleared the former refrigeration plant of debris on D day, that Cpl Worrall would have been useful if we had encountered a possible Improvised Explosive Device, or needed to consider blowing anything else up. So, at 0130Z with our Bergan back packs, and armed just as we were when we first landed, we climbed aboard one of the raiding craft. It was a still night, the wind having dropped, so the sea state was quite calm. The coxswain manoeuvred the craft out of the bay, opened the throttle and we sped off.

We were progressing very well, and it was good to take in some fresh air. After some time, we ran into thick 'pea soup' fog. The coxswain carried on without easing off the throttle, and I was just thinking how remarkable it was that this chap had such confidence in the bearing we were headed, when we crashed ashore on a pebble beach that was clearly the eastern side of San Carlos water, and not the Northern Port San Carlos side. The coxswain had mistaken a small cove for the mouth of San Carlos river estuary. We were still about a mile from what is known as Hospital Point which is at the river mouth, although it is actually very much part of the huge San Carlos Water Inlet. The tide was low and that had not helped. We examined the hull and found no damage, so we got the craft back afloat, and continued on our way, but the coxswain was far more cautious, and the final couple of miles probably took another 40 minutes.

We finally arrived at the jetty and climbed the steps from the bottom – reflecting the low tide. It was still dark, so we waited for daylight before taking a look at the settlement. This was my third visit, but the previous occasions were in 1977/78 when as part of NP8901 OC's patrol group we had crossed to West Falkland from the jetty, and returned several days later, having visited Port Howard, Fox Bay, the Shepherds Hut which the Argentine Pilot had taken refuge (and was in 1977 lived in by an ex-pat shepherd), and even crossed to Pebble Island using the MV Forest.

A rigid raiding craft at full throttle in San Carlos Water.

Despite 3 Para and L coy 42 Commando having moved forward; Port San Carlos was a hive of activity and there were no suitable buildings or land that a tented facility might be established. The settlement had also been earmarked as a landing site for Harrier jets should they need to operate ashore, and this was the final factor that put paid to the possibility of utilising Port San Carlos as a site for a medical facility. We returned to Ajax Bay and I briefed Surgeon Commander Rick Jolly of my conclusions, as well as the 'difficulty' we had encountered en-route. He fully accepted the situation, and we turned our focus on to supporting 2 Para who had started their assault to liberate Darwin and Goose Green.

The Battle to Liberate Darwin and Goose Green.

We had been climbing the steps of the small wharf at Port San Carlos when, unheard and unseen by us, the Frigate HMS Arrow began firing its 4.5inch gun at Argentine positions around Darwin and Goose Green. From 0335Z until 0505Z (0035 to 0235 local) the ship fired 22 star shells, and 135 high explosive shells. 29 Commando RA also fired 105mm shells. This was to enable 2 Para to move to their start line just to the North of Burntside pond, at the North end of the Darwin and Goose Green Isthmus, roughly 4k from the small Darwin settlement. This Isthmus is barely 2k wide and significantly less wide at some pinch points. From the 2 Para start point, to the South of the Isthmus, is about 9k. (So, 1.25 miles wide, 5.3 miles long). Like most of the Falklands it is a treeless landscape, with dense gorse bushes in places, and very low undulations.

As they moved to the start line, none of 2 Para had any idea of the scale of the Argentine forces they had been sent to dislodge. Estimates from an SAS patrol were reassuringly low, but the Brigade Commander Julian Thompson had also received intelligence indicating the area could have the equivalent of 3 fighting companies dug in. In fact, at the end of this battle, which was to last 14 hours, and was to prove the longest single engagement of the war, it transpired, according to Argentine figures, there were 1083 Argentine troops on this narrow isthmus.

Argentine Forces and Defences. Three Companies from two different Argentine Infantry Regiments had been combined and deployed to the isthmus. Each Company had 3 platoons of about 45 men, and a support section with two 7.62 general purpose machine guns and 4 recoilless 3.5" bazookas, plus the company HQ.

Firstly, there were two companies from Infantry Regiment RI 12. These were mostly conscripts, from sub-tropical Corrientes in Northern Argentina. These troops had only received the minimum basic training, with only a few months service, and they were not used to the Falkland weather. Their third company was on Mount Kent, thus the integration of RI 25 which was considered an elite force, with around 50 of its men having attended an Argentine commando training programme known as Halcon 8.

These Companies formed the main forward defence of the location, and despite their very different levels of experience, they are reported to have been well motivated and committed to their task. With respective HQ sections and support platoons their total number was probably around 600.

The site was additionally defended by two 35mm Oerlikon anti-aircraft radar-controlled cannon, which had already hit a Harrier on 2 May, causing it to crash, killing its pilot. These cannon were capable of being deployed in a ground support mode. There were also three 105mm howitzers (the same number of 29 Commando 105mm light guns available to 2 Para should they choose to request close fire support).

The ground had been prepared with interlocking trenches, and, ominously, was shielded with multiple beds of anti-personnel and anti-tank mines. The largest mine bed was at the northern entry to the isthmus, South of the mere known as Burntside pond. Others were positioned to prevent amphibious landings from the East and West onto the land around the settlements. It was a well determined defensive position, and in addition to the forces identified above, there were around 500 other Argentine military personnel, all (except possibly their priest) armed. Argentine Airforce cadets for example guarded the Airfield which lay about 500 metres WNW of the main Goose Green settlement.

2 Para assault. The BBC had apparently alerted the world of the impending attack on Darwin and Goose Green by 2 Para, in a news broadcast the day before, and this might have enabled the Argentine forces to ensure their defences were honed to the maximum. However subsequent post war Argentine accounts indicate their Senior Commanders believed it was a ruse, (just as British Intelligence had managed to persuade Hitler in WW2 that the D Day landings 38 years earlier were going to take place around Calais!). Nonetheless, whether they believed the BBC or not, the naval gunfire and artillery bombardment will have caused them to ponder whether this was still a ruse or a very clear signal of imminent attack.

Two forward Argentine platoons reported 50% of their men killed or severely wounded as 2 Para's 4 companies pressed forward. During these early encounters L/Cpl Gary Bingley and Pte Barry Grayling from D Company were hit attacking a machine gun position just 10 metres in front of them. Gary Bingley had a head wound that was to prove fatal. He was posthumously awarded the Military Medal. Barry Grayling was hit in the hip. Surviving, he was awarded the Queen's Gallantry Medal.

One of the Argentine platoons put down delaying fire, to enable them to fall back to Darwin Ridge. From here they directed their 105mm howitzers and 120mm mortars onto 2 Para who continued to press home their attack. It was now about 1030Z (0730 local) and daylight was breaking. Alpha company 2 Para were pinned down at the bottom of Darwin Hill and Col H Jones, led a charge up a gully with his close escort Sgt Barry Norman, adjutant Captain David Wood, and the 2ic of A Company, Captain Chris Dent, and Cpl David Hardman. All but Col Jones and Sgt Norman were killed. With a 148 Forward Commando Observation Post hidden with eyes on this position, capable of bringing in direct artillery and naval gunfire support if the Battalion had sought it, these deaths were controversial, as some felt they were avoidable.

Col Jones and Sgt Norman moved West at the foot of this small hill, and Col Jones again turned up the hill towards the Argentine trenches. He was hit with two rounds and died within minutes. He was posthumously awarded a Victoria Cross.

A Scout helicopter from 3 Brigade Air Squadron flew forward to evacuate Col Jones. Piloted by Lt Richard Nunn RM the helicopter was shot down by two Pucara from Stanley Airfield, killing Richard Nunn and injuring his aircrewman, Sgt Bill Belcher, with penetrating bullet wounds to both legs. Sgt Belcher was fortunate to survive. Richard Nunn received a posthumous Distinguished Flying Cross. Two Gazelles went on to evacuate some of the wounded casualties, that had managed to be evacuated back to the Battalion Aid Post further to the rear, and a second Scout rescued Sgt Belcher and brought back the body of Richard Nunn.

As the weather deteriorated only one of the Argentine Pucara, that had attacked Richard Nunn's Scout helicopter, returned safely to

Stanley. It would be a further 4 years before the wreckage of the other aircraft was found.

2 Para mortars had fired 1,000 shells to this juncture, helping to minimise further losses being inflicted upon the Battalion, but was this a missed opportunity to also use 29 Commando's light guns, which had been used with such accuracy during the unfortunate 'blue on blue' incident involving 3 Para?

The Argentines were to experience a massive blow to their morale when an air strike involving 5 Skyhawks, which they had summoned to hit 2 Para, instead hit their own lines, and resulted in their own anti-aircraft cannon returning fire and damaging an aircraft.

2 Para continued their advance just before 1500Z. Major Chris Keeble as acting CO, and Major Dair Farrar-Hockley's A company cleared the East flank of the Argentines, forcing a way past their trenches. Major John Crossland's B Company overcame equally heavy resistance at Boca Hill. Both company commanders were awarded Military Medals, reflecting their steadfast determination and leadership, and a Cpl David Abols was awarded a Distinguished Conduct Medal for daring charges at Darwin Hill.

Now C and D companies made their way to the airstrip, and towards Darwin School, about 500 metres East of the airstrip. B Company headed towards the southerly end of Goose Green.

At this point the Argentine 35mm anti-aircraft cannon were targeted at C Company, and it was extremely destructive, hitting a fifth of the company, and killing Signaller Mark Holman-Smith. D company also took casualties when they were ambushed by members of IR25 in yet more trenches, who shot Lt Jim Barry and Cpl Paul Sullivan, repeatedly. They seriously wounded Pte (Brummie) Mountford. L/Cpl Nigel Smith fired a 66mm rocket, which he aimed towards the trenches, but it exploded upon firing, fatally wounding him in his chest and face.

Pte Carter rallied the survivors of 12 Platoon and led them forward to capture the airfield. Carter was awarded the Military Medal for his actions. Some of the Argentine RI 25 managed to slip away, but only because an Argentine, Sgt Sergiio Garcia, had covered their withdrawal, and he himself was mortally wounded. There were unbelievable acts of heroism displayed at Goose Green by both sides of this conflict, and that served to demonstrate just how courageous the young Paratroopers were, because they were pitted against a determined adversary.

3 Harriers had been called in, and they attacked the 35mm cannon and smaller 20mm anti-aircraft weapons that had been trained on the C Company with such deadly effect. There is some dispute about the effectiveness of this intervention, but the combination of this air strike and more mortar rounds laid the cannon silent, and that was clearly a major boost to the assault. The Argentines responded with a Napalm armed Pucara from Stanley, which was shot down by small arms fire from the Paratroopers – drenching them in Napalm which fortunately did not ignite but must have been freezing as it slowly evaporated off their kit. The pilot survived the crash and was captured. An Aermacchi jet was also shot down by a Blowpipe missile fired by the RM air defence troop. The pilot of this aircraft, Sub Lt Daniel Miguel, was less fortunate.

C company were in a bad state after their encounter with 35mm cannon and IR25 forces. Their OC was wounded, the 2ic was missing, and the platoons were spread over a 1.2 square km area. D Company had regrouped to the West of some agricultural sheds, but all the Paratroopers would have near empty water bottles and meagre rations had to be shared between them.

Casualty Treatment. 2 Para will have used a similar 'buddy care' system as Commando Units, whereby the nearest individual, situation permitting, will strive to administer immediate first aid care, including maintaining an **airway** to ensure the casualty is **breathing,** applying the victims own shell dressing to cover a wound and stem **bleeding,** and maintaining a healthy **circulation**

of oxygenated blood, whilst administering pain relieving morphine if required, which each individual carried round their necks. Administering any care under these circumstances, is extremely difficult. You struggle to remove clothing to enable a dressing to be well applied and find you often can't get at the individuals own shell dressing because it's been taped to their webbing for example, or their webbing is preventing access to the top pocket, where they were advised to stow it. You yourself are beyond tired, and being shot at, whilst trying to do your level best for your oppo' (opposite number). You do this because you know your mate may well die if you don't, and you carry on until hopefully relieved by a combat medic (or RN Commando Medical Assistant -Cdo MA- in the Commando Units), or until you have to leave your mate to carry on the advance. This is the reality of first line casualty treatment. They will strive to evacuate the wounded to the Regimental Aide Post (RAP) which is the first point they are likely to see a doctor, but such aid posts also have to focus on the basics of airway and bleeding, if necessary, inserting an airway or intubating. If treated by the Combat Medic or Commando MA at point of wounding, they similarly strive to maintain the airway, stem bleeding, and set up infusions to maintain reasonable blood pressure. It is unlikely many men were able to make their way back to their RAP at Goose Green.

3 Brigade Air Squadron - Casualty Evacuation. Despite this precarious situation, 3 Brigade Air Squadron mounted an unprecedented casualty evacuation rescue mission that has been totally underestimated in its feat, and barely mentioned in any literature, save those that refer to the arrival of the casualties at Ajax Bay. At 1900Z (1600local), at great risk to the pilots and aircrew, having already lost a Scout Helicopter earlier that day attempting to retrieve the body of Col H Jones, every helicopter that 3 Brigade Air Squadron could muster from their remaining 12 (having started the campaign with 15), flew into the carnage that was Goose Green, and each helicopter, flying rations, water and ammunition forward, then often collecting 2 stretcher and one walking casualty, flew them back to Medical Squadron at Ajax Bay, with their large forward beam lights blazing. They did this continuously until, as light was rapidly fading, they had conveyed all 2 Para's casualties and significant numbers of Argentine wounded too. At Ajax Bay, we thought we had received the last of the wounded, but in the distance came the sound of one more Scout, and so it was that with a torch lit T on our improvised helicopter landing site, Captain John Baker was the last casualty received from Goose Green that evening. He required 4 units of blood – the most I can recall given to any casualty on either side of the conflict, and then underwent a successful operation undertaken by Lt Col Bill McGregor of 6 Field Surgical Team, to remove a 7.62mm round (i.e., bullet) that had penetrated the patient's torso on the right side, within a hair's whisker of his liver. The 7.62 round was identical to those used by British forces, as the Argentines were, somewhat ironically, equipped with the same British made Self Loading Rifles (SLR's), and unlike smaller, higher velocity rifles such as the US Armalite which used 5.56mm rounds (as was used by the Commandos Mountain and Arctic Warfare Cadre throughout the conflict), the 7.62 rounds would cause maximum internal damage, and often leave a huge exit wound. The Armalite would often incapacitate, whilst the SLR would also severely mutilate. Field surgery was miles apart from modern keyhole surgery. It required wounds to be cut wide open, bleeding stopped, dead tissue excised (debridement), and the removal of offending foreign bodies. Wounds would not be closed, as this could seal in infection, allowing wounds to fester and gas gangrene to flourish. The wounds would require a second exploratory operation aboard the Hospital Ship Uganda, to ensure all dead tissue had been excised, and that no infection was present. Such secondary operations, known as Delayed Primary Closure (DPC) needed to take place within 7 days of the initial procedure. (I do not pretend to be a Surgeon nor even have a civilian recognized medical qualification however, and emphasise these details are based on the knowledge that I had gleaned as a Commando MA in the 1970's – rather like RN and RM Pilots, none of which had a civilian licence to fly! My role was no longer hands-on clinical provision, except when the situation demanded. It was normally more that of medical facility provider, from siting, to setting up, equipping, supplying, and ensuring adequate staff provision, standards of care, and external and internal communications to receive and evacuate casualties, defence of location, heating, lighting, cooking; and such like).

But for the actions of 3 Brigade Air Squadron, a significant number of these casualties, who all survived to be evacuated to the Hospital Ship Uganda, would have had significantly reduced odds for a positive outcome. Many casualties owe their lives as much to the pilots and aircrew who flew them rearward, as they do to the medical teams at Ajax Bay. This was to be a familiar story that was repeated time and again as 3 Brigade Air Squadron were to establish a forward arming and refuelling operating base at **Teal Inlet** as the war advanced, and **One Troop Medical Squadron** were to move forward early, later supported with members of **5 Field Surgical Team,** at what was to become 3 Commando Brigades **Forward Brigade Maintenance Area.**

Last Light at Goose Green. At last light, Argentine helicopters, a Puma, a Chinook, and six Hueys, landed to the South of the isthmus with the RI company B members that had been on Mount Kent.

A company 2 Para were still occupying Darwin Hill 3km North of the airfield. B company were however much further South having initially progressed along the Western edge of the isthmus, they had then moved East to the South of Goose Green Settlement, and for them the arrival of more IR12 Argentine troops was not what they had hoped for, but they called in 29 Commando artillery support, causing some of the IR12 to re-embark on the helicopters before they took off to avoid the bombardment. Other remnants of IR12 dispersed in the darkness and according to Argentine accounts, managed to get back to their own Regiment, now all sheltering within the Goose Green settlement.

The reception of Casualties at Ajax Bay.

The first casualties to arrive back at Medical Squadron, Ajax Bay, were from the initial assault on Darwin Ridge that caused the death of Col H Jones, his Adjutant, the 2ic of A Company, and 3 Paratroopers. There were a further 11 wounded from 2 Para to this juncture and the Argentines had also suffered 18 dead and 39 wounded, and some of these wounded were also arriving, whilst others had been able to struggle back to Goose Green Settlement to receive treatment from their own medics. At Ajax Bay in and around our medical facility it was 'all hands to the pumps' as everyone was focussed on the reception and treatment of the casualties, as well as properly recording and managing those that were dead on arrival, though most of the 2 Para fatalities would arrive over the following 2 days, and Argentine fatalities were to be interred at a cemetery North of Darwin.

It took 4 men to unload each stretcher case. Most needed to be placed on a stretcher, having simply been placed either on the deck of the limited rear cabin space, or, in the case of Scouts, sometimes being placed inside 'flying coffins' - actually casualty pods - fitted on either side of the exterior these tiny rotary wing aircraft and used for both fatally wounded and salvageable casualties. These side boxes were the aviation equivalent of AA or RAC motorcycle sidecars, or car top boxes, except they were fitted on both sides and, as the name implies, were similar in size to a coffin. For the salvageable wounded however, these were not a stairway to heaven but the fastest route to ensuring a speedy recovery.

As was now very routine, the casualties were carried the 75 to 100 metres, initially across rough ground, then down the slight gradient to the facilities entrance, and into the Reception area for triage and any immediate (stop gap) care that might be needed. Again, less serious patients were immediately sifted across to the Minor Treatment section, and the more serious moved through to Major Treatment resuscitation section. All patients had a medical Form

(FMed) 28 raised and attached (if this had not been done at First Line); the field equivalent of an A&E case note.

The triage status of individual patients was fluid and constantly reviewed, insofar as a patient may, for example, have a piece of shrapnel lodged in their trachea, which might easily be removed in Major Treatments, restoring the airway and taking away any immediate threat to life, such a case could be down-graded from Priority One, (P1 – requiring immediate lifesaving care) to Priority 2 (P-2 requiring ongoing care but can wait) or even to Priority 3 (minor case requiring treatment within 24 hours). In reality minor cases received very prompt treatment, and in the case of friendly forces the goal was to return them forward if possible. Similarly, a P2 casualty could deteriorate and be upgraded to P1 – requiring immediate treatment.

Arguably many P2 casualties, and those P3 cases who were not capable of recovering sufficiently to be returned to their parent Units, could have been casevaced to the Hospital Ship Uganda, but because the weather was highly unpredictable and increasingly wasn't conducive to running the risk of flying over raging seas with minor patients, there was always a risk of clogging up the facility with a backlog of patients that could have been dealt with promptly. The upshot was that we tended to treat everything that we were presented with, but this is surely something that might have been worthy of scrutiny by eminent clinicians when the war ended.

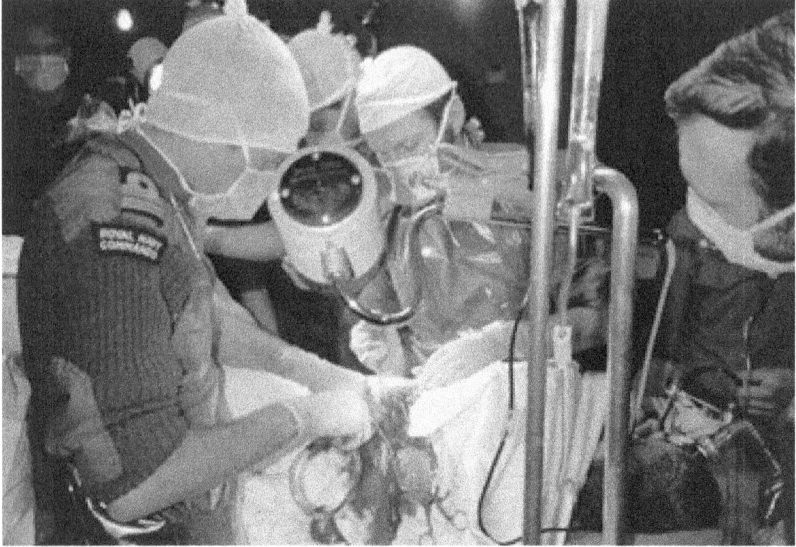

RN Commando Surgeon Nick Morgan from the RN Surgical Support Team (SST) 2 operates on a British casualty at Ajax Bay. A second operation can be discerned in the background to his left.

At around 1900Z (1600 local) we were advised that Darwin was captured, and Goose Green surrounded, and more casualties would be inbound. All this was happening within 16 hours or so of ourselves having been on the receiving end of Argentine Skyhawks, and the continuous bombardment that ensued as ammunition stocks exploded for some hours, necessitating our clinical teams to work throughout the night. Also of course having personally had a somewhat more adventurous journey to Port San Carlos than intended, along with Marine Steve Gosling and Cpl Cy Worrall.

Cpl Jon Clare adds his personal recollection of events: *Just a day after we had ourselves been bombed and buried our own friends, we dealt with the aftermath of the brave 2 Para attack at Goose Green, prepared all their dead and treated all the injured. We also received injured Argentines who were treated with compassion and dignity. Some had self-inflicted injuries, with the aim to be evacuated and sent home. Among their possessions we found distasteful and plainly ridiculous propaganda along with family photographs and personal letters. Most were relieved once they realised that they were not going to be eaten or shot. Some were professional soldiers, but many were obviously conscripted and little more than civilians dressed like soldiers. During that period, we committed too many young men to the peaty Falklands earth'.*

D Day+8 29 May 1982
The Argentine Surrender at Goose Green

The acting CO of 2 Para, Major Keeble, met with A and C company commanders and indicated he felt it would be best to call for the Argentines to surrender, and if this was not forthcoming, to 'flatten Goose Green' with all available fire power. Brigadier Thompson flew J Company 42 Commando and the remaining three 105mm light guns forward to reinforce the Paratroopers. He agreed with Major Keeble's plan and issued an 'Unconditional Surrender' ultimatum by the settlement CB Radio system, via Mr Eric Goss, the Goose Green farm manager, and it was passed to the Argentine commander by two Argentine air force POWs to Piaggi at around midnight local time (0300Z). The Argentine Infantry Regiment Commander, Piaggi, was to confirm his agreement or non-agreement by 0830 local (1130Z). In the event of non-agreement, he was warned he would be held responsible for the fate of civilians, 'by the terms and conditions of the Geneva Convention and Laws of War .... and by these terms we give notice of our intention to bombard Darwin and Goose Green'

An Argentine Air Vice Commodore, Wilson Pedroza, was actually the senior officer at Goose Green. Piaggi rightly advised him the game was up and he agreed to discuss the unconditional surrender, which was confirmed by daybreak on 29 May. They formed up outside with all their men. Pedroza briefly addressed them. They burnt a regimental flag so it would not be taken as a trophy of war and laid down their weapons. Each carrying just a few personal effects, they were taken into captivity.

Around 45 Argentine dead were later interred just to the North of Darwin. 140 of their casualties were evacuated to Medical Squadron at Ajax Bay of which 80 needed more serious treatment interventions. So, 45 dead; 80 seriously wounded and 60 less so, who would be returned to captivity; there were around 960 prisoners of war.

With the loss of Atlantic Conveyor, and with it all the POW holding facilities, most of the POW's were placed in the Tank Deck of the Landing Ship Sir Percival, where they would at least be out of the elements, warm, dry, fed and hydrated. A Royal Marine, L/Cpl Garcia, who was a fluent Spanish speaker of Gibraltarian origin, suddenly found his language skills rocketed him to VIP status within 3 Commando Brigade, as there was a need not only to communicate with this large number of Spanish speaking POW's for humanitarian support, but to also glean as much Intelligence from them as possible. Those aboard the Percival were taken to San Carlos Water, and over the next week as much intelligence (intel) as possible was gathered by simply interviewing as many as possible. The sole Brigade Intelligence Officer was later to record in his book, 'Nine Battles to Stanley', that this process revealed that 400 of the personnel at Goose Green had only been flown there on 27 May, to avoid the repeated bombing and artillery attacks that were being inflicted at Stanley airfield. So, prior to that, 3 Commando Brigade intelligence that the settlement was occupied by something approaching Battalion strength had been remarkably accurate.

Reception of 2 Para dead from Goose Green. As the Brigade push to break out of San Carlos Water was well underway, most of 2 Para's dead were flown back to Ajax Bay in a single Wessex 5 from 845 Naval Air Squadron. 11 bodies had to be removed from the helicopter, providing yet another gruesome task for our quartermaster staff and other volunteers to record and prepare these, the victims of a bloody battle, to be laid to rest. A medic verified every UK death and recorded the cause on a Field Medical Card (FMed 28), (but it has subsequently become clear to me that this process was not applied to Argentine fatalities who were also sometimes flown back for burial, and without exception had no means of identity. Such fatalities were confirmed as dead by a Medic and prepared for burial, but no FMed 28's were raised. Indeed, only those Argentines who died in our care were reflected in the Admission and Discharge Log). All the details are passed to the Field Records Office, and on this occasion Captain Roy Hancock, who is responsible for such records and reporting, visits the Squadron to obtain the necessary details, and help to reduce the task for our staff. It was not until the following day that the final five dead from 2 Para were recovered to Ajax Bay.

Night Artillery Warning at Ajax Bay. I cannot recall the exact date, but one night, most likely immediately after the Argentine surrender at Goose Green, we were all shaken to alert us to the risk of a possible Argentine artillery counter attack, from Port Howard. Just as with potential night bombing information, it sent a chill through my body, but given that there was really nowhere to seek proper shelter, and regardless of unexploded bombs, it seemed silly not to catch up on some much needed sleep, so I rolled over and thought no more about it. I was in good company, as it seems everyone else who was not tending the wounded did exactly the same. Fortunately, no counter attack came.

D Day+9 30 May 1982

Goose Green. The Battalion had lost 15 officers and men. A Sapper, and the Scout pilot brought the total lost to 17. Given the intensity of the fight for Darwin and Goose Green, it seems remarkable that the losses were not greater. Indeed, considerably more men had died in just 20 minutes when HMS Coventry had been bombed in Falkland Sound a couple of days earlier. Given that this was a brutal battle against dug in, established troops, this was frankly a miracle of professionalism and courage, tinged with much sadness. Moreover, the Argentine losses and casualties were three times greater.

By far the largest single burial ceremony whilst One Troop Medical Squadron were at Ajax Bay, as the British fatalities from Goose Green are laid to rest.

RIP:

Pte Steven Dixon

Pte Mark Fletcher

Pte Mark Holman-Smith

Pte Stephen Illingsworth DCM

Pte Tam Mechan

L/Cpl Gary Bingley MM

L/Cpl Tony Cork

L/Cpl Nigel Smith

Cpl David Hardiman

Cpl Michael Melia RE

Cpl Stephen Prior

Cpl Paul Sullivan

Lt Jim Barry

Lt Richard Nunn RM

Capt Chris Dent

Capt David Wood

Lt Col H Jones VC OBE

All these men were laid to rest in a shallow grave at Ajax Bay, with a brief ceremony, attended by about 200 of all ranks and all arms. It was a fitting but sad affair, and when it concluded we replaced our berets and carried on, each man contributing in their role, with the job of winning this war.

The Award of the Victoria Cross. With regard to Lt Col H Jones' Victoria Cross, there has been much debate about whether he and his small group of tactical HQ officers' should have been leading an attack. It is of course legitimate to study the strengths and weaknesses of tactics employed in battle, but the criteria for the award of a VC sets no requisite standard for tactics. It is an award for bravery, made to persons who… **'in the presence of the enemy, display the most conspicuous gallantry; a daring or pre-eminent act of valour or self-sacrifice or extreme devotion to duty',** and on that basis it was surely awarded to Col H Jones posthumously, on behalf of all who had fought that day with 2 Para.

Disposition of Friendly Forces 30 May 1982.

2 Para remain at Goose Green, consolidating their positions and recovering from their hard-fought victory. The settlement is a complete mess, with heavily mined areas, and the trenches still full of dead Argentine soldiers, who need to be retrieved and properly managed ready for burial, just to the North of Darwin.

D Squadron SAS had moved to Mount Kent on 27 May, and successfully countered an Argentine Unit known as 602 Commando Company 2 days later on 29 May. Two D Squadron men were injured with gunshot wounds, but it would be a further 2 days before they could be casevaced back to Ajax Bay, and they are reliant on their own medics to sustain them.

HMS Glamorgan shelled Stanley Airfield overnight with her twin turret 4.5 inch guns and fired a Sea Slug anti-aircraft missile, destroying an Argentine Skyward Fire Control Radar installation.

40 Commando continue to provide cover to the San Carlos area of San Carlos Water.

42 Commando were to have flown to Mount Kent on 29 May, but the loss of Atlantic Conveyor was continuing to bite, with great pressure on the Brigade support helicopter assets. With 2 Para consolidating at Goose Green, the 42 Commando move was postponed and they remain at Port San Carlos until 31 May.

45 Commando have 'yomped*' to **Douglas Settlement,** which is simply a rest point for them, and already confirmed secure. The ground en-route was very challenging, certainly amongst the worst on the Archipelago. They are due to depart for Teal Inlet today, 30 May. (*The origin of the term YOMP is 'Your Own Marching Pace').

3 Para have 'tabbed*' to **Teal Inlet** where the SBS are well established (see below) and have endured the same testing ground conditions experienced by 45 Commando, with deep wet peat bogs interspersed with stone runs that present formidable barriers. They are due to depart for Estancia today, 30 May. (*The origin of the term TAB is 'Tactical Advance to Battle').

SBS are operating in force, patrolling the hinterland of **Teal Inlet** which is to become a **Forward Operating Base** for 3 Brigade Air Squadron with refuelling facilities, and the **Forward Brigade Maintenance Area,** to support and enable the main assault towards Stanley, from the North, including **Logistic Resupply and Medical Assets** from the **Commando Logistic Regiment RM** (including One Troop Medical Squadron).

Arrival of Maj Gen Jeremy Moore. As the Scots Guards and Welsh Guards, together with the Gurkha Rifles are due to arrive at San Carlos Water the following day, they are preceded by Maj Gen Jeremy Moore, who takes up the role of Commander Land Forces, Falkland Islands. He will be responsible for coordinating both 3 Commando Brigade and 5 Infantry Brigade in the push to Stanley that is already well in train.

Medical Squadron. Number One Surgical Support Team, normally based at RN Hospital Haslar (which used to be situated in Gosport), arrive at Ajax Bay, resplendent in their clean combat kit, and all sporting Red Cross arm bands. They have been landed from the Aircraft Carrier HMS Hermes to re-join Medical Squadron, with which they are trained and established to function with. However, the Hospital Ship Uganda is now struggling to keep pace with the Delayed Primary Closure surgical requirements, as a result of all the casualties in recent days, and it is quickly agreed with the Medical Officer i/c on Uganda, that the bulk of this team could be best utilised on the Hospital Ship. Having seen the state of Ajax Bay most of SST1 seem pleased that they will be joining the Uganda team, but Surgeon Lieutenant Commander Ian Geraghty who is an anaesthetist, and four Senior Ratings, are selected to stay with Medical Squadron ashore.

Yet another, and surely the last Argentine casualty of Goose Green, is found clinging precariously to life, buried under his dead mates in one of Goose Green's defensive trenches. Pte Donato Ruiz is flown back to Ajax Bay and, looking as close to a corpse as is possible whilst still having a discernible pulse, he is collected from his rotary wing saviour, and brought down to the medical facility, 2 days after being severely wounded. Like so many of his unfortunate mates, his kit had to be removed, cutting off anything that wouldn't come away easily, and he desperately needed cleaning up, as he had defecated where he lay wounded. This was a typical picture that presented before us. Warm soapy water, sponges and plenty of paper towelling was a prerequisite for such cases. With a core body temperature around 4 or 5 degrees centigrade below what it would normally be, the cold had again proven an ally to these severely wounded casualties, inhibiting bleeding that might otherwise have caused some to exsanguinate i.e. bleed to death. This young man had a penetrating wound of the right eye, and fractures of the right hand and left thigh. The low hypothermic body temperature does not make the administration of anaesthesia easy however, and he required manual ventilation for two hours whilst he was operated on. He was a very fortunate survivor that went on to be casevaced to the Uganda and was eventually repatriated to Argentina.

17 Argentine and 8 UK personnel were admitted on 30 May 1982, and a further 5 UK personnel were flown to Ajax Bay to be certified dead on arrival, and to receive an appropriate burial.

Late in the night we all were alerted to the possibility that the Argentines might use a Canberra aircraft to try to bomb us. This information must have been as a result of our ships detecting an aircraft that was larger than the usual fighter bombers, as it was not too long afterwards that an aircraft passed over the area of San Carlos. Fortunately, its bombs were dropped but ineffective, probably because the pilot had no visible light or other indication where to bomb. It was a strangely more frightening experience than actually facing very effective air raids in the daylight though. Aging former British Canberra aircraft went on to make 43 bombing missions against UK assets.

D+10 31 May 1982
Brief Summary of UK Special Forces
Actions during this period.

In order to understand how the disposition of the breakout from San Carlos Water was being forged, it's worth outlining at this point a summary of some of the key Special Forces actions that have taken place. Whilst the SBS were dominating the ground in and around Teal Inlet, it is necessary to introduce a further UK Specialist Force that was on the ground, namely the Royal Marine Mountain and Arctic Warfare Cadre. This small group of about 60 men were, in the 1980's, responsible not just for nurturing and training specialist Mountain Leaders within the Royal Marines, but primarily played a strategic role within the UK and Netherlands Landing Force, (UKNLLF) for the defence of NATO's Northern Flank in Arctic Norway, and further afield as required. Led by a Royal Marine Captain, Rod Boswell, the North of East Falkland was a terrain that they thrived in. 3 Commando Brigade used the Cadre as a Brigade reconnaissance asset, and Capt Boswell had established a number of covert Observation Posts (OP's), some having been in situ for several days, as well as rigorous patrolling of key areas, to monitor enemy movement. (The M&AW Cadre were effectively utilized and deployed as an SF asset throughout the Falkland war and are thus appropriately recorded as such in this account).

Meanwhile D Squadron and Boat Troop, SAS, were similarly placed on Mount Kent, and in particular to facilitate the arrival of 42 Commando which had been scheduled to take place on 29 May, but was postponed due to insufficient support helicopter assets, not least reflecting the requirement to resupply 2 Para at Goose Green, and the loss of helicopters on Atlantic Conveyor. Mount Kent had been clear of enemy activity when Argentine troops had departed to help repel 2 Para at Goose Green, on the evening of 28 May.

Now however, at about 0900Z 29 May another Argentine Troop of commandos, comprising a 5 man HQ and two fighting sections of 12 men each were being flown to Mount Kent by helicopter from Stanley, and more were expected in subsequent waves. But the weather was appalling, with white-out snow blizzards, and so the subsequent waves were cancelled. What's more, one of the two fighting sections was landed at the wrong site, namely Bluff Cove Peak, and their landing was observed by an M&AW patrol led by Sgt Stone.

The other Argentine commando section had landed on the Stanley side of Mount Kent, and were engaged by Boat Troop, SAS, two of whom were injured in the exchange. Boat Troop moved to higher ground, and by the following morning of 30 May, the Argentine commando section had moved off Mount Kent and were headed for Mount Estancia, less two men, who had lost contact with their Section, and eventually linked up with the 5 man HQ team, which had to abandon an unconscious NCO who had fallen badly, and was subsequently treated and casevaced by UK SF medics.

The Argentine commando section that had been dropped off at the wrong site, were trying to head from Bluff Cove Peak towards Mount Kent, and at about 1400Z on 29 May suffered two fatalities as they were suddenly hit with gunshots from the East, causing the surviving 10 Argentines to also head for higher ground. At the same time a Puma full with Argentine reinforcements, had left Stanley, only to crash near the Murrell river bridge, when two Harriers had forced it down too low, killing 6 and injuring the remaining 8.

These actions paved the way for 42 Commando Unit to eventually start to fly in to Mount Kent in Sea Kings of 846 Naval Air Squadron when the weather abated in the early hours of 31 May, initially with K company, who secured the position ready for a section of 7 Commando Battery 29 Commando RA to be lifted in by the sole Chinook available to the Landing Force. By first light 42 Commando had consolidated the position and Stanley was just 11 miles to their East. The wounded SAS men were flown out to Ajax Bay together with the unconscious Argentine NCO, and the area was steadily strengthened over the following 2 nights, including the remainder of 7 Commando Battery RA; L Coy 42 Commando; and 2 Troop 59 Commando RE; who were flown to Mount Challenger where, yet another OP was established.

The Argentines had not given up, and yet another group set off from Stanley using local Land Rovers that they had requisitioned, and motorcycles. They were spotted by 42 Commando and mortared, causing them to vacate the Land Rovers but they kept heading towards the lower reaches of Mount Kent. They were again mortared and left an injured man on the slopes with a young officer to care for him, as they made their retreat. Argentine accounts subsequently reported that the young officer spent the next 2 nights helping his wounded man back to Argentine positions in Stanley.

Meanwhile, the Argentine section that had been trying to link up from Bluff Cove Mountain with the other section (that had now abandoned Mount Kent), were keeping their heads down on Mount Simon to shelter from the British Forces. They decided their best bet was to try and link up with members 601 Combat Engineer Battalion who were at Fitzroy Bridge, and in doing so they waded waist deep across Malo River which was a raging torrent due to the weather. More snow swept in and they then instead headed to the shelter of a house at Top Malo. They made it to the house and were relieved to find it unoccupied and started to recover from their freezing situation. Unfortunately for them, the M&AW Cadre had set up an Observation Post just 200 metres from the house, and 2 hours before first light on 31 May, Captain Rod Boswell seized the initiative, landing close by, again in a Sea King from 846 Naval Air Squadron, 18 men, including a fire support team, assaulted the building with fixed bayonets, firing light weight hand held

66mm anti-tank rockets, and then moving forward, unleashing a continuous volley of Armalite rounds, before pausing, firing more rockets, and again moving forward. The building was immediately ablaze, causing the occupants to leave from the rear, and to head for the cover of the swollen river about a 200 metre dash away, having already suffered 2 dead, a further 6 were wounded; the remaining 4 knew it was time to throw in the towel, and surrendered.

The M&AW Cadre also had 4 injured, 3 requiring casevac to Ajax Bay, with 2 chest gunshot wounds (GSW's) and an upper arm gunshot wound, whilst a 'lesser' injured case was a GSW to the hand.

These actions that unfolded over 3 days, serve to demonstrate how the ground had to be won and dominated, as the war moved forward, with many acts of individual and collective bravery, the vast majority of which go unrecognised beyond the South Atlantic Medal and Rosette that was subsequently awarded to us all.

The Special Forces operations help to demonstrate how there was no respite for Medical Squadron or its attached Parachute Clearing Troop colleagues at Ajax Bay, which lay about 45 miles to the West – a 90 mile round trip for the support helicopters, and this was to underpin the decision to deploy One Troop Medical Squadron forward to Teal Inlet. By the standards of recent days, it had been a relatively quiet day for Medical Squadron at Ajax Bay, but this translated into receiving and treating 8 UK and 10 Argentine casualties, but there were no UK fatalities.

One of the UK casualties that day was a RN Lieutenant Commander from 846 Naval Air Squadron who had an eye laceration that necessitated his rearward evacuation to Uganda with the other wounded men; and another was a 42 Commando JNCO who had developed festering pustules on his legs and abdomen, who was able to re-join his Unit 2 days later. The SF M&AW Cadre SNCO who had a GSW injury to his hand was not evacuated to Ajax Bay for treatment and soldiered on following treatment by the Cadre's Leading Medical Assistant.

The world's television and press descended upon Medical Squadron, as did the new UK Land Force Falklands Commander, Major General Jeremy Moore. Surgeon Commander Rick Jolly rightly manages all these visits, something he particularly revelled in. The media positively lapped it up and I doubt anyone could have executed a more media savvy display than Rick Jolly. I sensed a degree of jealousy or even resentment among some of the more senior clinical staff however, as his interviews could give the impression that he was the leading clinical 'hands on' practitioner, as opposed to the Officer in Command - albeit with a clinical background. Nonetheless this impression remains to this day.

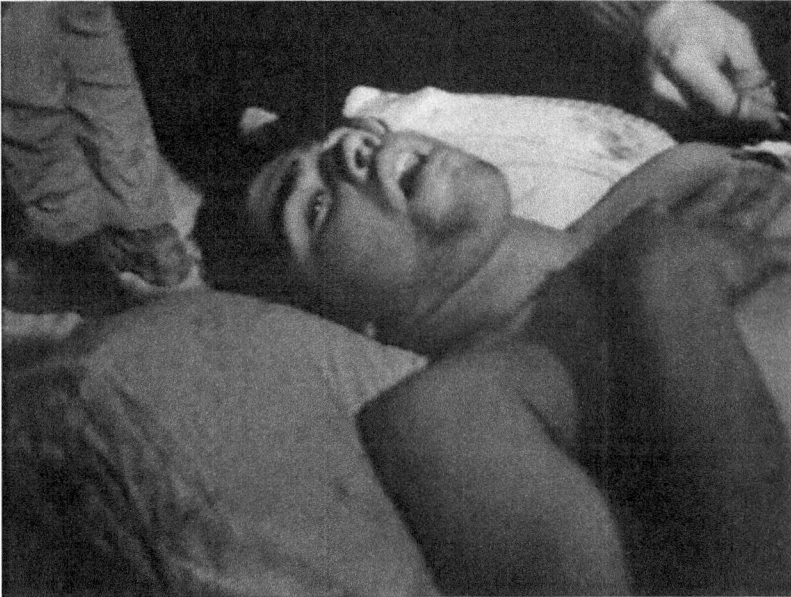

A seriously wounded Argentine upon his arrival in the Major Treatment section at Ajax Bay.

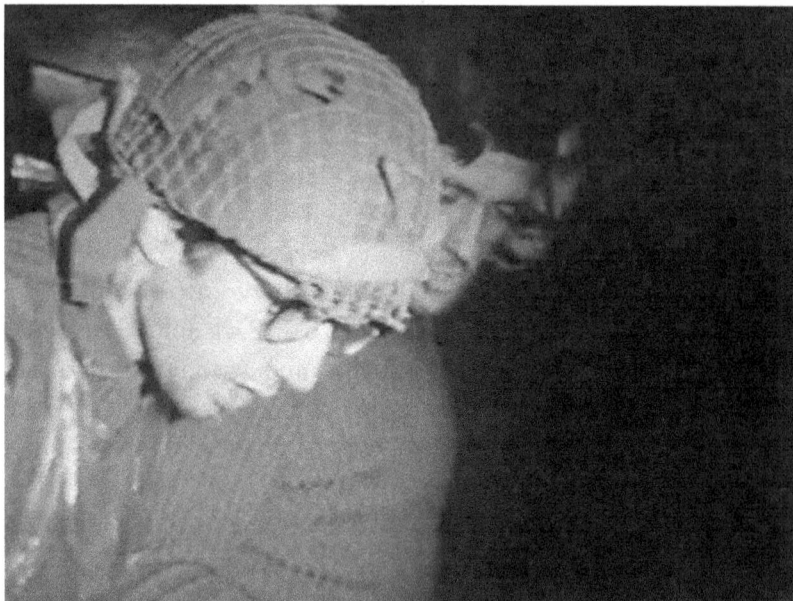

With their faces etched with fatigue, Marine Jim Giles, (far right) who is a Spanish linguist, speaks with the casualty and clarifies that the Argentine's wound is two days old, as Chief Medic Graham Edwards checks vital signs and Doctor Howard Oakley (wearing his 'trademark' helmet) determines the priority for surgery and the initial requirement for intravenous infusions and pain relief.

Immediate notice to reconnoitre Teal Inlet to move One Troop Medical Squadron Forward

Much later in the day, I receive a very brief order to sail on the Assault Ship HMS Intrepid round to Teal Inlet that evening, 31 May 1982, to reconnoitre the Bunk House (normally used by single farm hands and also provides temporary accommodation for sheep shearers and other transient farm labourers) with a view to establishing a 25 bed forward medical facility (still referred to as a dressing station, but with more advanced resuscitation and treatment capabilities). I gather Marine Steve Gosling and Corporal Cy Worrall together, ensure they are aware of the task afoot, and we set off to join Intrepid for the short night transit, with our Bergan backpacks again fully laden, including 3 days rations and armed sufficiently to at least boost our morale.

D+11 Tuesday 1 June 1982

Teal Inlet. As day breaks, we are at the mouth of the estuary to Teal Inlet. It's a cold but clear day, with some sunshine, but accompanied by the usual relentless wind, blowing at its typical average of 20 mph. We know the SBS have confirmed the Inlet is clear of enemy activity, but it's a considerable channel of water and as such they have been unable to conduct a thorough diving reconnaissance to confirm it is clear of mines, so our Assault Ship, HMS Intrepid, will not enter this natural harbour. Instead, we have to transfer to a Landing Craft Utility, which will be at significantly less risk than Intrepid, and should also provide some assurance that the channel is clear for subsequent Landing Ships Logistic (LSL's) to navigate up these waters.

It's a choppy voyage of about 12 miles from Goat Point to the North, to the landing slip just to the East of Teal Inlet settlement, and the journey takes us a couple of hours, but it is a surreal pleasant experience after the repeated air raids, casualties, fatalities, and bombings at Ajax Bay, as we take in the vast uninhabited treeless landscape. The Falkland Islands cover a land mass the size of Wales, but with a population of barely 2,000, most of whom live in the capital Port Stanley, it is mostly a desolate and lonely place.

We arrive at the landing slip and are able to step ashore, keeping our boots and feet dry, without difficulty, and we make the short walk of 500 or 600 yards up a gradual rise to the Bunk House. The ground around us is well grazed by sheep, so the grass is like a lawn, and there are no large stones littering the settlement as there are at Ajax Bay and across most of the North of East Falkland. There are also what look like Cyprus Pine hedges in places, and these Macrocarpa (to give them their correct name) help to act as wind breaks. The Bunk House is a large two storey building, with multiple small bedrooms upstairs, and a large combined recreation and dining room downstairs, The ablution area is also quite a large space and its immediately apparent that Major Treatments could easily be set up in the large recreation and dining room, and minor treatments could be shoehorned into the ablution area. We would need to establish Reception within a 24 x 18 feet standard tent, and similarly the Holding/ Evacuation Ward in another, but there was ample space to accommodate this tentage requirement in the immediate grounds. There was already a small kitchen, but it would be too tiny to cater for over 40 men, and so a 12x12 feet tent would be erected for this, and One Troop's cook-set would be required.

The Bunk House was actually full to the brim at this point however. The SBS were using it as their opportunity to recuperate from endless coastal reconnaissance tasks, and Captain Rod Boswell's men of the M&AW Cadre were also using Teal Inlet to recuperate from yesterday's assault on Top Malo House. Rod Boswell was in a jubilant mood as he recounted the previous days exploits to his friends in the SBS. I wait quietly until he departs before making myself known and establishing that the SBS expect to remain at Teal for at least another day or so, and we quickly broker an agreement whereby if and when my Troop arrive, the SBS will move upstairs as we set-up below.

Marine Gosling opens up his radio and we notify the Commando Logistic Regiment and our own Medical Squadron Command Post, using the Land Force Admin Net, (LF Admin) that the building and its local area is suitable for a 25 bed Forward Dressing Station. We specify our tentage, cook-set, and generator and light set and cable requirements from our own (G1098) Field equipment scale, and our own Troop CP equipment, and Medical (I1248) equipment and medicines. The Troop have a very busy 8 hours ahead of them, preparing to re-pack kit now sat in Chatham Containers at Ajax Bay. Normally we would have been able to simply redeploy using our own designated vehicles and trailers, none of which had accompanied us on this 8,000 mile mission.

The work to move forward is supervised by two highly capable and reliable Chief Petty Officer Medical Assistants, Graham Edwards and John Smith, and by last light they will have loaded everything into the designated Landing Ship Logistic, LSL Sir Percival, that was to sail that night, to beach at Teal Inlet the following morning. When you have Senior Ratings of this calibre and experience, with a similarly dependable team below them, the whole task becomes much easier, and is based more on organic mutual respect and trust rather than some overly hierarchical distorted image that the general public might think is the norm for such organisations. Everyone strived to be supportive of each other, and like a wall, it was recognised that those at the bottom were needed to support others above, and with the loss or reduced effectiveness of any individual there was likely to be a commensurate reduction in cohesion and effectiveness across the whole organisation. Every man counted. It was a team effort.

Teal Inlet Bunk House that One Troop Medical Squadron utilized, with additional tentage at the rear, showing the nose of a Wessex Mk5 commando helicopter on the left.

Forward Brigade Maintenance Area and 3 Brigade Air Squadron Forward Operating Base

We familiarise ourselves with the rest of the settlement, and it's now clear to us that Teal Inlet is being rapidly ratcheted up to be the Forward Brigade Maintenance Area for 3 Commando Brigade, with ammunition, ration supplies and water, being moved forward from here. 3 Brigade Air squadron are establishing a helicopter arming and refuelling facility, with two teams to operate around the clock and a Command Post (CP) co-located. We are able to discuss and agree rigging a landline direct to them when our CP kit arrives with the Troop the following morning. The Air Squadron are happy with our proposals for a Landing Site just 30 or 40 yards from where the entrance to our Reception tent will be sited, and clarify that there is no need to routinely light the landing site at night as the pilots are using Night Vision Goggles – an innovation that has represented a step change in the capability of helicopter operations in this war.

Some elements of 3 Para are still leaving the settlement, heading South in the direction of Stanley, with a forward base established a couple of miles West of Estancia the day before, and one of their patrols have captured several of the survivors of the original Fanning Hill Mob or 'Combat Team Eagle' who had been in situ at Port San Carlos, and escaped as 3 Para and 42 Commando came ashore on D Day. These were the enemy responsible for shooting down the two helicopters from C Flight 3 Brigade Air Squadron that had flown off LSL Galahad as the landings commenced. They had managed to evade capture until now, but they were in a terrible state as they were taken back to HQ 3 Commando Brigade for questioning. Alpha Company 3 Para crossed the Murrell River and secured Mount Estancia on 1 June 1982. Mount Longdon will be their next objective and the Battalion has already assessed they face an enemy force on Longdon similar to their own strength, including elements of the Argentine 601 Commando, and able to call in close artillery support from the vicinity of Moody Brook, just a mile or so to the West of the centre of Stanley.

45 Commando are arriving and bivouacking wherever they can, having yomped from Ajax Bay via Douglas, fully laden with their weapons, ammunition, fighting order, and personal kit. But there is to be little rest for their Recce Troop as the Unit seeks to gather as much intelligence as possible for their subsequent objective Two Sisters, a significant twin peak 900 feet high feature, that looks down over Moody Brook and Stanley just beyond.

Condor Troop 59 Commando Royal Engineers are here alongside 45 Commando with whom they are normally embedded. Their support in dealing with anti-personnel mines (and later some anti-tank mines) will soon be sorely tested.

Teal Inlet is a hive of activity, as a scout helicopter has received some minor maintenance in a sheep shed and is hauled outside. The pilot climbs aboard and the ground handler indicates he is clear to start up. These scenes are reminiscent of the Bi-Plane days of the Royal Flying Corps in France in the First World War, when words such as Hanger (French for a large farm building) and Sortie (French for going out) became part of the common language of our aviators.

My small recce trio head back to the bunk house, which has a very small but warm kitchen, heated as it is by two peat burning Rayburn cookers. The journalist Max Hastings has found a cosy corner to rest himself, and the lady who was normally the Bunk House cook, Mrs Gloria Anderson, made myself, Cy Worrall and Steve Gosling, an ordinary instant coffee, but for us it was the best coffee we had savoured for what had seemed like an eternity, but it was still less than two weeks since we had gone ashore. Mrs Anderson kept the peat stoves burning 24 hours a day whilst we were deployed there. She was truly an unsung hero.

There were three Falkland Islanders accommodated in the Bunk House at the time, namely Jimmy McCullen who was a farm hand at Teal; Henry Smith who was a shepherd who normally lived at Lower Malo House. Henry would usually winter at Teal Inlet, and had his own room allocated in the Bunk House. His neighbouring Top Malo House had fortunately been uninhabited before the invasion and was of course completely set ablaze during the M&AW operation to dislodge Argentine commandos. Last but not least there was a 16 year old farm hand called Neil Rowlands, who was to often come to our assistance with his tractor and trailer, and generally help us whenever he could. Yet another unsung hero of this war, Neil had only been at Teal inlet since the invasion, after his mother had suggested it might be better if he were to head out of Stanley. He needed no prompting and the next morning he set off on his small motor bike. With his rucksack packed, very little money, and armed only with a camera, he rode towards Moody Brook, and thereafter cross-country to Teal Inlet, passing numerous Argentine troops as he went, none bothering to stop him. I doubt his mother would have been quite as keen for him to leave Stanley if she had any inclination of the exploits that awaited him.

Medical Squadron – rear (Ajax Bay). One Troop were now busy preparing to move forward, and all the equipment and stores were being loaded under the direction of CPO's Graham Edwards and John Smith. The Canberra had arrived back in San Carlos Water yesterday evening, enabling Three Troop Medical Squadron to disembark (as well as 5 Brigade's Scots Guards; Welsh Guards; and Gurkhas). The Medical Squadron has been busy at Ajax Bay, with 25 admissions, comprising 10 UK and 15 Argentine casualties. Ominously 8 of the UK admissions are 2 Para and J coy 42 Commando (Naval Party 8901 1981 and 1982 detachments re-instated and attached to 2 Para) with cold weather injuries i.e., Frostbite and Trench Foot.

Some POWs had been kept back at Goose Green to help as best they could to restore the settlement to its original condition as a farmstead and rural community. Four conscript POW volunteers were also clearing up the debris, including artillery shells, in and around the School House, when the shells exploded – in a similar manner to what had occurred at Ajax Bay on 27 May. Two of the victims were hauled out – possibly by a 2 Para medic – but a third was beyond reach and died in the blaze. The fourth victim had both his legs blown off and was casevaced back to Ajax Bay. He sadly became the first, and one of the very few casualties to die at the medical facility, but the truth is, had he survived, he would have been severely disabled and require care for the rest of his life. Nonetheless I don't doubt that his family will grieve his loss for eternity. Medical Squadron were to have a remarkable 'Deja vu' situation almost nine years later to the day, when in the middle of Kurdish Northern Iraq, a US Paratrooper from the US 105th Airborne Unit was brought in, having stepped on an anti-tank mine and lost both legs right up to his pelvis. The RN Surgical Support Team operated successfully, and he had seemingly recovered, only to die from an air embolism travelling to his heart and killing him 36 hours later. Unfortunately, air embolisms are a significant risk factor following traumatic amputation, particularly involving blasts, and both losses stay with those who fought to save them, like a hammer blow.

Jon Clare adds his own insight as 5 Brigade arrived at San Carlos Water: *The tempo across the Brigade had been increasing daily as Paras and Marines were marching across very difficult ground, in increasingly wintry conditions, to their new objectives. 5 Infantry Brigade were landed elsewhere in San Carlos Water, but a company of Welsh Guards were landed at Ajax Bay and as they marched, with a spring in their step, sporting what looked like brand new kit and rucksacks, up the hill past our trench positions, a few of their group quipped that the Royal Marines could relax now as they were here. Later, perhaps even the next day, they appeared again, this time coming back down the hill, quietly, with no spring in their step and heading to the waiting shipping for the easier sea-transit to their destination. This was not to be one of their finest moments. The absolute horror of what was to happen to them in the forthcoming few days, for which the ordinary soldiers bear no blame nor could have avoided, was a terrible shock to us all. Here and now, they were already visibly physically (and probably mentally) nowhere near as battle ready as 3 Commando Brigade's marines and paras.*

We went about our duties accordingly until it was confirmed we were to move to Teal Inlet, where a Forward Brigade Maintenance Area was being established. Malcolm Hazell with Cy Worrall and Steve Gosling had already gone forward. A move away from this place for me was exactly what the doctor ordered!'

Disposition of Friendly Forces 1 June 1982

Forward patrols of 3 Para and 45 Commando, advance on Mount Simon and Malo Hill, where they take into captivity 14 Argentine Red de Observadores (ROA) Air Force ground observation teams who had witnessed much of the action to capture Mount Kent and Top Malo. These Argentine Observation Teams had clearly been operating in a highly professional manner, and like the Argentine Lieutenant Commander who had been captured by 40 Commando RM on 27 May at San Carlos (see D+6 Disposition of Friendly Forces, 40 Commando RM) they probably played a key role in directing their fixed wing aircraft assets with great accuracy; only for their pilots to be frequently let down by their bombs failing to explode....thank goodness! These new POW's will no doubt be interviewed by 3 Commando Brigade's Intelligence Section.

Most of 45 Commando are resting up at Teal Inlet at this stage however, whilst 3 Para are now forming up around the area of Estancia.

42 Commando dominate the ground on and around Mount Kent. By this stage the weather has deteriorated and the conditions on this high strategic rocky ground, with significant wind chill factor, are totally inhospitable and not conducive with static defensive positions. This is the South Atlantic equivalent of establishing a dominating Unit presence on the highest rock of Gutter Tor Dartmoor at the coldest mid-winter point.

29 Commando RA 7, 8 and 79 Batteries are now being flown forward by support helicopters with their 105 mm light guns underslung, and subsequent flights with 105mm shells underslung. The aim was to ensure 1000 rounds per gun, 18,000 rounds in total.

40 Commando are essentially a rear Force Protection Asset at San Carlos, ensuring the offload of 5 Brigade troops is protected and unopposed.

59 Commando RE are having to be deployed forward in increasing numbers, and inch by inch, probe the ground in front of them to ensure it is clear of anti-personnel and anti-tank mines. At this stage it seems like random indiscriminate unmarked mined areas, but this analysis has to be radically changed by the end of the conflict.

2 Para remain at Goose green. Out of 30 casualties who were evacuated to Ajax Bay on 28 May, all but 4 were casevaced further to the Hospital Ship Uganda. One of the 4 who were deemed fit and able to return to their Unit, which they all did by 2 June, was Pte Dave Parr who suffered 'a superficial gunshot wound of the abdomen'. It had been made clear to Pte Parr that he could be Casevaced to the Hospital Ship Uganda, but he chose to return to his mates. He was to later be killed whilst fighting to recapture Wireless Ridge.

Special Forces. All 3 SF Units i.e., SAS, SBS, and M&AW Cadre return to their 'bread and butter' tasks of patrolling, setting up Observation Posts, and carrying out forward reconnaissance. Between them, they had ensured a corridor was clear to the last few peaks surrounding Stanley, going toe to toe with the enemy, with the least possible cost in terms of casualties. Moreover, **Teal Inlet was secured and would provide vital rotary air, logistic, and medical support. Unhindered by Argentine air raids that had come very close to destroying us at Ajax Bay, and were to prove so destructive at Fitzroy, far from playing 'a minor role in the war'** (as is stated in Wikipedia), **Teal Inlet was the secret**

air, logistic, and medical base, that helped to ensure we won the war.

RAF - Black Buck 5. The RAF are still doing their utmost to disrupt if not disable Argentine operations on Stanley Airfield, as news filters down that the fifth Vulcan bomber raid hits an enemy radar installation. It is the first news of further raids we have heard since the initial raid was announced on the BBC World Service news whilst we were still en-route to the Islands.

D+12 Wednesday 2 June 1982
One Troop Medical Squadron at Teal Inlet

Landing Ship Logistic (LSL) Sir Percival passed Goat Point at first light and continued its way slowly down toward Teal Inlet. It was another cold day, as Cpl Cy Worrall and I went down to greet One Troop Medical Squadron. We had been able to procure the support of the 16 year old lad, Neil Rowlands, who drove a tractor, and with the help of other Islanders we loaded all the equipment onto the trailer up to the Bunk House. (It was to be 38 years later in 2020 that I was able to be in contact with Neil by the innovation of the internet and be reminded that he had also been living in the Bunk House, throughout the time we were deployed there).

Had we not had the tractor we would have had to man handle everything up to our new location, as we had none of our vehicles or ambulances, and the 18 x 24 tents alone would have taken the entire Troop to get them the few hundred yards up the gentle slope.

After a quick briefing the team had set up the tentage and were moving equipment inside. If there was a Guinness World record for organising the setting up of these large tents Corporal Tim (sometimes aka Tom) Robinson would probably have held it. He had 3 years seniority as a full Corporal and knew every inch of the Squadron's canvas. It was a laborious task to have to set it up, and even more to strike it down, but he could be depended on to organise the team and get the job done.

CPOMA John Smith, our Troop Quartermaster, guided our young 'chef' Marine Neil Blain, who set up all the tented galley facilities, and John Smith organised all the medical facilities ancillary equipment, such as the generator, lighting, and heating equipment and additional water in a bowser, whilst his 'opposite number' CPOMA Graham Edwards, had to ensure all the medical equipment and stores were being set out in a workable manner. The Reception tent would also hold a large number of air portable stretchers on which to place casualties who would be arriving in the light helicopters, often just on the deck, or, as previously mentioned, in the casualty pods (also known as flying coffins). The Evacuation Ward, just as at Ajax Bay, had no beds, and the casualties would remain on their stretchers all the way back to the Hospital Ship Uganda if they were casevaced.

As the clinical areas were rapidly being established, our command post was similarly being set up, under the guiding hand of the Troop Sgt, John Simmonds. He was pleased to get his teeth into this important part of the organisation and was always well on top of all situation reports, casevac requests rearward to the hospital ship Uganda, and such like. Marine Steve Gosling was our only professional signaller, but Marine John 'Tojo' Hughes was very conversant with the Clansman PRC 320 radio from his former service with 41 Commando Unit, and volunteered to be Steve Gosling's opposite number, on a shift about basis. Everybody was well capable of routinely using the radio if required however, and from recollection we utilized the Land Force Administration Net for communication back to our parent Commando Logistic Regiment at Ajax Bay, as well as to Medical Squadron rear at Ajax Bay. The field telephone line was established up to 3 Brigade Air Squadron, and this was to prove invaluable. Cpl Bowes was attached with us from the Field Records Office at Ajax Bay, and this helped considerably reduce the casualty and fatality reporting burden that otherwise would have absorbed much time in the CP when trying to monitor the arrival of casualties, or organise rearward casevac, or, equally importantly to return casualties forward, and such like.

We were just a 25 'bed' (i.e., stretcher patient) facility, but we were extremely thin on numbers to sustain this. At this stage there was just one doctor, Surgeon Lieutenant Howard Oakley, and he would be hard pressed to do more than the Regimental Aid Posts would be able to achieve in terms of casualty treatment – in fact many of the RN Commando Medical Assistants at Teal Inlet had amassed more practical casualty care experience than Dr Howard Oakley, as they had benefitted from multiple tours in Northern Ireland and elsewhere. Howard's main interest was in the medical management of non-freezing cold injuries however, and he was to find this field of medical specialism was to be in much demand as the winter progressed, and men were exposed to the elements for a considerable protracted period, without any respite.

Blood requirements. We have no stocks of whole blood at Teal Inlet, nor a suitable storage facility. To-date the need for whole blood has been mercifully low due mainly to the increasingly cold weather conditions inhibiting the peripheral circulation of casualties, but some will inevitably be required, and instead we will rely on seeking volunteer donors, as and when required, taking into account intended operations, and thereby anticipating requirements. We have Baxter bags that enable donors to give blood and then transfuse this to needy recipients. There was little risk in 1982 from more recent threats such as HIV, CJD, or the various types of Hepatitis that were to become prevalent, and we generally transfused blood of the same blood group, as everybody ashore should have had their blood group on their 'dog tags'. So, the absence of a Laboratory Technician at Teal Inlet did not prove problematic. Similarly, all our surgical instruments, whether just a pair of forceps, or a comprehensive set of post-operative instruments, were all able to be liquid sterilized, something that contamination with 'Prions' associated with CJD would absolutely rule out today.

First Fatality at Teal Inlet. At this stage we are barely established as a Forward Dressing Station, with no more clinical (doctor) expertise or capability than Unit Aid Posts we are meant to be supporting. Unfortunately, we learn that a member of the SBS, Sgt Ian 'Kiwi' Hunt has been fatally wounded in a 'blue on blue' patrol incident involving another SF patrol of SAS Troopers. The SBS were tasked with patrolling beach and coastal areas, whilst the SAS were tasked with patrolling an inland area. The coastal features are often impassable without venturing inland, sometimes by some distance, and the inland patrol's intended routes are often disrupted by stone runs and, increasingly, potential mine threats. With poor visibility, and the terrain limitations outlined, the SAS patrol fired on the SBS patrol, with the tragic loss of Sgt Ian 'Kiwi' Hunt. His body is recovered to Teal Inlet, but he is dead, and nothing can be done for this brave warrior. His body was cleaned up inside the Major Treatment area in the Bunk House, placed in a body bag, and what seemed like the entire SBS team carried him off. I assumed they were carrying him down to a Landing Ship for refrigerated storage and subsequent burial elsewhere, but only recently learnt that they had actually carried his body several hundred metres away to the South East of the settlement and conducted a burial and service there. This site is where a memorial now stands and includes the names of other British fatalities we received from the forward areas.

As a result of this first fatality coming back to us at Teal Inlet, and having consulted with our superiors at Ajax Bay, an Engineering Request (known as an Engquest in military shorthand) was submitted to dig a burial trench adjacent to our facility just 40 or 50 metres from the small outhouse building we went on to use as our mortuary, and discreetly hidden behind a row of conifer trees. A large military digger, probably a Combat Tractor from Condor Troop Royal Engineers, who are permanently attached to 45 Commando Group and now also at Teal Inlet, arrived from the West end of the settlement where large row farm buildings stood. It came down past the trees in view of the Bunk House, and I directed it to the other side of the trees, to the spot we had selected.

A deep trench was dug to a depth of two metres, and sufficient to hold around 30 fatalities laid alongside each other.

It was increasingly clear that we lacked sufficient clinicians with resuscitation expertise, to deal with the sort of casualties we will surely be expected to manage as the push towards Stanley continues. Surgeon Commander Rick Jolly had been keen to hold on to his resources at Ajax Bay, but he had to acknowledge that the additional flying time to cover the 60 mile minimum round trip for Scout and Gazelle helicopters to convey casualties to Ajax bay was not sustainable, and I was later notified we would receive a number of members from the Parachute 5 Field Surgical Team, including their Surgical Registrar, Major Charles Batty RAMC, and Anaesthetist Maj Dick Knight RAMC, and WO2 Fritz Sterba RAMC and 2 operating technicians/assistants (whose names cannot now be discerned on our nominal and the full FST including those at Ajax Bay is therefore reflected in the Order of Battle in the appendices). These would be further supported by Surgeon Lieutenant Commander Tim Riley, a very proficient Commando trained resuscitation RN doctor, and three Medical Technician 1 RN CPO's, all from the Surgical Support Team no.2, drawn from RN Hospital Plymouth, namely Steve Davis, Trevor Firth, and Tony Byrne. This was good news, and we were advised they would join us with all their necessary additional equipment and stores by 4 June, which is subsequently what happened, and we were a Light Forward Surgical Facility thereafter, even if the name had never been used before!

Jon Clare adds his personal recollections of the move to Teal Inlet: *'Uprooting and packing away One Troop's stores at the Ajax Bay facility was not as onerous a task as it could have been. The whole troop were excited to be moving to a new location. Preparations complete, we embarked on LSL Sir Percival for a welcome overnight passage around to Teal Inlet and because we were all very aware of the significant air threat, it was a very quiet and sombre sail around. Despite this we leapt at the opportunity to give our kit the once-over and shower and real bunk for the night. Although Ajax Bay had been busy, there always seemed enough people around for the required jobs and sometimes even had to hunt to find things to do to relieve the occasional boredom. Anyone who has been to war will tell you that it's not all action all the time and once it's all over you very quickly forget the times spent doing nothing! Our time at Teal Inlet was to prove anything but boring. If establishing our own Forward Surgical Facility was what was required and given this was to be the nearest Medical Facility to the front line, this seemed a sound plan. Yet we had to work hard to prove this was the main receiving facility to those at Ajax Bay! Eventually we got our surgical support but, meanwhile, the casualties had started to roll in and we did our best with the limited medical support available'.*

The Logistic Build Up at Teal Inlet. Teal started to receive substantial logistic supplies to support 3 Commando's final assault of the remaining peaks around Stanley, including Mount Harriet, Mount Longdon, Tumbledown, Two Sisters, Wireless Ridge, Mount William, and Sapper Hill. Landing Ships Logistic (LSL's) are brought in to Teal Inlet, having been laden with stores from Ajax Bay, via Mexi Floats in San Carlos Water. They are able to offload at will, from ship to shore, unhindered by the threat of enemy attack. Despite being well forward from Ajax Bay, the absence of enemy air activity made Teal Inlet feel like a very secure second line facility, where, certainly for the first 10 days, Ajax Bay had felt like the epicentre of the war. Indeed, it would not be inappropriate to describe the 'Battle of San Carlos Water' as being an Air to Ground battle executed by the Argentinian Air Force against the UK Landing Force….and but for their duff bombs the Argentines might well have won!

The Commando Logistic Regiment benefits from the arrival of 81 Ordnance Company who had sailed South with 5 Brigade. This organisation was placed within the Commando Logistic Regiment's organisation because they had no experience or assets to support amphibious logistic operations. This meant that the Commando Logistic Regiment had to assume logistic responsibility for both Brigades.

It was apparent that a perhaps unforeseen benefit of succeeding to defeat the Argentinians at Goose Green and Darwin, had emerged, in that the Argentine forces now expected the assault of Stanley to come firmly from the easier going trail along the southern West to East axis from Darwin, and possibly also including a direct amphibious assault on Stanley; but Teal Inlet was not on their radar, and the entire 3 Commando Brigade were now pouring assets, equipment, and troops through Teal. This Axis was to prove decisive, and a lot of it was in place before 5 Brigade had barely started to come ashore.

D+13 Thursday 3 June 1982

One Troop Medical Squadron. Having set up our facility yesterday, this was to be our second and final day at Teal Inlet without surgical and resuscitation clinical assets. A daily pattern would all too soon emerge of receiving multiple casualties and, within a few days, fatalities too, for the duration of our deployment at this location:

Land Mines. Marine Curtis from L Company 42 Commando suffered what was to be recognised as the typical injury sustained by stepping on an anti-personnel mine, after his patrol inadvertently found themselves in one of the deadly unmarked Argentine mine fields. Such injuries typically presented with the foot and ankle having been protected by the victim's boot, but almost totally amputated traumatically by the impact of the blast, from the lower leg. Commonly leaving just 3 or 4 inches of skin and other soft tissue keeping the booted foot loosely dangling. The cold weather consistently ensured the peripheral circulation of such cases was minimal, so none exsanguinated (bled to death).

These mines were designed to debilitate, and in so doing, to tie up men and resources to treat and evacuate them; and above all to sap morale and instil fear. Marine Curtis had to be evacuated further to Ajax Bay because at this stage we had inadequate resuscitation capability, i.e., no better than a Unit/Regiment Aid Post might be able to provide, and zero professional surgical capability. Of course, it would have been feasible to cut the remaining tissue away, and to have dressed the wound, but it would have been far from ideal and might well have required diathermy (sealing blood vessels by heat) of potential bleeding as a result of such an intervention, so without access to surgery, the preferred course was to apply a temporary dressing and splint the whole injury, give analgesia, and evacuate rearward. If we could have got a support helicopter (see the paragraph below) we would have sent him straight back to Uganda Hospital Ship, but it would have incurred an unquantified delay. 3 Brigade Air Squadron were able to immediately casevac Marine Curtis to Ajax Bay, and this was to be the first and last case we could not adequately care for.

With regard to this particular mine field, 59 Command RE spent the next 24 hours clearing it, and thankfully none were injured doing this dangerous work, but mine injuries were to become an increasing problem, as this was to prove far from being an isolated incident.

Support Helicopter Tasking. Some have subsequently been critical of the availability of support helicopters (Sea king 4's, Wessex 5's, and Chinook) for tasking, including tactical, logistical, and medical, but it has to be remembered that 845 Naval Air Squadron (Wessex 5's), and 846 Naval Air Squadron (Sea King 4's) were configured to support 3 Commando Brigade RM with 3 fighting/manoeuvre Units (40, 42 and 45 Commandos), the Commando Logistic Regiment RM; 29 Commando RA; and 59 Commando RE. During the Falkland War these two Naval Air Squadrons had to support a Brigade with 5 manoeuvre Units (i.e., 2 and 3 Para additionally), and a plethora of other Units, (such as the Rapier Batteries, and the Blues and Royals), and not least support Special Forces operations, often being mounted from ships of the Task Force, sometimes hundreds of miles away). Moreover, by this stage, the Commando Helicopter Force were supporting 5 Brigade, who were struggling to play catch up, and only one Chinook was available, as we must remind ourselves, because Atlantic Conveyor was lost to an Exocet missile, losing three chinooks and six Wessex 5's. Thus 845 and 846 Naval Air Squadrons were being pulled in many directions, and even Pilots have to sleep!

With regard to casualty evacuation, the Sea kings and Wessex were almost exclusively used for the rearward evacuation of the casualties we had treated, back to the hospital ship Uganda. There were however some exceptions to this when the support helicopters also flew casualties back to us from the forward Units, usually having flown supplies forward and being tasked whilst on the ground in the forward areas to take casualties or fatalities rearward on an opportunity basis. The fact that Teal Inlet had a helicopter refuelling facility within a few hundred metres of our location made it easier for all helicopters to undertake such casevacs.

Argentine Fatalities. A familiar pattern that was to emerge at Teal Inlet, was that fatalities from both sides of the conflict were brought back to our facility by helicopter. In the case of UK fatalities, as a minimum, they should have dog tags to identify them (there were two exceptions to this), but in the case of Argentine casualties it was impossible to identify them, and so our Troop Quartermaster, CPO John Smith, found himself having to do the best he could for them, cleaning them up and placing them into body bags ready for burial. Because we had no Unit details, and no known name, and no number, the fact of burial of an unknown Argentine soldier was passed to the Field Records Office. These were not recorded as patients as they were dead on arrival (DoA), killed in action, and had not gone into our Reception for admission.

On one occasion in particular, a Wessex Mk5 helicopter brought back multiple dead Argentine conscripts, and the aircrewman in the rear cab could barely bring himself to handle these poor dead souls, as I organised their movement straight to our makeshift mortuary. They were in a dreadful state and clearly all very dead, and, as with a group of Argentine fatalities received at Ajax Bay, and others at Teal Inlet, they had no identity. They were prepared for burial and the Field Record Office was notified. A burial ceremony was organised liaising with the Commando Logistic Regiment for the provision of a Priest or Padre. As had happened at Ajax Bay, none of these fatalities were logged into the admission and discharge book because they never went into the medical facility. Whilst technically correct, I was not aware this was occurring, and would have preferred that they were logged as unknown Argentine fatalities, received Dead on Arrival.

All Argentine fatalities were laid to rest in the same trench as our own troops, with a brief but proper ceremony. The reality was that our primary task was saving lives and having to also shoulder this responsibility for the dead was a significant additional pressure. Quite simply there was no one else to take on this task however, and all these poor souls, regardless of whether they were Argentine or British, were treated with the utmost dignity, as were all the wounded casualties.

Only one Argentine casualty died in our care. He was only barely alive when he arrived at our location (which was later on 12 June 1982) and died very soon afterwards before anyone could attempt to save him, at a time when we were inundated with a group of Argentine casualties. He was named by his other wounded Argentine comrades, with whom he had been casevaced back to us, and he had multiple gunshot wounds. This fatality had been admitted to our location and was therefore recorded as an admission who was Discharged Dead (DD). For CPO Smith, and his occasional helpers, the task of preparing the fatalities for burial was an unimaginably horrific job; the stuff of nightmares; and for me John Smith showed remarkable diligence, impartiality, and deference to duty, in this unenviable aspect of one of his many tasks.

The above details are a sensitive but factual reality, and it is my own first hand witness account which I never expected to be challenged. That is however exactly what happened on the weekend of Saturday

1 August 2020, with considerable consequences, as will become clear later.

Letter Home: On the evening of 3 June, we received mail and I finally managed to pen my second letter since coming ashore:

'Dear Bev, Many thanks for letters 1 & 2 dated 16 May which I received this evening....I have now moved forward with my Troop to a new location and am no longer with Eddy (Petty Officer Middleton HQ Medical Squadron). We are in a farm settlement and are working in and around the Bunk House. It is reminiscent of 1st World War movie scenes, with chickens around the place and pilots coming in for a cup of tea whilst their aircraft are refuelled. The only difference is we are using helicopters and not bi-planes but their speed and navigation aids are very similar.'

'The weather at the moment is exceptionally mild compared to my last time here (i.e in 1978). The wind has been very subdued. Of course I am aware that it can and will no doubt change dramatically. There has been a lot of mist around because of unseasonal conditions. This has given us good cover, but impeded our advance by restricted flying. With luck it will all be over by the time you receive this letter.'

'I dream of having a bath and having a clean change of clothing but at least I am dry and relatively comfortable and cannot describe the grief I feel when we receive dead and wounded casualties – some terribly maimed for ever. I pray it all ends soon!'

'In the mean time my love, take care.....All my love and kisses.'

Trench Foot – A Serious Threat.

Trench Foot is categorised as a non-freezing cold injury, and the wet peat bogs and saturated grass of the cold Falkland winter with its incessant wind, were to prove to be the ideal ingredient for this World War One phenomenon to reignite. Over the next two weeks we were to admit 52 severe UK cases suffering from this debilitating condition, that reduced some of the strongest, fittest, most elite troops, to disabled casualties, unable to walk unaided. 3 Para suffered the highest proportion, with 19 cases admitted through Teal Inlet and eventually casevaced to the Hospital Ship Uganda. They were closely followed by 42 Commando, with 17 cases similarly casevaced to Uganda, and 45 Commando with 11 cases. The remainder came from 29 Commando (3); 2 Para (1) and Special Forces (1). It should be noted that 2 Para casevac route would have mainly been through 5 Brigade's system – thus the apparent difference with 3 Para.

The Argentine forces were far from immune from this predicament, and the following picture reflects a typical image of Trench Foot in an Argentine patient treated at Ajax Bay, with Marine O'Donovan from 3 Troop Medical Squadron in attendance.

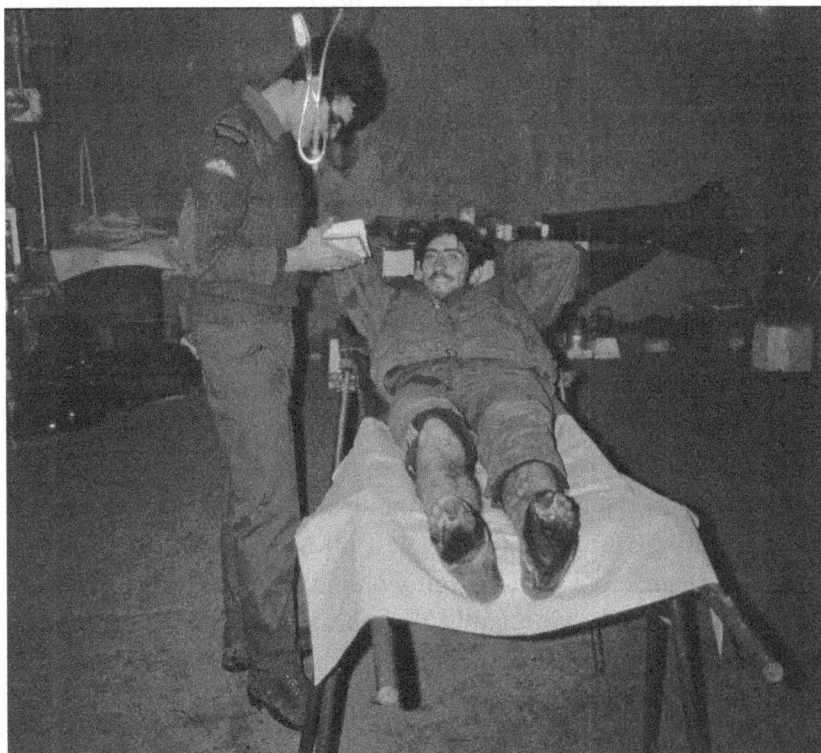

Some operational officers felt this was a minor problem and that individuals were making more of the condition than their symptoms merited, but that is not just unkind to the individuals afflicted, it ignores the true disabling physiology of this condition. Many others were understandably quick to blame their boots, but that may also have been far too simplistic.

Until tomorrow when we are reinforced from Medical Squadron at Ajax Bay, our sole Troop Doctor is Surgeon Lieutenant Howard Oakley. Howard was not a surgical or other specialist registrar, he was a recently qualified doctor who had finished his 'houseman' training at the RN Hospitals, and was a similar age to me, around 26 years old. He was however almost certainly the only clinician in this theatre of war, truly concerned and interested in the physiology of trench foot, and no one could have done more than him to try to revive the feeling of normal sensation in the feet of these afflicted individuals, and to remove their pain, not simply abate it temporarily with analgesia. He would hold these cases in our tented evacuation 'ward' for days, striving to ensure the temperature was as conducive as possible to their recovery, and exploring every possible treatment avenue. But it was all largely to no avail, as the significant majority would end up being evacuated to the Hospital Ship Uganda. I was very unkind to Howard one evening after the war, having had one beer too many, to describe his endeavours as useless, as in this respect I was surely looking in the mirror, as none of us were able to do any better.

It's important to reiterate that in the Royal Navy the term Surgeon originates from the 18th century when the Ship's Surgeon was also the butcher, who had to combine his knowledge of cutting up meat, with the business of saving lives. By 1982, and for many, many years before, and to this day, all Medical Officers have a Medical Degree, but the term Surgeon did not confer a professional surgical status. The 'Surgeon' title indicates 'Doctor', and perhaps it would be better replaced with the latter, because it was then, and must remain today, a source of misunderstanding – not least with the wider medical fraternity.

After the war Howard Oakley was to spend many years researching non-freezing cold injury at the Institute of Naval Medicine, but to this day there is still no treatment for Trench Foot, other than to allow those affected to recover in the most conducive climatic situation possible, and their recovery can take many weeks.

In 2013, Surgeon Rear Admiral Francis (Frank) Golden, (with Thomas Francis, and Deborah Gallimore) wrote a 'Lessons in History' review of the morbidity of cold injury during the Falkland Conflict, using 3 Commando Brigade as the 'study group', based on surveys conducted after the Brigade returned home in 1982, the paper concluded that whilst 'just' 70 cases were evacuated to Uganda, 16% of the Brigade sought treatment at RAP or Medical Squadron level for non-freezing cold injury. 76% of the fighting Unit troops (40, 42 and 45 Commandos) had some degree of affliction. In 29 Commando RA and 59 Commando RE it was lower, but still 59%, and even in the Commando Logistic Regiment it was 42%. Most significantly, the report noted that the Brigade troops, incredibly, wore 46 different types of boots, but 75% wore either DMS, or Cairngorm Mountain Boots. 80% of the Brigade used the standard issue plastic insole. **Not one single type of boot was shown to have afforded better protection against Trench Foot. Trench Foot afflicted troops regardless of the type of boot worn, in proportionate numbers.**

So, was something else going on? The following statement within the paper gives deeper insight:

'If one fell, it was a major effort to get up, which involved the assistance of several comrades who themselves were struggling under their own appalling loads and fatigue. They 'yomped' (marched) all the first day and half that night before bedding down in the open for the remainder of the night. Unfortunately it rained heavily before dawn and, without tents, with only ponchos (waterproofed capes) for protection, they were soaked through. The following morning they set out again but this time took only ration packs and weapons in anticipation of enemy contact.'

'That night they reached their objective, the small settlement at Teal, where they adopted defensive positions around the settlement. There, they were able to relax and bed down for 2–3 days while 'recce groups' surveyed the surrounding countryside. But without the benefit of sleeping bags on a bitterly cold night, many, despite their exhaustion, kept walking in a circle to help maintain body heat. The ambient temperature was below 0°C. At this stage, some noticed numbness of their feet with paraesthesia on weight bearing. Most had blisters. Once contact with the enemy was made, the men moved forward again often through driving rain and falling snow. As the enemy positions were predominantly on the upper regions of the mountains, it was necessary for a series of assaults over steep gradients to occur, frequently at night, often in sub-zero temperatures with very strong winds—survival conditions.'

'After several days of these horrific conditions, with fluctuating temperatures, precipitation and high wind speeds, many lost all sensation in their now white toes, and paraesthesia made it difficult for some to sleep at night. For these, weight bearing first thing in the morning was particularly painful. On occasions, the weather improved, in that it stopped raining, but [it] froze instead.'

Certainly, troops were coming back to us, often soaking wet, always freezing cold if not clinically hypothermic (i.e., unacceptably low core body temperature) from the incessant wind chill; whereas those with good leg and body weather protection, and also a good bivouac when resting up, would have good peripheral circulation and so had a far better chance of avoiding Trench Foot. But it was a lottery, and if someone's boots had shipped water over the top of the boot when they went ashore, or during one of the long marches, the more waterproof boots simply retained the water. The thick loop stitch arctic socks worn next to the skin were also a recipe for terrible blisters that were avoided by those who wore thin smooth socks beneath them – many a boot was blamed for blisters caused by these loop stitch arctic socks.

What Surgeon Rear Admiral Golding's paper shows us very clearly is that Trench Foot was a ticking time bomb among many forward troops and among nearly half of the more rear troops too, and those who thought otherwise simply were not in possession of the facts. If the war had gone beyond mid-June, the numbers that were being evacuated would have multiplied exponentially.

Disposition of Friendly Forces

Black Buck 6. The RAF carried out yet another bombing mission, again hitting Stanley runway. The fact that the Argentines were able to effect temporary repairs and the runway was never totally delivered a knockout crater, is more a reflection on the bombs available to the Vulcans at that time, without going 'nuclear', which is what these long-range cold war bombers were designed to deliver. What should never be underestimated is the degree of fear and morale sapping effect these bombing raids must have had on the largely conscript young Argentine men, and also on their regular officers. Few if any would have envisaged that the UK would be able to mount successive bombing raids against them, conducting the longest bombing raids in history at that point, seemingly with impunity. It must by now have been crossing their minds that their home towns and cities might be at similar risk from these cold war vintage bombers, not to mention the UK's ability to ratchet up operations with the strategic deterrent SSBN submarines that had long replaced these bombers in that role.

79 Battery Royal Artillery and 3 Para. 105mm light guns are flown forward to support 3 Para who now dominate the ground in and around Estancia. 3 Para are conducting rigorous night patrols of their next objective, Mount Longdon.

42 Commando has similarly dominated the ground on and around Mount Kent and is also conducting night patrols of their next objective, Mount Harriet. The purpose of these patrols is not just to determine the disposition of the enemy, but to discern the preferred axis of the attack, and in this respect Lt Col Nick Vaux seems to be ahead of everyone, as he has concluded that he will hit Mount Harriet from the South East side i.e. the Stanley facing side, as the Argentine main defences are, understandably, facing West towards Goose Green.

45 Commando had mostly been resting up at Teal Inlet since 1 June, but their CO Lieutenant Colonel Whitehead, had not been wasting this time. Recce Troop, and elements of Condor Troop 59 Commando RE who were embedded with the 45 Commando Group, had been patrolling their next objective, Two Sisters, and the presence of Condor Troop Royal Engineers with Recce Troop is yet more indication of the growing awareness that there is a serious threat from unmarked and indiscriminate sowing of mine fields.

M&AW Cadre similarly remain at Teal Inlet whilst conducting patrols and inserting OP's. In between these demanding operations, these men volunteer their services to help us at our facility, collecting casualties from 3 Brigade Air Squadron helicopters and bearing their stretchers into our reception tent, 30 metres from the designated Landing Site - any closer and the tentage was at risk of being blown away by the helicopter downdraft on landing and take-off.

SBS. We have been sharing the accommodation in the Bunk House with the SBS who had moved upstairs, and most of our team were kipping where they worked. Now the SBS leave, taking the body of Sgt 'Kiwi' Hunt with them, and it is the last contact we have with them during this war. Sgt Ian Nicholas Hunt's body was repatriated to the UK and his last resting place is at St Michael's Churchyard, Hamworthy, Poole. Despite undertaking numerous covert beach reconnaissance and other special operations, this was to be their only loss of the conflict.

SAS. The location of neither D nor G Squadron is known to One Troop Medical Squadron at this juncture, but it cannot be ruled out that elements will be conducting reconnaissance in Stanley in 'plain site', masquerading as civilians. A future objective for the SAS is the low hill feature immediately opposite Stanley, across the North side of the bay, known as Cortley Ridge. This feature holds large fuel storage tanks once mainly utilised by RN ships and now largely for the Power Station. These are situated to the East of the former NP8901 base at Moody Brook, and the bay is well under a mile across from the water's edge of the feature to Stanley on the South side, so it is not an altogether insignificant target.

5 Brigade

2 Para are now operating within 5 Brigade for the final push, on the southerly West to East axis, towards Stanley. They have been flown forward to Bluff Cove with a battery of 29 Commando 105mm light guns in support.

The 1/7 Gurkha Rifles have taken the place of 2 Para at Darwin and Goose Green, having marched from San Carlos.

The Welsh and Scots Guards are still situated around San Carlos. There is disquiet and rumour circulating about their physical fitness and 'grit' for the task ahead.

D+14 Friday 4 June 1982
One Troop, Medical Squadron, Teal Inlet.

Kelp Water 'Trots'. One Troop Medical Squadron start to receive another group of Medivacs (Medical patient evacuations) with which it becomes very familiar, and the Treatment's Section boss CPOMA Graham Edwards is already very familiar with this from his NP8901 days in the Falklands- Kelp water 'trots'! 45 Commando were the worst affected with over 30 men evacuated to the facility over the next 10 days, but all the main Units were affected in 3 Commando Brigade. The main problem being the need to draw water from streams and rivers. Some of the unfortunate individuals mention they had ran out of water sterilisation tablets. This may have played a part, but as former NP8901 members, both Graham Edwards and I can recount that the peat content of water in the field (or camp as the countryside is known to the Islanders) can cause very severe 'trots', and bacteria need play no part. Indeed, even the well treated water in Stanley can have a high peat content which triggers severe diarrhoea in an unsuspecting and unconditioned digestive system. This may sound amusing to some, but this 'bog standard' medical condition could easily prove fatal in troops having to live and fight in the middle of a Falkland Island winter. The afflicted can become severely dehydrated in just a few hours, not to mention the debilitating limitations of practicing 'cat sanitation', with a minimal supply of toilet paper, whilst suffering from severe trots in a war zone. The Unit Aid Posts can of course administer a limited quantity of appropriate medication, but the most severe cases needed not just rest and a gradually reintroduced diet with plenty of clean water, but initially intravenous infusion to rapidly rehydrate them. A 12 x 12 feet Unit Aid Post tent could at best manage and hold a couple of such cases and nothing else. Thus, the most severe cases were all Medivaced by 3 Brigade Air Squadron, back to Teal Inlet, often in the middle of the night when it was safest for helicopters to fly and usually combined with re-supply flights forward.

Having been initially booked in to the system in the 24 x 18 feet Reception Tent, these patients will have been sent through to Graham Edwards small team in Treatments within the Bunkhouse, to receive a full assessment and appropriate treatment regime, and then be taken into the Evacuation 'ward' 24 x 18 feet tent to begin their recovery, which fortunately was usually within 48 hours of admission, and resulted in such cases being Returned to Unit (RTU'd) without further interventions.

Clinical Support. To this point Howard Oakley has been our only doctor. We have been here at Teal Inlet with fewer doctors than a single Commando Unit Aid Post, all of which had been reinforced with a second doctor for this war, and they benefitted from a dentist also. Now he is joined by Surgeon Lieutenant Commander Tim Douglas-Riley from the Surgical Support Team 2 at Ajax Bay, who has substantial experience as a Resuscitation doctor, and was one of two Commando doctors (the other being Surgeon Lieutenant Nick Morgan) to treat 3 Para's 'blue on blue' casualties aboard the Assault Ship HMS Intrepid, shortly after the initial landings at Port San Carlos. The prompt and appropriate endeavours of doctors Tim Douglas-Riley and Nick Morgan is surely one of the key reasons none of the 8 seriously wounded paratroopers died, and they were all subsequently successfully operated on and further managed at Ajax Bay. Tim has three of the highest qualified Medical Technician 1 CPO's with him. Tony Byrne and Steve Davis are to be deployed with Tim Riley in Graham Edwards Treatment section, and now with LMA Jock Winton, MA's Mick Greaves and Taff Barlow, and general duties Corporal John Clare with marine Jim Giles, the treatment section can handle just about anything that confronts them. Jim Giles was fluent in Spanish which proved particularly useful when treating Argentine casualties. MT1 Trevor Firth provides welcome additional clinical support to the tented Evacuation ward, joining POMA John 'Jacko' Jackson, LMA Andy Ellis, MA Nick Vrettos, and marines Jock Ewing, Taff Price, 'Wal' Wallace, 'Robby' Robinson, and Kev Frankland.

In addition, Major Charles Batty RAMC Surgeon, and Major Dick Knight RAMC Anaesthetist, with Warrant Officer Fritz Sterba, and other members of 5 Field Surgical Team, join us with their operating table and equipment, to set up next to our Command Post, and co-located with Major Treatments/Resuscitation in the main room of the Bunk House.

Our Reception tent has no newcomers, and relies on LMA's to prioritise patients into Major or Minor treatment cases, and to feed them through in order or their priority. LMA's Dave Cook, Dave Poole, and Rod Cain share this considerable responsibility, assisted by MA Derek Whitfield, Cpl Tom (aka Tim) Robinson, and marines John Thurlow, Chris Thornton, and Taff Evans. Dr

Howard Oakley often provided additional support to this team at times of pressure.

Somehow HQ Medical Squadron had managed to retain 5 of my Royal Marines who had journeyed from the UK with One Troop and worked with the team at Ajax Bay. My Troop strength at Teal Inlet was just 34 (against a Peace Establishment of about 50), plus a handful of additional staff comprising most but not all of 5 Field Surgical Team. Our reinforcements were very welcome and much needed, but we would still be a very thinly spread staff, running a 24/7 facility.

Our revised facility is quickly set up and we notify the Commando Logistic Regiment and Medical Squadron at Ajax Bay on the Land Force Admin net of our new found surgical capability and much enhanced resuscitation capability. Sgt John Simonds similarly then picks up the land line phone and relays the same information to 3 Brigade Air Squadron.

None of our newcomers are ever found wanting at Teal Inlet. The three CPO MT1's are not Commando trained, but they are capable professionals who fit in well and act as good clinical mentors to our team.

Troop changes at Teal Inlet. 45 Commando has largely vacated Teal now, and forward elements of 3 Commando Brigade HQ and Signals Squadron are moving in, between our facility, and 3 Brigade Air Squadron. An assortment of what are known as B echelon or second line elements of various Units are now working from Teal, receiving all their supplies by regular Landing Ship Logistic (LSL) voyages from San Carlos Water, from potable drinking water to rounds (bullets), shells, mail, and rations, and moving them forward to those now on the outer high ground ring, which is like a choke, keeping the Argentine troops within.

Civilian Aid to the Military Community! This is the reverse of a well-established military term, i.e. Military Aid to the Civilian

Community. The young 16 year old Neil Rowlands, and his 2 chums in the bunk house found themselves elevated to **Key Worker** status (to use a 21st century term), and Neil's tractor and trailer were frequently sought to help move stores, ammunition and jerry cans of water up from the beach at Teal Inlet, up to the farm buildings, and sometimes beyond that. He conveyed Argentine prisoners of war from the Malo Hills; and helped us with stretcher bearing casualties to and from helicopters!

D+15 Saturday 5 June 1982

One Troop Medical Squadron is alerted by the land line from 3 Brigade Air Squadron at first light that another casevac helicopter is inbound. The Reception team was alerted in their tent and, with a couple of the team away snatching a bite to eat at breakfast, Cpl Tom Robinson and myself, with LMA Dave Poole and Marine John Thurlow, go out to await the small helicopter, but Marine Gosling in our Command Post receives a land line call from 3 Brigade Air Squadron to stand us down, as the helicopter is on its way to Ajax Bay. Whether this was because somebody had been unaware of our upgraded capability as a surgical centre, or because of some other reason, we do not know, but the extended flight to Ajax Bay was not in the best interest of the wounded patient.

Marine Kevin Patterson, 42 Commando, had been on a patrol led by Sgt Nev Weston, and the first indication they had that they are in the middle of yet another mine field is when an explosion shattered the silence of their stealthy night patrol, and Kevin Patterson gave out a cry of pain, as one of his feet and ankle are all but totally torn from his leg. The nightmare scenario of trying to care for a wounded patient, and extricate the patrol from an unmarked minefield, with a seriously injured casualty, whilst summoning a helicopter to rescue him, is frankly unimaginable.

Despite the casevac having been diverted to Ajax Bay, this story is more relevant than other mine incidents, not just because it acted as a good preparatory exercise for our newly attached 5 Field Surgical Team, but because, as Nick Van Der Bijl's excellent book 'Nine Battles for Stanley' records, half of the 42 Commando patrol that Marine Kevin Patterson had been with that fateful night, actually continued its mission. Another Sergeant, also with the patrol, Tom Collins, led 3 men to the western edge of Mount Harriet, their Unit's next objective. They were spotted by an alert Argentine patrol but managed to go to ground and avoided an engagement in the midst of the enemy. They were able to clearly see the route that the Argentine patrol took when it finally gave up its search and headed back towards their own lines. This route was noted down by Sergeant Collins and passed to Lieutenant Colonel Nick Vaux when they returned to 42 Commando. This route was to be the basis for the axis of 42 Commando's successful attack on Mount Harriet, approaching on its South side from the direction of Stanley, several days later.

Later in the day, we received another mine victim at Teal Inlet, who was whisked straight into our Reception tent, where he was tagged with his FMed 28 Field Medical Card, and his vital signs were assessed by LMA Dave Cook, and found to be quite reasonable considering the circumstances of this traumatic amputation.

He was taken into the rear door of the Bunk House, through the minor treatment centre into the door immediately on the right, into the Major treatment and Surgical operating area. Surgeon Lieutenant Commander Tim Douglas-Riley was ready to prepare our latest casualty for surgery, and Anaesthetist Dick Knight is similarly hovering to assist. The Operating Team are ready, buzzing around with an air of enthusiasm that cannot hide that they actually relish their task. If I were to suggest to them that this casualty was going straight from the resuscitation table to Uganda instead of being operated on here and now at Teal Inlet, I think at least one of them would have wanted to put me under the knife instead!

Sadly, as with all such cases we were to receive, both at Ajax Bay and Teal Inlet, all that could be done was complete what the traumatic blast had failed to achieve and fully amputate the leg from its dangling ankle and foot, ensuring the wound was surgically cleaned up and dressed. We did not incinerate such body parts at Teal, in case the resulting smoke literally sent the wrong signals to our foe, giving our location away. We buried all such amputations, in the large slit trench which 59 Commando Royal Engineers had prepared for us to bury the dead, just behind the line of evergreen trees to the South West of the building, probably about 40 or 50 yards from the Bunk House.

Casevac to Hospital Ship Uganda. At around mid-day we have our first support helicopter land at Teal Inlet to take patients from our Evacuation ward to the Hospital Ship Uganda. During the two weeks we are at Teal Inlet we receive 217 casualties and medical cases for treatment.

Most casualties, having received appropriate care, including surgery when necessary, are flown out to Uganda. For them the war is over, and this includes 9 Argentine casualties who have survived their injuries and been cared for. Some UK casualties and medical cases were able to re-join their Units from Teal Inlet, and this is estimated to have been around 50 cases, which includes the vast majority of medical cases, in which event around 165 cases were subsequently flown back to the Hospital Ship Uganda.

The Uganda was supported by 3 smaller vessels, HMS Hecla, HMS Hydra, and HMS Herald, which were also formally declared to the International Red Cross as Hospital Ships. The role of these three smaller vessels was to 'decant' patients who had been treated on Uganda and to ferry them to Montevideo where they were passed ashore. UK casualties were flown home via RAF VC10. So these three smaller vessels were perhaps more accurately Ambulance ships.

Uganda shared the honour of being one of our oldest vessels in the 200 mile exclusion zone, having been completed in 1952, but it's a matter of interpretation as the aircraft carrier Hermes had actually been laid down during WW2 in 1944, but never entered service until 1959. Uganda had been in the Mediterranean when Argentina invaded the Falklands. She was then an education cruise liner for school children who were put ashore at Gibraltar. Uganda was converted to its new role in under 60 hours, including a helicopter pad, and refuelling at sea capability. Reverse Osmosis water plants were added later on 15 May by the ship's engineers, whilst in the South Atlantic. The ship had 82 medical staff including surgical consultants including general, orthopaedic, burns, and maxillofacial specialists, and other consultants in anaesthetics, medicine, psychiatry, radiology, and pathology. There were a number of junior medical officers, 2 medical service officers (for administration and public health responsibilities), 14 nursing officers, and 32 male and 23 female nursing staff. The medical staff were almost entirely provided by the two RN Hospitals at Haslar in Gosport, and Stonehouse in Plymouth. They were supported by 23 Royal Marine Bandsmen, and numerous volunteers among the ship's crew. The conditions on Uganda were as close to perfect as it was possible to achieve for its patients, and Surgeon Commander Mike Beeley who was aboard the vessel later noted that 270 British casualties had suffered from penetrating injuries (gunshot wounds) and represented 46% of the British casualty caseload. The medical team on Uganda performed over 500 operations under anaesthetic using 2 operating tables for 12 hours each day and requiring 361 units of blood to be transfused.

Yes, the Hospital Ship medical team had superb accommodation at sea, but Uganda was absolutely key to ensuring the work that had been started ashore in very different, difficult circumstances, went on to save all but 3 casualties (from both sides of the conflict) that were evacuated to the ship. Moreover, the small Ambulance Ships, Hecla, Hydra, and Herald, ensured Uganda never exceeded her bed capacity.

D+16 Sunday 6 June to D+20 Thursday 10 June 1982.

By a quirk of fate, it is 6 June 2020 as this is being written, exactly 38 years after the events, which that day at Teal Inlet marked exactly 38 years that 'the other' D Day landings took place over the beaches of Normandy. Then as now, with 3 Commando Brigade being critical to the success of the landings, and the subsequent breakout into the surrounding hinterland.

The Brigades Tactical Headquarters is now also here at Teal Inlet, and Leading Medical Assistant (LMA) Pat Parsons is providing their medical cover. Like my Troop, and all Medical Assistants of all ranks forward with the fighting Units and Companies, Pat is Commando trained, and our Royal Marine counterparts all refer to such individuals as 'Doc' which is testimony to the esteem in which they are regarded, and the faith that our Royal Marine brothers have in our abilities to look after them in their moment of need. Whether it's a plaster for a blister, or an infusion to maintain satisfactory blood pressure when someone is wounded, or medication for a particular condition, they know these men will do their utmost for them. Pat has found our location, and visits to seek a small number of resupplies for his medical and first aid stores. He also offers to help us whilst he is in Teal Inlet and for several days he provides a welcome addition to our strength on an ad hoc as needed basis.

We are now waiting for 5 Brigade to catch up and move into position and we hear that Landing Ships Logistic (LSL's) Sir Galahad and Sir Tristram are now both ferrying elements of the Scots and Welsh Guards forward to Fitzroy, largely because these two battalions had been unable to repeat the long marches that the Royal Marine Commandos, and Paratroopers from 3 Para, had achieved over the tougher Northern terrain.

All the forward Units within 3 Commando Brigade, not least 3 Para, had by this stage experienced contact with the enemy that had given the strongest possible indication that the Argentine troops were still manning viable Observation Posts on the high ground they still held. Indeed a 3 Para probing patrol of Mount Longdon two days earlier had been subject to artillery shell fire that had caused them to withdraw. 42 Commando, 45 Commando, and 3 Para, as well as the M&AW Cadre, were rigorously probing and patrolling not just their future objectives but also those that would subsequently be given to 5 Brigade assets. The upshot of this is that there were daily contacts with the enemy, resulting in both casualties and fatalities, and the victims of these encounters came back through Teal Inlet. A typical day would see some Trench Foot and Kelp Water Trot diarrhoea medivacs, along with some battle casualty casevacs, and some fatalities. Fatalities were always a low point, regardless of whether they were UK or Argentine. Each victim still required four men to carry them from a helicopter, and it still required preparing them, albeit before placing them in a body bag, and it then required more men to carry the bodies over to the burial area when a burial team had been arranged, including a Priest and/or Padre.

All the time the weather was deteriorating, and the days were at their shortest. The Brigade had wintered in Norway, and now it was wintering in the Falklands having only benefitted from a brief UK spring before sailing with the Task Force. This was something that former 8901 members were all too familiar with – a double winter whammy.

We typically were receiving between 10 and 15 casualties and medivacs daily during this phase, which supposedly represented a quiet phase of the war. All arrived by light helicopter, and the majority being subsequently evacuated to Uganda by the much larger support helicopters – typically arranging two or three such flights each day, and always unescorted as we could not afford to lose any of our staff to being stuck on Uganda. None of us from One Troop actually went on this floating paradise that was absolutely crucial to the survival of so many casualties from troops on both sides of the conflict. If either the medical facility at Ajax Bay, or here at Teal Inlet, had been permanently knocked out, Uganda could have come in closer and the situation could have been worked around; but if Uganda had been sunk, it would have represented a much greater catastrophic blow to the Casualty Evacuation Plan.

Chemical Attack Threat. During the course of what was otherwise a typical day, our Command Post was alerted to be prepared for the possibility of a chemical attack. Collective Protection for field medical facilities did not exist at that time, and some individuals expressed concern that they had left their personal chemical protection equipment i.e. S6 gas respirator and protective clothing, boots, and gloves, at Ajax Bay. The threat report was clearly driven by hard intelligence, but all of us were relieved that nothing transpired. Those who had left their kit at Ajax Bay were no doubt the most relieved however.

(By the time Medical Squadron deployed to the First Gulf War, with 200 reservists and bandsmen whom we had trained, and 60 regular Squadron personnel, initially in support of 32 Field Hospital RAMC during Operation Granby, Medical Squadron was particularly proficient in utilising full collective protection, but little was utilised by 32 Field Hospital. All personnel with 32 Field Hospital grew accustomed to living, eating, and sleeping in individual personnel protection, and wearing the improved S10 respirators. Fortunately, at the end of Op Granby, when Medical Squadron was re-deployed to Northern Iraq only days after returning to the UK, with 160 personnel, for Operation Haven, chemical protection never proved necessary – given the high ambient temperatures that was a huge relief).

Visit heralds Mail. Major Gerry Wells-Cole RM **is** 3 Commando Brigade HQ's lead officer for Logistics who continuously liaises with the CO of the Commando Logistic Regiment, Lieutenant Colonel Ivar Hellberg, and they both work tirelessly, striving to ensure the Landing Force's share of 100,000 tons of supplies that have been shipped to support Operation Corporate , are moved forward to their Units. Major Wells-Cole visits Teal Inlet and takes the opportunity to look in on our medical facility to 'ensure we are not forgotten'. He is reassured with what he sees, as Tim Douglas-Riley just finishes working on a patient who is passed back outside, and into the tented Evacuation ward. It's literally a brief drop in visit, but he advises we may have mail and other deliveries, so Tim and I take the opportunity to walk back up the settlement towards other Brigade assets.

Despite the cold it's good to get out of the medical facility for 5 minutes, there are no helicopters buzzing around and for a brief moment life feels almost normal, as we three enjoy a pleasant chat. In the large farm sheds that 3 Brigade Air Squadron had been working on a Scout helicopter when we first arrived at Teal Inlet, there is now a Wessex Mk 5 Commando helicopter, as it seems a flight of four Wessex have now also been deployed to this Forward Operating Base. Tim and I pick up a couple of mail bags and head back down to the Bunk House, where morale is already good, and now it has been lifted further, as the mail is handed out – just letters from family and loved ones, but somehow its better than Christmas!

D+18 Tuesday 8 June 1982. News filters back to us at Teal Inlet that 3 Ships and a Landing Craft Utility have been hit whilst trying to offload Welsh Guards and Scots Guards at Fitzroy. The details are initially vague, but we learn that it includes elements of 16 Field Ambulance RAMC who were to have supported 5 Brigade. Initially we are told there are 55 dead (5 from HMS Plymouth; 48 from the LSL Galahad; and 2 from the LSL Sir Tristram). We then are told that there were also 6 Royal Marines killed when a Landing Craft was also hit. There are apparently about 150 burns cases, who are all being casevaced back to Ajax Bay, where they typically will receive the application of Flamazine burns cream, with a sterile plastic sheet overlay (like 'kling film' in its consistency), and the more serious cases would receive a regime of intra-venous fluids.

Teal Inlet is the only Second Line Medical Facility unaffected by this disastrous situation and able to accept casualties from across the Landing Force as usual.

Nobody in One Troop seemed really surprised by the news. Having been on the receiving end of bombs ourselves at Ajax Bay, we were saddened but not surprised. Also, we had been hearing from casualties and medivacs that a 3 Para patrol had been subject to accurate shelling and gunfire that must have been directed from an Argentine Observation Post. The ships were in such exposed positions that it was inevitable if any enemy Observation Posts were still functioning in the vicinity and the Argentines were capable of mounting an air attack, they would do so, not least because this had been an air corridor for their aircraft between Goose Green and Stanley.

Much later after the war it transpired that an Observation Post manned by Argentine 602 Commando on Mount Harriet had indeed summoned the raid, which involved three waves of aircraft. The first two waves comprised 4 Skyhawks each, and the final wave was 6 Daggers.

Harriers shot down 3 of the Skyhawks, and some accounts state as many as 10 Argentine aircraft were brought down in total but suffice to say it was not a walk in the park for the Argentine pilots. The Argentine land forces were unable to exploit this hard-won advantage that the Argentine Air Force had achieved however, and the main strategic consequence was a few more days delay was created in launching the attack on the outer positions still held by Argentine Forces around Stanley.

D+19 Wednesday 9 June 1982 We have some quite poorly Argentine casualties awaiting treatment in the Reception tent at Teal Inlet, along with a Sergeant from 3 Para and two young Paratroopers who are awaiting minor treatment. Unfortunately, it becomes clear that the two young Paratroopers think it would be fair game to have a go at the Argentine wounded who are in a sorry state. I have to intervene and explicitly tell the Paratroopers that the Argentine casualties are no longer combatants, they are unarmed casualties, and if either of them lay a finger upon them I will ensure they face appropriate charges. The Sergeant from 3 Para also intervenes to voice his support for my stance, which was very welcome. It was fortunately the only time during the whole conflict that I had to exercise use of my executive responsibility in such a way.

D+20 Thursday 10 June 1982 Patrols to harry the enemy intensified as the delay in attacking the outer positions ensued. Unfortunately, there was then a Blue on Blue, early on Thursday morning, well before first light. A so-called friendly fire incident that caused the death of four Royal Marines, Sergeant Robert Leeming, Corporal Andrew Uren, Corporal Peter Fitton, and Marine Keith Philips, and three further casualties. A 45 Commando patrol and the 45 Commando Mortar Troop mistook one another for Argentine forces. Surgeon Lieutenant David Griffiths and LMA Paul Youngman were dispatched to the scene in their 45 Commando Aid Post BV tracked vehicle, but by the time they arrived the three surviving casualties had already been evacuated. Paul Youngman placed the fatalities into the outer covers of their sleeping bags and into the back of the BV, where they were transported back to their Aid Post, but Paul recollects there was no room for him in the BV and he made the journey back on the roof of the vehicle, in freezing conditions. This was a low point for us at Teal Inlet, as many in the Troop knew the victims of this terrible mistaken encounter.

Letter Home: On 10 June I managed to pen my third letter home, since coming ashore:

'Dear Bev, It is now nearly three weeks since we moved ashore, and I have been in this location for as long as I had been at our first location. There is talk of us having to move further forward soon to compensate for an Army Med Unit that was hit during the air attacks at Fitzroy. My Troop are obviously lucky as none of us has been hurt throughout,

despite many around us being less fortunate. We intend to stay lucky! We don't really want to move from our present location because we have good air cover and our position has not been compromised by the BBC announcing it to the world as other locations have been'.

'I have lost track of money situations (at home) but there should be no problems. I will sit down and do some sums later today. On the gloomy side it looks as though my Access (bank) card, RAC card, driving licence, cheque book, history books, etc., have all been destroyed when the Galahad was badly damaged. Really I should have left the cards at home but we had no way of predicting this would happen. As soon as I can get some sort of confirmation about my kit I'll let you know so you can inform Access for me Bev.... we will have to ask Access to issue new cards'.

'I have also received a Motor Cycle News with a short letter dated 19 May thank you, but mail is very slow getting down here'

'Well honey, I will write again soon and let you know about my kit problems on Galahad, but thank God I wasn't on it!'

'Take care my love and hopefully we will be back together by the end of July for our birthdays! Lots of love to you'...

Brigade Plans for Phase One of the Final Assaults Towards Stanley.

We learn on 10 June that tomorrow, the night of 11/12 June 1982 is the planned opening phase of the final assaults to re-take Stanley. What has been termed The Argentine Outer Defence Zone, comprising Mount Harriet, The Two Sisters, and Mount Longdon, will be attacked by 3 Commando Brigade, including 3 Para, who will attack Longdon. 45 Commando will attack Two Sisters, whilst 42 Commando is to lead the attack on Harriet.

These 3 fighting Units have been exposed on the toughest terrain on the Archipelago, but have been rigorously probing their respective objectives, and the three Commanding Officers have been able to develop their planned assaults based on the intelligence gleaned by the patrolling, as well as gathered by covert Observation Posts.

D+21 Friday 11 June 1982

It's still dark as a number of us are huddled around our Galley Tent to get an early breakfast before we face another busy day, and perhaps the last we can refer to as typical, as anti-personnel mine victims, shrapnel wounds, trench foot, and kelp water trots, as well as an assortment of all other injuries and illnesses, have kept us busy since our move from Ajax Bay to Teal Inlet. We have remained on Greenwich Mean Time (Zulu Time) since our arrival, but at Teal we have adjusted our lifestyle so as not to be eating breakfast in the middle of the night, so it's probably around 1000Z or 0700 local as a Wessex fires up to the West of us in the settlement, it ground runs for a few minutes before taking off, clattering a few feet above our heads. It was just normal. Hardly anybody even looked up.

Later that day, some hours after sunrise, we learn that Wessex 5 Yankee Hotel, flown by Fleet Air Arm pilot Pete Manley and his navigator Arthur Balls, and armed with two wire guided anti-ship missiles, designated AS12's, had flown a daring lone raid in a bid to strike an enemy target in the heart of Stanley. Flying ultra-low until the Wessex was just North of Wireless ridge which is the high ground feature that runs West to East on the opposite North side of the bay from Stanley, the helicopter had climbed to about 200 feet and hovered in order for the wire guided missiles to be fired at the Town Hall, which abuts the bay lengthways, and the main Stanley road passes on the other side, with the Police Station adjacent on the opposite side of the road, just a few yards further down.

UK Special Forces had gleaned intelligence that the Argentine Land Force Commander. General Menendez, usually held an early morning meeting with his senior officers, in Stanley Town Hall, which in more normal times would host a variety of events, ranging from films – which were always well attended due to the lack of television on the Islands in those days – to regular badminton, and even the Island's National Darts contest – which was something akin to the national sport of the Islanders and taken very seriously with competitors traveling from across the Islands to participate. But now, from over 2 miles away, Wessex Yankee Hotel was hovering at 200 feet when its first wire guided missile was fired. These had to be brought on to the target by the fire aimer, and in this instance, with what appeared to be tracer coming towards them, the missile passed just a yard or two to the West side of the Hall, and smashed into the roof of the Police Station, which had also been taken over by the Argentine forces. The second missile was also then fired but the Wessex was barely above Wireless Ridge, and it is thought that its wire guided system snagged with the hillside and had to be jettisoned.

An SF Observation Post advised Yankee Hotel that their first missile looked like a strike, but as we learnt, that proved incorrect as the sun rose. Moreover, it transpired that Menendez had cancelled his morning meeting that day, so perhaps it was a good thing for the Islanders that their Hall had been left unscathed.

Had Menendez been in the Hall with his officers, and the strike been successful, the attack may have caused an early end to the war. This was an important exploit, launched from Teal Inlet, and yet another example of the important role the settlement had contributed towards securing the recapture of the Islands.

The police station had been occupied by an Argentine Major named Dowling who was despised by the Falkland Islanders, and he made good his escape back to Argentina before the Argentine surrender. He had also been responsible for interrogating the Naval Party 8901 captives, and apparently relished his task too much.

Harrier jets also hit Argentine Air Defences on 11 June, and ships began bombarding targets in and around Stanley. Unfortunately, the bombardment caused the only deaths of local people when a house in Stanley was inadvertently struck.

RN ships also bombarded the Phase One objectives with their 4.5 inch shells, in an effort to weaken the resolve of the Argentine Troops tasked with defending these positions.

Fatality reporting: Cpl J Smith from 42 Commando was casevaced back to us, but sadly was Dead on Arrival. He was buried shortly afterwards in our burial trench, with proper ceremony.

The Night Assaults on Mount Longdon, Two Sisters, and Mount Harriet, 11/12 June 1982

Tonight, would see the combined Units of 3 Commando Brigade, including 42 Commando, 45 Commando, and 3 Para, attack their designated high ground objectives. The assault of each objective, was organised around these fighting Commando Units and in the case of Mount Longdon, the 3rd Parachute Battalion. Each had substantial additional resources, and thus the term 'assault group' is an appropriate appendage to the individual Unit or Battalion tittle. The fighting troops of each assault group faced a lengthy foot slog from their existing bivouac positions to the assault start lines, and all three assault groups included Royal Engineer Sappers who had worked tirelessly with their respective group during the preceding days, patrolling with them, to strive to clear their assault approaches of anti-personnel mines – or find their way around them – but clearly it had not always been possible to achieve this in the final approaches that they were to make closing in on their foe. 9 Para RE provided sappers to 3 Para group, and 59 Commando RE provided sappers to 42 and 45 Commando (Condor Troop was embedded within 45 Commando).

Artillery Support. Each of the three assault groups had a battery of 105mm light guns in support from 29 Commando Royal Artillery, and 148 Commando Forward Observation Battery from RM Poole provided dedicated observation posts to each group. (This is a 29 Commando RA asset but based with and commonly deployed operationally with the SBS).

Naval Gunfire Support. Each group also had an RN ship dedicated to providing naval gunfire support, and 148 Commando provided the vital communication and co-ordinate details for such support.

3 Para assault group included HMS Avenger. Avenger was a modern Type 21 frigate. It had a single turret Mk 8, 4.5 inch gun and quadruple Exocet launchers. (Avenger was sold to the Pakistan Navy in 1994, when she was just 20 years old and remained in Service with Pakistan until very recently – finally being sunk in April 2020 when she was used for live firing target practice).

45 Commando assault group included HMS Glamorgan, a County Class Destroyer (which by most world navy definitions was a Cruiser). Glamorgan had Mk 6 4.5 inch twin turret guns, and quadruple Exocet launchers.

42 Commando assault group included the older HMS Yarmouth, which was a Rothesay Type 12 class frigate launched in 1959, and armed with the same Mk6 Twin 4.5 inch gun as Glamorgan, but just a single turret . (Yarmouth was also instrumental in the recapture of South Sandwich Islands with the Ice Patrol ship HMS Endurance).

Argentine Artillery. All three Argentine held positions could call upon 105mm howitzer support, and in the case of Mount Longdon they also had the much larger 155mm guns in support. Moreover, because they were in static defence, they could call in such support to hit pre-designated areas, without having to establish grid references.

In contrast the UK assault groups would have to determine exactly where both they and the enemy were, whilst moving and in contact with the enemy, which is not easy, especially in the dark in a pre-GPS world. This is why 148 Commando Forward Observation Battery were to prove invaluable in pin-pointing positions and bringing down artillery and naval gunfire support with incredible accuracy. The CO of 3 Para Lt Col Hew Pike had already witnessed this during the unfortunate Blue on Blue incident involving two of his companies just a couple of days after the Landings at San Carlos Water, and he was not about to squander this morsel of an advantage on Mount Longdon.

The move to respective start lines.

Both 3 Para and 45 Commando's Yankee and Zulu companies and Tac HQ moved to their start lines by crossing the Murrell Bridge. This was inevitably slow but thankfully this choke point was not spotted by the enemy, who, although alert to the high risk of an attack, did not expect it to come at night, and believed they would be mounted from the West Goose Green axis. Once across the Murrell River the going was still very tough for both 3 Para and 45 Commando, but 45's Yankee and Zulu companies were just a few hundred yards from their start line, code named 'Pub Garden', which they reached at 2359Z or 2100 local time, and they then waited for Xray company to reach its start line.

45's Xray company, with the 40 Commando Milan Troop (as 45's Milan were destroyed at the Ajax Bay bombing on 27 May, so the 45 Milan Troop had been re-rolled as a machine-gun troop), had moved to their start line by wading the Murrell River further downstream. They had started their march at 2000Z (1700 local) and reached their start line to the East of Mount Challenger at 0230Z (2330 local).

3 Para's companies crossed their respective start lines at around the scheduled time of 2300Z (2000 local).

Meanwhile 42 Commando, who were utilising the Welsh Guards Recce Troop to secure their start line, were concerned when the Guards fulfilled this task in daylight, and radio communication with the Guards failed after nightfall. Kilo Company 42 Commando were guided by Sergeant Collins along a route through the minefield that he and his small patrol had witnessed an Argentine patrol use, several days earlier. They crossed the Stanley - Goose Green track and moved safely to their form-up position to the South East of Mount Harriet. 42 Commando's Milan Troop had (like 40 Commando Milan Troop attached to 45 Commando) found the Milans really tough to move over the East Falkland terrain. The Welsh Guards Recce Troop were late to their final start line, and so it was secured by 11 Troop, who subsequently spotted the Guards sheltering slightly off grid and closer to the enemy. Lima Company 42 Commando set off towards their start line at 2130Z, 1830 local time, and the Unit was ready to start their assault at 0100Z, (2200 local).

The Assaults

3 Para Assault on Mount Longdon. B Company had either decided to adjust its final approach from North West to West, or perhaps found the terrain had funnelled them slightly South? They were advancing stealthily to contact and were within a few hundred yards of the enemy positions, when the silence was shattered. Cpl Ian Milne had stepped on a mine, as a significant part of the western approach to Mount Longdon had been sewn with mines. The 3 Para assault group battle had begun, and Lieutenant Colonel Pike did not hesitate calling in the support of 105mm light guns of 79 Commando Battery to shell the Argentine positions. Despite this 3 Para faced well-placed machine-gun fire from defensive positions that had to be assaulted, and Sgt McKay's hand held, lightweight, 66mm disposable anti-tank weapon proved effective in despatching a difficult to rout machine gun emplacement.

Meanwhile A Company had maintained its Northerly axis and had been making their own stealthy approach. After the mine detonated however they were diverted round to the West to support A Company who were facing formidable resistance having attacked from the expected axis. 3 paratroopers who were attempting to lift Cpl Milne into a BV, were themselves injured as they detonated yet another mine. The BV202's were provided to all Aid Posts within 3 Commando Brigade. They were a tracked articulated vehicle built in Sweden and in service with 3 Commando Brigade; BV denoted Belted Waggon in English or Baltes Vagn in Swedish or Beltet Vogn in Norwegian. These vehicles proved every bit as useful and dependable in North East Falkland as they were in Arctic Norway.

B Company had effectively stirred the hornets' nest and were facing a wall of deadly machine gun fire. Lt Bickerdike was brought down as his Platoon drew closer to yet another Argentine gun emplacement. Sgt McKay, by this time alone, continued forward. He succeeded in silencing the gun before himself being struck down, mortally wounded. He was posthumously awarded a VC and his tactical actions and his courage were beyond reproach.

3 Para had organised their Support Troop into a back-pack team, and a vehicle section. The back-pack team consisted of 6 General Purpose machine guns and one Light machine gun, and 5 Milan firing teams. It also included 18 designated stretcher bearers who would soon learn that 4 men were required to carry a stretcher over this demanding terrain and would use the 3 Bde Air Sqn strategy of ammo forward, casualties back. The vehicle section was a motley but welcome mix of Falkland Islander aging Land Rovers and Tractors, as well as 3 Para allocated vehicles.

Colonel Pike again sought to use all the fire power at his disposal, and HMS Avenger joined the fray, firing her 4.5 inch gun, directed by 148 Commando Battery, and slowly but surely the 3 Para assault group began to turn the tide. Their man-pack team and vehicle section worked forward, continuously resupplying ammunition and bringing casualties back to the forward Aid Post which was organised by a resourceful C/Sgt Brian Faulkner, who was awarded a Distinguished Service Medal for his endeavours. Once casualties were patched up as well as possible, they were evacuated to the Battalion Aid Post (known as Regimental Aid Post or RAP in both the Army and the Marines) where the first RAMC medics were deployed. This contrasts with the Commando Units who all had RN Commando Medical Assistants at company level, but 3 Para's overall casualty evacuation plan reflected that a lot of thought had gone into recovering casualties.

From the RAP all those requiring further treatment were evacuated to Teal Inlet by 3 Brigade Air Squadron. The fact that battle casualties were receiving surgical intervention at Teal Inlet may not have been widely known among forward troops because all helicopter casevac rearward from RAP's was handled by 3 Commando Brigade Ops and usually passed to 3 Brigade Air Squadron.

Casevac Comment A great deal of rubbish has been written about patients making their own way back to second line medical facilities and other fanciful tales. The reality is that casualty evacuation was excellent, and only delayed if the tactical situation was unsafe, or the weather very bad, and in both cases the situation had to be extreme to cause a delay in 3 Brigade Air Squadron carrying out a casevac mission. Numerous books and publications have been oblivious to the vital role of Teal Inlet as the 3 Command Brigade Forward Maintenance Area, and its One Troop Medical Squadron facility with resuscitation and surgical support. What's more, because 3 Commando Brigade's Medical Squadron was advantageously embedded within the Commando Logistic Regiment, neither it, nor its other service provider Squadrons (Ordnance, Workshops, and Transport) have tended to be reflected on any Order of Battle subsequently published. From the medical standpoint this has encouraged stories of Field Surgical Teams deploying forward as if on their own, when all such assets were deployed to either Medical Squadron assets or, for the final few days of the war, 16 Field Ambulance at Fitzroy. Finally, with regard to mobility, Medical

Squadron and its Surgical Support Teams normally would deploy with their equipment packed into their vehicles. Few vehicles were taken to the Falklands because of the harsh terrain, particularly around the northern half of East Falkland, thus they had to be moved amphibiously. They had no more nor less mobility than the Field Surgical Teams that were similarly reliant on Force assets for mobility.

Argentine positions continued to be cleared, often by lobbing grenades into their sangars. It was not until around 0930Z, (0630 local), that the Argentine defenders decided to withdraw whilst it was still dark, and they could slip away. Nearly 300 Argentine Troops had occupied Mount Longdon. Around half managed to slip away, of the remainder 36 were dead, and 80 wounded, and others were taken prisoner. The injured lay where they fell until 3 Commando Brigade was able to evacuate them. 10 hours after the assault began 3 Para had 17 paratroopers and a Sapper dead, and 48 wounded paratroopers.

42 Commando Group Assault on Mount Harriet. Compared to 3 Para, the 42 Commando assault was a walk in the park, but mainly because of the inspired plan of Lieutenant Colonel Nick Vaux, to launch the assault from the Stanley side, and the determined patrolling, with an element of good fortune, that led Sergeant Collins to track the route an Argentine patrol had taken back into Stanley, through a mine field. 42 Commando faced a similar threat to 3 Para, including around 300 enemy troops, with interlocking machine-gun arcs of fire, securing the high ground, and 105mm Argentine howitzers with pre-determined coded shelling targets.

As Kilo Company made their way up the South East slopes of Mount Harriet, a diversion raid was launched from the Western slopes to simulate the main attack and draw the Argentine fire – not an enviable task given that many of the Argentine troops on Harriet were equipped with modern lightweight night sights! This diversion raid was the task of 11 Troop Juliet Company, who were the former Naval Party 8901 commandos who had been ousted when the Argentine forces invaded. This was a fitting turn of fortune for them.

HMS Yarmouth was relentlessly bombarding the Argentine positions, directed by 148 Commando Battery, Naval Gunfire observer 3. The Argentine forces retaliated with 155mm guns hitting the 1/7 Gurkhas at Bluff Cove, and in doing so indicating they still had an observation post somewhere in the vicinity of Mount Kent.

Peter Babbington's men were making stealthy progress up the South East slopes, and eliminated two sentries en-route, silencing them with knife assaults. Their element of surprise had been total, and working in small teams, sometimes just pairs, they took out trenches and sangars. Such was the element of surprise, assaulting the Argentine positions from the direction of their own lines that within 45 minutes some of the Argentine troops confronted by Kilo Company had begun to surrender, but One Troop were still taking fire from machine-gun bunkers which Corporals Steve Newlands, Sharkey Ward, and Mick Eccles assaulted and overran. One of the assailants (Steve Newlands I believe) was wounded in his legs. All 3 were awarded military medals.

One Troop Kilo Company went on to capture the Argentine Command Post (CP) of the Argentine 4th Infantry Regiment. The Argentine CP's vehicle caught fire as a result of the assault.

Lima Company 42 Commando, commanded by Captain Wheen, had followed Kilo company and similarly scaled Mount Harriet from the South East, just on the left flank of Kilo Company. Once the stealthy advance to contact had erupted into a full-blown fire fight assault on machine-gun bunkers and rifle sangars, Lima Company also entered the fray. At one stage their arcs of fire were encroaching on Kilo Company, and they had to stop firing for fear of causing a 'blue on blue' or 'friendly fire' incident. Lima Company were on the receiving end of very heavy fire and unable to respond without jeopardising marines in Kilo company, forward of them on their right flank. The situation was remedied when Captain Wheen called in support from 7 Commando Battery (29 Commando RA) 105mm light guns, who again demonstrated the deadly accuracy of these tactical field weapons – often shelling positions barely 50 metres from 42 Commando marines, with deadly accuracy. Another Argentine platoon came forward in an attempt to salvage their position, but no sane person would have remained in a zone being pummelled by shells from a battery of guns, as 7 Battery 29 Commando continued to give a masterclass demonstration of extremely close gunfire support. The surviving Argentines broke contact and made their way towards Goat Ridge on the North side of Mount Harriet, beyond which were 45 Commando's designated objectives on Two Sisters.

Captain Wheen's Lima Company took the Argentine Aid post, and, now on the high open ground of the summit, moved towards Goat Ridge (code named Katrina). 5 troop came under fire, so they withdrew to a safe distance, requested 7 Battery 29 Commando RA support, who pounded the Ridge, and the objective was cleared. 4 Troop moved forward, to put 'boots on the ground' thus ensuring it would not be exploited again by the Argentines.

At about 0900Z, (0600 local), whilst still very dark, Lieutenant Colonel Nick Vaux moved his Tactical Headquarters onto the Mount Harriet summit, with Juliet company – the RM Poole 'Naval Party 8901' 1981/2 and 1982/3 detachments - in defensive positions around him. The tables had been turned!

Footnote: Cpl Eccles was later to serve as Sergeant Eccles MM, in Medical Squadron, and like most, he rarely spoke of his Falkland exploits (unless he'd had a drink). I was also later privileged to serve with Peter Babbington, on the staff of the Commodore Amphibious Warfare, and we neither of us were aware, let alone spoke about, our respective roles in the Falkland war. I was immensely proud to find myself standing by him and Major General Nick Vaux (as he was later to become and under whose command I was privileged to serve in HQ Commando Forces). At the 25th Anniversary Fly Past, at Horse Guards Parade, Harriers roared overhead, and I said *'It's alright! They're ours!'* which drew a wry smile from the General. The objective code words on Mount Harriet were Nick Vaux's wife and daughter's names! He always enjoyed a good joke.

45 Commando Group Assault on Two Sisters

The Two Sisters feature is so called because it is a twin peak, one peak on the South side and the other to the North, both of similar height over 1,000 feet, and separated by a slightly lower saddle between. It is a steep, craggy, rock-strewn feature that ought to be akin to an impregnable castle. It lies between Mount Longdon to its North, which has its access to the North limited by the Murrell River, and Mount Harriet to its South, which has its access limited from the South by the significant sea inlet known as Harriet Harbour. The Two Sisters is the plug in the middle, and if captured, the Argentine forces will be hemmed into the Stanley isthmus, with only the much lower features of Tumbledown, Wireless Ridge, Mount William, and Sapper Hill providing cover.

The stakes could not have been higher as X-ray Company 45 Commando moved due East along the south facing rock strewn slopes of Two Sisters, towards the western edge of the South Peak objective code named 'Long Toenail' (perhaps because it bore a resemblance to a toe digit), the base of which lay just a few hundred feet below the tip of the southern 'turret' of this seemingly impregnable feature. One Troop initially led, then paused as 3 Troop passed through, and made their way to the South West base of the objective. However, being at the base of objective Long Toenail was one thing; getting to the top and fighting along it was quite another and would require men of exceptional verve and courage.

Leadership would prove critical, as 3 Troop headed up the ridge, and an Argentine heavy machine gun spat its high velocity rounds out among them, as an Argentine flare exposed all the 3 Troop commandos. Incredibly, nobody had been hit, as the troop went to ground, and crawled their way to safety, wherever they could shelter. The 29 Commando gunners of 8 Battery were already engaging elsewhere, and the Mortar Troop had found that they needed to re-seat the mortar baseplates after firing just a couple of rounds. Like the Sennybridge ranges in Wales, the Falkland Island peat was proving a poor foundation in wet conditions for mortars. Milan troop stepped up, firing two missiles to despatch the guns.

Two Troop then also advanced and made their way to the base of Long Toenail, where they were promptly pounded by Argentine 105mm howitzers, but fortunately without the lethality of the British 105mm light guns in the hands of 29 Commando and directed by 148 Commando forward fire control.

Meanwhile Yankee and Zulu Companies had begun their advance towards the West side of the North Peak of Two Sisters. Code named Summer Garden (in keeping with their Pub Garden code name for their start line), and despite Argentine shells falling randomly in front of them, it seems their advance was actually undetected until they were within 400 yards of their objective, and similarly had to go to ground.

To their South, in X-ray Company, Marine Nowak was fatally wounded when he was struck by machine-gun fire. Mortars were also falling around the lead troops in Yankee and Zulu Companies assault, killing a 59 Commando sapper from Condor Troop, Chris Jones, (who was not wearing dog tags but was identified by his Troop Officer), and wounding several others. Col Whitehead called in 29 Commando RA's 8 Battery to pummel the Argentine positions on the South Peak, and to the North Zulu Company's Lieutenant Dytor, 8 Troop commander, realised that they could not just lie low in a defensive mode taking hits at the foot of the Northern Peak. It was a do or die situation. He got to his feet, and moved forward, urging his men to follow, they too moved forward, firing as they went, and others followed. Lt Dytor's initiative had provided the momentum required, and now 45 Commando's Mortar Troop was pounding the Argentine positions. Two of the Troop commanders were wounded in this phase of the assault.

X-ray Company succeeded in pushing their foe off 'Long toenail' by around 0545Z or 0245 local. Yankee Company had pushed East across the south side of the North peak, and Zulu company had pushed East from the North side of the Peak. All 3 Companies had to clear enemy machine gun and rifle positions in the same manner as 42 Commando and 3 Para had done, whist being subject to enemy mortar fire and shelling, requiring many acts of individual and collective bravery, often passing without special mention or notice. Well before daybreak the Argentine command post was captured with the senior officer, and a number of mopping-up missions took place, but Two Sisters had been captured. Colonel Whitehead established his Tactical HQ on Two Sisters and was planning to move on toward Tumbledown when the Brigade Commander directed him to hold fast where they were.

HMS Glamorgan had remained on the gun line with Yarmouth, and Avenger. She was now about to leave and re-join the main Carrier Task Group, to which she was providing vital air and surface defence with her Sea Cat, Sea Slug and Exocet missile systems, but was struck by a land launched Argentine Exocet from the occupied Stanley Airport. Fortunately, the missile struck above the waterline, skidding across its helicopter flight deck, through to the hanger, and smashing into the ship's anti-submarine Wessex. Glamorgan had little indication of the attack and had just managed to fire one Sea Cat missile in defence, which had insufficient time to prime, and narrowly missed the Exocet.

When the Exocet hit the Wessex there was a massive fireball as aviation fuel exploded. Glamorgan had a large hole in her aft end on the Port side, and fires raged, as the ship's company fought to save the ship. After four or five hours the situation was brought under control, but 13 sailors had died when the missile struck, and another of the many wounded also subsequently died of his injuries. HMS Yarmouth came alongside and assisted Glamorgan, which had to jettison some Sea Slug missiles that had been pre-loaded.

Glamorgan was able to head back to the main Task Group, which was about 50 miles further to the East, and she re-joined them at about 1530Z (1230 local) and received further makeshift repairs to strengthen her battered structure. She remained on station, as all her weapon systems were viable, albeit less one Seacat launcher which was lost over the side. She was the first ship in history to survive a strike from an Exocet. The fatalities and the injured were managed afloat.

HMS Glamorgan was yet another example of the heavy price the Royal Navy paid whilst deploying ships in direct support of the landing force, and rarely mentioned.

Footnote. Glamorgan was sold to the Chilean Navy in 1985. She finally sank in 2005 when being towed to a breakers yard. Her losses in 1982 brought the 45 Commando assault group fatalities to 18.

The Arrival of casualties at Teal Inlet

One Troop Medical Squadron were by now more than used to receiving mass casualties, and this was to prove a day of running faster to stand still. Waves of mainly Scout helicopters started to arrive at first light, landing one at a time, with others hovering in a Teal Inlet horizontal version of a Heathrow stack, at 30 or 40 yard intervals, waiting to come in. The visibility was not good, and Teal was the only destination they were flying to, as there was a thick morning mist – the sort that blankets the English countryside after Guy Fawkes bonfires and fireworks, only this time the culprits were weapons of destruction. The usually bracing fresh air of the Falkland Islands had a slightly musty tinge, and it was uncommonly still. Literally the fog of war.

The scenes below were captured on someone's camera – although few if any of One Troop had brought cameras or other personal effects ashore as a result of the briefings we had received in this respect. The first such picture shows Petty Officer Medical Assistant Taff Evans carrying a casualty from a scout. This picture was correctly captioned as Teal Inlet in Surgeon Commander Rick Jolley's book Red and Green Life Machine, and clearly shows a second Scout hovering to land. It also reveals to those with eagle eyes, a third Scout beyond the second. A sequel of this picture was subsequently wrongly reported in the Royal Marine Globe and Laurel publication of July 1982 as being at Ajax Bay, but Taff Evans had not been deployed to Ajax Bay as he was with a forward Unit with 3 Command Brigade. The picture of the second helicopter landing was subsequently doctored to be used as the basis for an official artist's depiction of casualties arriving at Ajax Bay.

POMA Graham'Taff' Evans (front left) leads a stretcher bearing party at Teal Inlet, as a second Scout can just be discerned, hovering behind with more casualties.

The second Scout is unloaded with Cpl Jon Clare (front right) leading, and the same men shown in the previous picture take the rear of the stretcher having returned the 40 yards from the Reception tent.

Re-fuelling the helicopters took place just a few hundred yards from the medical facility

Everyone was working flat out, and we tried to move minor cases through to Minor Treatments immediately to get them out of the way, but the Unit/ Battalion Aid Posts had of course casevaced their most serious Priority One cases first. We were able to get the early arrivals through our Reception triage tent and straight into Major Treatments, where Surgeon Lieutenant Commander Tim Douglas Riley, with Chief Medical Assistant Graham Edwards and his team, worked quickly to ensure we weren't about to lose anyone. More intravenous fluids, dressings, and such like, were passed through to the Reception tent, so casualties who had arrived either with intravenous infusions that needed changing, or others with none inserted and needed cannulating with the fluid giving needle, could receive intravenous fluids that were of a reasonable temperature for their bodies to tolerate without inducing shock or hypothermia. Most airways were fine, there was rarely a need for airway interventions in the Reception tent. It was mainly gunshot wounds, shrapnel, and anti-personnel mine traumatic amputations. The cool climate was again proving to be an ally, even a saviour, to the casualties, and there was rarely a struggle to stem bleeding. That said, some casualties, including members of X-ray Company 45 Commando who had waded across the Murrell River, were already borderline hypothermic, and needed special blankets to help retain warmth and ensure their core body temperatures did not fall lower. Overall, though, despite some truly horrendous injuries, we were on top of the situation, and at no stage was there a panic that someone was slipping away. With reasonably warm tents, albeit only being heated with primitive 'Aladdin' paraffin stoves, and with Mrs Gloria Anderson keeping the peat Rayburn stove going in her small kitchen, ensuring the Major treatment area was a very comfortable temperature, not just for the casualties but for those working to fix them, the patients were kept in a stable but very serious holding state until it was their turn, in order of clinical priority, to be treated.

Major Batty and his small surgical team similarly just worked through a never-ending list of cases that needed field surgical interventions. They did the minimum required, and then passed each such case back for recovery, and into the Evacuation ward, where Dr Howard Oakley worked with Petty Officer 'Jacko' Jackson and LMA Andy Ellis to care for them until they could be evacuated. All instruments continued to be liquid sterilized after each case. There was not a single recorded case of medical acquired infection.

The Bunk House cook, Gloria Anderson, and our 'chef' Marine Neil Blain, would ensure there was copious hot water for the numerous tasks that benefitted from clean water (in addition for tea to keep us all going), and we were able to grab a bite to eat to sustain ourselves. Most of us were just grateful that we had not had to endure what these men had been through, and that we were not facing continued nights in the open, on the coldest windswept places on the Islands. None of us envied any of them. We recognised how fortunate we were, and we were privileged to be able to help these injured men. Moreover, we benefitted from a large peat burning boiler in the Bunk House that was being stoked by two of the local residents, Jimmy McCullen and Henry Smith.

As the day went on the visibility improved and we had some success in getting patients evacuated to Uganda, using Wessex from the Teal Inlet Forward Operating Base. A few less serious cases were also flown to Ajax Bay, who at this time were having a comparatively routine day. We began to dare think we were working through the back log, when yet more patients arrived, and this time as a result of the newly won positions being shelled. Two more 155mm guns had apparently been flown in to Stanley by the Argentines that morning, and had started to shell the positions that 3 Commando Brigade had just captured. Also, sappers were clearing positions, searching for booby traps and unsafe munitions which they would detonate. During these searches they would find more wounded, mostly Argentine casualties, and many of these also came back to us. We received an Argentine commando officer who had a gunshot wound through his foot that was almost certainly was self-inflicted and was almost exactly the same as two others that had been processed through Ajax Bay before we came to Teal Inlet. I wondered if they had been taught to do this, perhaps as a tactic to avoid interrogation?

Fatality reporting: On 12 June 1982, we reported the sad death of the only Argentine conscript who died shortly after arriving in our Reception tent. He was called Ramon Quintana and was identified by other Argentine casualties whom we were striving to triage and treat. Almost 40 years later, in early 2022 I was told by the doctor who had seen Quintana that one of his ears had been cut off. Why the doctor had taken 40 years to divulge this is, for me, inexplicable, but I have no reason to doubt the doctor's recollection.

We also received the following British fatalities Dead on Arrival whom we subsequently laid to rest with proper ceremony: Pte M J Dodsworth 3 Para; Sapper C Jones RE Condor Troop 59 Cdo RE (45 Commando Group); Mne M J Nowak 45 Commando Group; Mne G M MacPherson 45 Commando Group; Cpl I F Spencer 45 Commando Group (without dog tags, identified by his friends in our facility).

All fatalities, from both sides of the conflict, were treated with the utmost respect and dignity, and Ramon Quintana was laid to rest in the same trench as the British fatalities, but I recollect we laid British fatalities starting from one end of the trench, and Argentine fatalities from the other end.

Patient Holding Capacity Crisis: By late afternoon, as darkness fell, we had been sending regular situation reports (sitreps) to HQ Medical Squadron, at Ajax Bay, but we had to express concern that we were *'at our crisis capacity expansion limit'*, to which came the reply *'Do not understand. Say again over'. 'We are at our crisis capacity casualty limit'* was sent again, and the reply again *'Sorry still don't understand what that means?'* to which I replied, *'we are f***ing full'.* This is a fondly remembered moment of our time at Teal Inlet, despite everything around us being a pressure cooker of indescribable scenes. Surgeon Lieutenant Commander Tim Douglas Riley went on to be head of the RN Medical Branch, holding the rank of Surgeon Rear Admiral, and he always reminds me about my succinct communication that day; albeit it never brought us any relief.

The Refrigeration building at Ajax Bay offered endless scope for holding casualties, and it seems their experience of receiving 150 burns cases on 8 June, who mostly needed Flamazine cream and analgesia, and 70 of which were passed to the fleet in San Carlos Water, had left some at Ajax Bay feeling we ought to be able to replicate their efforts, despite having just two 24 by 18 feet tents with Aladdin paraffin heaters for meagre warmth, with intermittent snow showers outside, and a fraction of the staff. We were established as a 25 stretcher-bed facility and were running at way beyond this number. As the weather clagged in, and flying was again limited, we got on with our task, and the long day was followed by a long, long night.

The next morning, Sunday 13 June, most of the Troop had managed to get a couple of hours sleep before first light, and joined by others from 3 Para, 45 and 42 Commando, we buried more dead.

The Final Assaults of Mounts William and Tumbledown, Wireless & Cortley Ridges, and Sapper Hill. Sunday 13 June – Monday 14 June 1982.

The fact that the Argentines had continued to shell the positions that 3 Commando Brigade captured yesterday, unfortunately indicated that they were still resolved to continue to fight. 29 Commando RA had returned fire, shelling the Argentine guns that were scattered around what was left of the former Naval Party 8901 RM Commando base at Moody Brook, but it was clear they were not ready to capitulate. Some were beginning to wonder if it would come to street fights through Stanley, in which case we surely would still overcome them, but there would likely be significant civilian casualties.

In the late afternoon, HQ 3 Commando Brigade were directly targeted by 2 waves of four Skyhawk jets. Their site had almost certainly been compromised by Argentine signal direction finding electronic equipment, and it was imperative they moved. The Tactical HQ element moved into a well sheltered nearby gully, but it was decided that the main HQ should relocate to Mount Kent, and this was not fulfilled until the middle of the night on 13/14 June.

2nd Scots Guards. It is perhaps fortunate therefore that it is now the turn of **5 Brigade** to capture the lower lying features immediately surrounding Stanley. **Mount Tumbledown** rises 600 feet above the surrounding terrain (around 800 feet above sea level) and lies just to the South West of Moody Brook, and will be assaulted by the **2nd Scots Guards** who will, as 3 Commando's Units had done, deploy as an assault group, including 4 Field Regiment RA 105mm light guns, and 148 Commando Forward Observation Battery (Naval Gunfire Officer 5). Sappers would be provided by 3 Troop 9 Para Squadron; and HM Ships Yarmouth and Active were available to fire their 4.5 inch guns in support.

The Guards were to launch a forward diversion attack along the Darwin to Stanley track, at a point just West of Pony Pass where the Argentine Marine Oscar Company was tasked with blocking the expected British advance. Scots Guards Major Richard Bethell MBE was tasked with leading this diversionary attack. Bethell had only recently re-joined the 2nd Scots Guards after a 12 year long stint with the SAS, so it's fair to say he was a man up to the task. He pulled together a small group that included 12 recce Guardsmen, a machine-gun fire support team, 4 Troop Blues and Royals Scorpion tracked reconnaissance vehicles, a mortar fire controller, and 2 sappers from 9 Para Squadron RE.

Meanwhile the main body of the Scots Guards had been flown to Goat Ridge by Sea Kings of 846 Naval Air Squadron, from where their 3 rifle companies would move East to assault Tumbledown.

At about 1600 local time (1900Z), with snow falling, tracked Scorpion armoured reconnaissance vehicles from Lt Coreth's 4 Troop, Blues & Royals, joined Maj Bethel's newly created diversion attack platoon of a dozen Scots Guardsmen, plus a light machine-gun fire support group, and 2 sappers from 9 Para RE, and a mortar fire control JNCO – Cpl Miller, at Harriet House. Sappers cleared the route, so it was 1830 local before they approached their target. The Scorpions moved into fire positions to provide cover for this divisionary assault, and a couple more hours passed as they crept forward. Using a night sight they then detected occupied trenches just 80 yards or so in front of them. Sgt Maj Braby took his LMG support team off to the right flank to establish a fire support position, as Maj Bethell advanced with his recce team. There were three trenches ahead and Sgt Danny White attacked the left; Bethell the centre; and L/Cpl Pashley RE the right. Both Sgt White and L/Cpl Pashley died in this first assault, as they lobbed grenades wounding some of the Argentine defenders.

Over the next two hours the effectiveness of the light machine-gun team grew, as did the fire support from the Scorpions. Bethell and his recce men went on to assault 11 machine-gun sangars before midnight local time. He had 4 wounded and 2 dead, but this was not just a 'create a few bangs and clear out' diversion. Bethell had assaulted a company of Argentine Marines, on a full-frontal axis, with guts, bullets, and grenades, but now, with ammunition all but spent, it was time to get his men out. They headed back to the first trenches, where Scots pipers were now forward, caring for the wounded. An Argentine stood up in a trench and lobbed a grenade – he was shot but the grenade caught Piper Duffy in the chest, and Bethell had shrapnel in his legs. Sgt Ian Miller then trod on a mine, and the blast caught four others. They were then shelled for 40 minutes, but Bethell was still very much in command, and they picked their way West, heading to safety.

Communication with the Scorpions had become difficult but was now improving and they were called forward to assist. The sky was then lit up by an Argentine flare, and they were again being shelled, when Lt Coreth's Scorpion went over an anti-tank mine, that caused the whole vehicle to lift off the ground and come crashing back down. Its tracks and wheels were useless, but the immobile vehicle continued to provide fire support to Tumbledown. 57 mines were cleared from around the vehicle by sappers at daybreak.

Bethell and his men made it back to Harriet House where 42 Commando A Echelon (first line of forward support) arranged for casevac, which was probably to 16 Field Ambulance at Fitzroy, which had established there a few days earlier with 6 (Para) Field Surgical Team that had been at Ajax Bay with Medical Squadron, since D+1.

This diversion attack had duped the Argentines into believing they were confronting a Battalion scale attack which they had then repelled, but at 2300Z (2000 local) G Company 2nd Scots Guards started to move forward from Goat Ridge on Mount Harriet, towards Tumbledown, and they were almost certainly unaware of the debt they owed Maj Bethell and his small team for drawing the focus of their coming advance. G Company advanced about 1.3 miles over exposed ground, unchecked by the enemy. As the snow came down and the wind increased, they reached their objective.

On their left flank Maj Kiszley's company was not to be so lucky, as the advance of two platoons was being watched by Argentine marines using night sights, who opened fire between 300 and 400 yards. The 148 Battery Forward Observation Officer for 105mm light gun support (and probably Naval Gunfire Support also) was separated from the company tactical HQ, and thus a vital component of the assault was impotent. 42 Commando's Mortar Troop provided some fire support from Goat Ridge, but they were a poor substitute for the loss of 105mm light guns. Guardsman Ronald Tabini's last words to Sgt Maj Nicol were 'I've been shot Sir' before falling silent. Nicol went to help Sgt Simeon who was also fatally hit, and Sgt Maj Nicol himself was then struck. Argentine artillery began to fall and the advance of the left flank ground to a halt. The CO, Lt Col Scot had to organise fire support and he ensured that was his focus.

At about 0230 local time, 14 June, the Argentine company that Bethell had assaulted moved up from the vicinity of Pony Pass to the saddle between Tumbledown and Mount William. The Scots Guards now faced 2 companies and responded with a standard 'fire and movement' tactic that enabled them to doggedly claw themselves slowly forward.

When 15 Platoon Scots Guards charged, some Argentines began to abandon their positions. Lance Sgts McGuiness and Davidson followed a field telephone cable and attacked the bunkers to which they were laid. Maj Kiszley and a small team of men reached the summit, but an Argentine machine-gunner hit 3 men, including Lt Alasdair Mitchel who was struck in the legs. His 29 strong platoon suffered 2 dead and 12 wounded.

Maj Kiszley held the summit with just 3 men! Below them Piper Ridges, the company medic, had his hands full treating the wounded.

A forward pincer operation followed on the East end of Tumbledown, when more Argentines were captured. The remaining Argentines left just before first light and the Scots Guards had secured Mount Tumbledown, largely without the benefit of 105 mm light guns or Naval Gunfire Support, which demanded courage and tenacity against a determined foe that was far from being a push over. Forward Observation Officer Captain Keith Swinton had been shot in the chest by a sniper at about 0230 local time. He survived the wound.

2 Para assault on Wireless Ridge. With a new CO, Lieutenant Colonel Chaundler also had 8 and 79 Commando Batteries, 29 Commando RA 105mm guns in support, with 148 Commando Forward Observation Battery Naval Gun Fire Officer 2; Three Troop Blues & Royals Scorpions and Scimitars; and Recce Troop 59 Commando RE.

Late afternoon Sunday 13 June 1982 2 Para, now back within 3 Commando Brigade, moved to a concentration area on the South of Murrell River, just half a mile North East of Wireless Ridge. C Company was to hold the start line, but it was on the receiving end of Argentine shelling, and they had to adjust their position to avoid casualties. Some Argentines abandoned their positions as C Company had moved towards the start line.

The Argentines were in defensive positions that stretched from just below Mount Longdon to beyond the fuel tanks on Cortley Ridge, which were to be the subject to a special forces diversionary raid. The Argentines were effectively located in an arc to the North of the former Naval Party 8901 RM Commando detachment base at Moody Brook that now lay in ruins.

At about 0200 local time (0500Z) D Company 2 Para assaulted an Argentine company with their machine-gun platoon and the Blues and Royals armoured vehicles, and their foe capitulated. The 30mm cannon of the Scimitars proved to be a major tipping point.

Argentine artillery had not given up however and D Company had to shelter wherever they could.

A and B Companies of 2 Para had met stiff resistance from an Argentine company, so they pulled back and let 29 Commando's gunners sap their morale by shelling the objective. When the shelling stopped the two Companies pushed forward and broke the resolve of the Argentine defenders.

The Special Forces diversionary raid on Cortley Ridge involved the RM Raiding Squadron and members of the SAS Boat Troop and the SBS. They were spotted before they got ashore as their raiding craft headed for the coast on the North side of the Ridge, and they took very heavy fire as they landed. One SBS NCO and 2 SAS troopers were hit, and the group were lucky to get off the beach. History often unravels to reveal unexpected outcomes however, and it later emerged that the failure of this small diversion raid persuaded the Argentines that a planned insertion of their own Commandos behind British lines should be abandoned. (Ruiz – Moreno, Commandos in Action).

Some Argentine officers tried to reinforce Wireless Ridge with conscripts they had gathered together in Stanley. They engaged D Company 2 Para and were immediately subject to shelling from 29 Commando's gunners and withdrew to Stanley. By 0500 local time (0800Z) it was over on Wireless Ridge. Argentine Commandos were isolated and cut off on Cortley Ridge.

1/7 Gurkhas had set off from Goat Ridge at 0230 local time, to a position below the North side of Tumbledown, to capture Mount William. The 5th Argentine Marine Battalion were withdrawing however, and Mount William was taken by the Gurkhas without a struggle – their reputation was seemingly enough to enable them to secure the objective without loss.

Welsh Guards with Alpha and Charlie Companies 40 Commando RM. At first light on the morning of 14 June 1982, with 29 Commando RA gunners still pounding Argentine forces on the western fringe of Stanley including their artillery pieces around Moody Brook which occasionally returned fire, a company of Argentine marines still held Sapper Hill – the last high ground feature to the right of the concrete road that runs from Moody Brook and the Power Station, into Stanley.

Following their losses when the Landing Ship Galahad was bombed on 8 June, the Welsh Guards now had two of their three fighting companies replaced by Alpha and Charlie Companies of 40 Commando Unit, Royal Marines. A troop of sappers were also attached from 59 Commando RE, but unlike other Units and Battalions who had used sappers to ensure routes were clear of mines, for some reason they were held at the rear. That was until the overnight freeze began to thaw and the Guards and Marines found themselves in the middle of a mine field. Two Royal Marines were seriously injured by exploding mines and this caught the attention of the Argentines who shelled and mortared the area. The engineers were called forward and spent 4 hours clearing a path through this deadly ground. Alpha and Charlie companies were subsequently flown forward to assault Sapper Hill, but 9 Troop Charlie Company were taken too far forward and immediately found themselves returning fire as they were engaged by the defending Argentine marines. After about 10 minutes the enemy fire stopped however, as it seems they had slipped away, back in to Stanley, and the final assault on the Falkland Islands was over, but the mine threat remained, and the scope of that threat was only to become clear long after the cessation of hostilities.

Fatality Reporting 13 June 1982: Private C E Jones 3 Para, was received at our facility at Teal Inlet. He was sadly Dead on Arrival and was prepared for burial in our trench, which took place with appropriate ceremony.

One Troop Medical Squadron, Teal Inlet 14 - 15 June 1982

Snow covered the settlement as yet more casualties were flown back to us in waves of flights by 3 Brigade Air Squadron's Scout helicopters. We received 12 casualties from 2 Para, and two fatalities for burial, including Paratrooper Colour Sergeant G P M Findlay.

9 Scots Guardsmen were also received, but none of their dead (unless the unidentified British fatality who had been blown to pieces and had no identity was a Scots Guardsman).

3 wounded sappers were also casevaced to us; as were 2 casualties from 40 Commando, probably from the above anti-personnel mine incident. Alongside these casualties were a continuing flow of medivacs (medical evacuations) for cold injuries such as Trench Foot, as well as sickness for the next 48 hours. **By the morning of 16 June we had admitted and treated 217 casualties and medivacs at Teal Inlet.** This figure is robust as it was in my

immediate post-operative report, but the surgical workload is somewhat more complex to unravel:

In The Journal of Naval Medicine Vol 69 1983 Surgeon Commander Rick Jolly noted 320 operations had been performed ashore, and 211 of these were at Ajax Bay, and this figure for Ajax Bay was 107 by 31 May 1982 when Cpl Worrall, Mne Gosling and I left for Teal Inlet, as recorded in the book 'The Red & Green Life Machine'.

Somehow, a 2017 Royal Navy medical paper entitled 'Medical Support to Operation Corporate' by J. G Penn-Barwell, which actually only focused on Surgical assets ashore, and in doing so seems to have reduced the number of operations performed ashore by 30 to 290, and totally ignores the vital role played by Medical Squadron, albeit it does acknowledge surgery took place at Ajax Bay and Teal Inlet. Does this discrepancy of 30 surgical cases exclude Argentine casualties? The report attributes 79 operations at Ajax Bay and Teal inlet to 5 FST, and it can be confidently asserted that this is the minimum figure, because Teal Inlet had received 27 gunshot wound casualties, 25 shrapnel casualties, and 23 assorted other cases including mine injuries, all requiring surgical intervention, and only a very small number of these may have been capable of waiting or were deemed better served to wait for appropriate Consultant care afloat on Uganda.

The 5 Field Surgical Team Surgeon, Charles Batty, was much later to record his arrival at Teal Inlet to have been as late as 8 June. One troop Medical Squadron had recorded their arrival as 4 June, in the immediate post operation report drafted 26 June 1982. Regardless of this, what can be asserted with confidence from the above is that between 45 and 55 patients received operative care at Teal Inlet and therefore between 162 to 172 out of 217 patients did not require surgical intervention ashore. This is an important point because it demonstrates that **3 out of 4 patients were not surgical cases.**

*The picture above, depicting most of One Troop Medical Squadron
with 5 FST was taken by 16 year old Neil Rowlands who forwarded
it to the author Malcolm Hazell in 2020. Others are still caring
for patients awaiting casevac to the Hospital Ship Uganda.*

Jon Clare records his recollections of effectively transforming at
Teal Inlet, from a General Duties (GD) Royal Marine Commando
JNCO Corporal, to a hands on 'honorary medic' saving the
lives of his comrades alongside professional medics: *'To me a lot
that happened at Teal Inlet was a blur. I don't know whether this
was due to events at Ajax Bay playing on my mind too much, or
perhaps that we were so busy at Teal Inlet that the time just flew
by? I recall receiving two injured friends from 45 Commando, my
previous Unit, Cpl's Ginge Davidson and Phil Tinsley. 'Ginge', a real
warrior from Reconnaissance Troop, was extremely disappointed to
have to be evacuated due to a large loose rock falling onto his heel. 45
Commando Recce Troop went on to conduct some of the most successful
and daring patrols of the war, passing vital information to their HQ.
Phil, from Y Company, had received a 7.62mm round through his
bicep because of an accidental discharge from one of his fellow marines
during the approach march. Our medical training was being used as
there was an urgent requirement to assist in the saving of lives, and
the medics' confidence in our newly acquired clinical skills grew. I was*

taking blood from volunteers one minute, then administering drips to the injured and cleaning and dressing wounds the next. A steady stream of Scout helicopters brought casualties from both sides to Teal Inlet. We dealt with many Argentine dead and wounded as well as our own. Unfortunately, mortuary duties were still an ongoing task and during what I think was my first full day at Teal Inlet we dealt with a colleague, whom I remember from the previous year when we were on our promotion course at the Commando Training Centre together, an SBS operative killed in a blue on blue. Quite a bit Later, perhaps on the 11 or 12 June, we had the sad duty of preparing two more Royal Marines, both from X Company, 45 Commando, again both friends of mine, Marine 'Blue' Nowak and Cpl Frank Spencer. Although they were my friends I didn't attend their funeral, perhaps because it was too busy, but regardless, I'd had enough of funerals by then. Two weeks after arriving at Teal and after the welcome news of victory and the cessation of violence, we departed for Stanley'.

On 16 June 1982 at 0010 Z (2110 on 15 June local time), whilst still managing the care of a number of patients, One Troop Medical Squadron with 5 Field Surgical Team attached, were ordered to redeploy to Stanley, as the Argentine forces had formally surrendered. We gathered at daybreak, outside our small facility, which had received a third of all the casualties treated ashore, and between us we had also received a third at Ajax Bay.

The un-folding Mine Situation

The Argentine mine warfare situation that had emerged was very different to the otherwise conventional warfare that had been waged throughout the conflict, and it left its victims incapacitated for the rest of their lives. It is important that the true extent of the Argentine intentions in this respect are recorded below.

It was only after the end of hostilities, when a full survey of the scope of the Argentine mine warfare activity was undertaken, that the horrific extent of this aspect of their invasion was exposed.

30,000 mines were sewn, including 25,000 anti-personnel mines, and 5,000 much larger anti-tank mines. These mines were procured from a variety of sources and included Italian SB33 mines; Spanish PB4 mines; and Israeli No 4 mines that are difficult to detect. They also used their own FMK 1 and 3 mines. The mining was systematic, and in depth. For example, if the UK Landing Force had been foolish enough to attempt a full-scale landing in the area of Stanley it would have been catastrophic – Surf Beach to the North of Stanley alone had 1,000 mines sewn across it. Stanley common, which is an open public access space, was similarly strewn with mines. An abandoned building near the Murrell Peninsula minefield was still fenced off in 2018 and serves to reflect that the 'sweep' we conducted of the abandoned Refrigeration Plant on D Day 21 May 1982, that went on to be Medical Squadron's largest facility throughout the war, had been a far more wise precaution than we had ever imagined. Some areas of Goose Green were cleared soon after the war, and around 80% were found in sand or peat, so very easily hidden.

York Bay, to the North East of Stanley, just above the airport, proved very difficult to clear, because its sand dunes drifted so much in the Falkland winds.

In 2016/17 seven teams were still employed on the clean-up task and cleared 3,000 anti-personnel mines and 150 anti-tank mines, from 47 separate mine fields, but 30% of known mines had yet to be removed 35 years after the war, and in 2018 27 known mine fields were still being cleared, and it was suggested additional surveys were still required, especially on West Falkland. The last recorded casualty from a mine was in 2017 when a mine exploded whilst being cleared. Fortunately, this was apparently not too serious an incident, but its serves to demonstrate that the mine threat still existed until November 2020 when the last mine was ceremoniously dispatched. It is repugnant that anti-personnel mines were potentially still viable death traps around the Falkland Islands for 38 years after the war, and sadly may never be fully cleared because of the proverbial 'needle in a haystack' nature of the problem. Moreover, it serves to underline the prudent decision that Brigadier Julian Thompson RM took in conjunction with the naval head of Amphibious Warfare aboard HMS Fearless, Commodore Michael Clapp, in acting upon advice from Major Ewen Southby-Tailyour RM to conduct the re-capture of the Islands from a Bridge Head secured at San Carlos Water. Major Southby-Tailyour had been the Officer Commanding the commando detachment known as Naval Party 8901 from 1978 to 1979. His detachment had relieved the one I had served with, and fortunately he was a keen yachtsman who had gleaned what proved to be a decisive insight into not just the navigable waters around East Falkland, but the beaches. Like the rest of us however, neither he, nor Brigadier Thompson or Commodore Clapp, would have been aware of this ugly dimension of the Argentine defensive strategy, that serves as a reminder of the lengths they were prepared to go to, to capture these remote Islands and their peace-loving inhabitants.

The Final Move to Stanley 16 June 1982

We evacuated the last of our patients at Teal Inlet and they were flown to the Uganda Hospital Ship. We struck the medical complex, repacking all our equipment, tentage, and stores, and the young Falkland Islander Neil Rowlands helped us load it all onto his tractor trailer. We headed down to the water's edge and loaded it all into the tank deck of the waiting RFA Landing Ship, and left as we had arrived, amphibiously.

Just a few hours later we were alongside in Stanley and had to organise transport from the jetty to get our kit up to the large community hall past the hospital, that had been occupied by the Argentine medical teams.

The clean, tidy, peaceful settlement of Stanley, that I had last set foot on in 1978 when I left with the Naval party 8901 Commando detachment from the same jetty, was now a snow covered, damp, dirty, cesspit of a place, full of the defeated Argentine troops being corralled as prisoners of war; their rusting weapons piled high, literally in weapons dumps! Further down past the hospital a large old white horse was wandering slowly up and down the road, as if in a confused state of shock.

We somehow managed to get our kit into the building we have been detailed to set-up within, but it is absolutely full of Argentine medical kit and rubbish, like a house awaiting a removal waggon. I head off to visit my old medical friends in the hospital where I used to work on many Wednesdays during my deployment in 1977 to 1978. We agree to provide a couple of One Troop Medical Squadron Staff in the entrance to the hospital and set up our Teal Inlet Admission and Discharge book with a small desk.

The following day, the horse was dead. It lay in the road below our building, and I was deeply saddened that I had not thought to try to put water out for it, albeit there was no running water to be had in Stanley at that time – it was something else that needed to be fixed. One last innocent sorry victim of this bloody war, let down by everyone, a poor old horse. It was not moved for at least another day, as many of our troops, both Paratroopers and Marines, were marched in to the full to bursting settlement, passing this poor dead nag as they were being urged to put some swagger in their step, as they were viewed by their vanquished forlorn foe whose freedom and future lay in the hands of the proud victors.

Jon Clare's recollections of moving into Stanley: '*My memories of arriving in Stanley are vague, but some things stick in your mind. The town was in a state of minor chaos. It reminded me of the photographs of Second World War towns in France that had been liberated. UK military personnel and equipment, Argentine POW's, piles of weapons and equipment. We took over a building that seemed to be a community centre, and had been used by the Argentines as a medical centre of some sort. It was filthy and appeared ransacked. We were careful when cleaning it out not to be too clumsy with the rubbish we were collecting as it contained all the detritus of a poorly run hospital. Once established we began familiarising ourselves with the local area and a couple of us came across a CH47 helicopter on the outskirts of the town. A UK pilot was trying to establish whether it was useable and got us to assist by pumping the hydraulic transmission pump. Needless to say, it didn't work. In the meantime, our chef Neil Blain had found a fridge containing some prime Argentine steak. He tested it and said it was still good to eat, so after a promise from Neil that the steak actually was 'beef' steak, we barbequed it and along with some miniature whisky bottles from some abandoned Argentine rations, a handful of us had a small BBQ celebration'.*

'The final official act of the Falkland Campaign for me and my team was a mission to recover the remains of an Argentine soldier from his resting place up on a small ridge above the town. We set off with a body bag. An edge of seriousness was applied when, after about 20 minutes, we found ourselves among an Argentine M67 grenade string minefield, akin to a cats-cradle with a little green ball at each corner. Delicately stepping past this, bearing in mind these were sometimes 'obviously' placed as to divert or channel you into more lethal mine fields (antipersonnel), we made it to our Argentine soldier. After some minor adjustments to his configuration, as he had obviously been hit by something big, we managed to fit him into the bag and make our way back past the grenade string and back down the ridge to the Medical Centre'.

'For the Marines of Medical Squadron, our personal experience in the Falklands Campaign was not what we had trained for, nor was it acted-out in a role we particularly wanted, but you can only play with the cards you are dealt. For my hand, I will be forever grateful, because you must be careful what you wish for. And for the few times that it was dangerous, very often it was fun, but mostly it was important, necessary and professional. After 38 years' service and many operational tours later, this is the operation which leaves the most indelible mark'.

Jon Clare's additional comments to my own account throughout this publication are entirely fitting and help to demonstrate the essential contribution that non-medical Royal Marine Commando's made towards the successful deployment of Medical Squadron at Ajax Bay, Teal Inlet, and Stanley. Jon went on to specialise as a Mountain Leader (ML) and attained the rank of Major. He has only recently retired from the Corps.

On 18 June 1982 I walked into the Government Offices just down the road from our location and managed to get a telegram sent to my wife. It simply said *'Dear Bev, now in Stanley, everything ok. Miss you. Love Mal.'* I passed Prince Andrew as I came out of the building, and he seemed quite surprised. I felt pride and respect for him that he had flown helicopters from an aircraft carrier throughout the conflict. Neither of us spoke, but he looked fresh and clean, and I certainly wasn't. My telegram arrived in Plymouth two days later.

2 Field Hospital RAMC were later, on 22 June 1982, put ashore in Stanley, and I was at the King Edward Memorial Hospital when their Commanding Officer arrived. A very pleasant gentleman who had been instructed to strive to set up an integrated facility with the hospital. 2 Field Hospital had no Admission and Discharge book and I therefore agreed to leave One Troop Medical Squadron's which we had instigated at Teal Inlet. Having left our previous book at Ajax Bay for continuity, which remained with Medical Squadron when we returned to the UK, it is regrettable that our Teal Inlet Admission and Discharge book was never returned to the Squadron. The recorded names of British Fatalities that came back to us at Teal Inlet has only been subsequently possible because Leading Medical Assistant Rod Cain recorded these names, and that of the Argentine who died shortly after arriving in our Reception Tent, in a letter home to his wife, and Rod was able to verify this when I contacted him in January 2022.

For One Troop Medical Squadron, our war was over. It had started for us as soon as the Argentinians had invaded the Islands at the beginning of April 1982, and now thank God it was over! Over, except that is to say that despite subsequently undertaking a number of other major operations in the future, including the First Gulf

War (US Dessert Storm; UK Op Granby) in 1990/91, and the subsequent Operation Haven in Northern Iraq until 15 June 1991, the Falklands War had left unique indelible and, in many cases, horrific memories. We had seen and treated casualties of all the major land battles and received and buried their dead comrades. We had also received a good many of the injured men from stricken ships, including the first fatality at Ajax Bay who was Hong Kong laundry man B K Kye from HMS Coventry which suffered more fatalities than any single land battle of the war, as she lost the battle to stay afloat, whilst fighting to protect those of us ashore.

These memories, and of preparing and laying men of both sides of the conflict in long trenches cannot be diminished nor overstated, and we will carry them with us for the rest of our lives.

The unresolved circumstances regarding the burial of the dead at Teal Inlet Bunk House.

This should have been the end of our story, but a twist of fate has dictated that it must continue, as an important post operation anomaly became apparent:

In addition to casualties needing treatment at Teal Inlet, as already mentioned earlier, we received a number of dead Argentine fatalities, and 11 UK fatalities in total. These fatalities included Sgt Ian Hunt, whose body was taken by his SBS comrades on 2 June 1982, to what is now the Memorial site at Teal Inlet and his body was eventually repatriated to the UK.

Of the 10 other British fatalities, only one, Cpl Ian Spencer I believe, who was a Commando Sapper Royal Engineer, serving with Condor Troop of 45 Commando Group, had died whilst in our care as we strived to save him. The remaining 9 British fatalities were all Dead on Arrival, and one of these was unidentifiable, having been blown to pieces and without his identity tags. Apart from Sgt Ian Hunt, the remaining 10 British fatalities were all buried in our trench adjacent to the Bunk House behind a single row of trees.

The trench was dug after we had received the body of Sgt Ian 'Kiwi' Hunt, whom the SBS had carried off. It was dug having consulted with our superiors at Ajax Bay and with their full knowledge and authority. Indeed, the Engineering Request (Enquest) was submitted through our Command Post (CP) back to the Commando Logistic Regiment CP, with our grid reference. Its primary function was for fatalities.

Only one Argentine casualty, whom I have recently been reminded was identified as Ramon Quintana by other Argentine casualties and was close to death when he arrived with multiple gunshot wounds, died shortly after his arrival whilst he was still in our Reception tent. All the other Argentine fatalities had been flown back to us Dead on Arrival, and they were all in a dreadful state and without identification.

All the fatalities received respectful ceremonies with a padre conducting each ceremony. Our Padre was the Reverend David Leighton (RiP) and he presided over most of the ceremonies, but not all of them, as he was often visiting troops at Ajax Bay and elsewhere. Unfortunately, David died just a few years after the war. I attended each brief ceremony, accompanied by just a few men, as we were continuously busy coping with live casualties, which was our primary role. All such ceremonies were requested and organised in conjunction with the Command Post at Ajax Bay. We sent Situation Reports every 8 hours to Ajax Bay, and these detailed casualties and fatalities.

Our burials at Teal Inlet were in stark contrast to those at Ajax Bay which had been attended by many individuals. Indeed, whilst we had been at Ajax Bay we had managed the reception and burial of 18 dead British and one Hong Kong British National, but the task at Ajax Bay had been spread across many more available personnel because of the presence of HQ Medical Squadron, and the fact that several of One Troop's marines had been retained at Ajax Bay when we moved forward. In contrast, at Teal Inlet the grim task of preparing bodies for burial, was largely managed by CPOMA John Smith, often at most with one helper, including myself on one or two occasions, and sometimes, when we were very busy, he did this task alone. I was never asked to provide nominations for awards at the close of the war, but if I had been, then the likes of John Smith would have been at the top of my list.

I much later read that all the fatalities interred at Teal Inlet were exhumed in October 1982 by the Pioneer Corps under the direction of Major John Robb, and I reflected that their task must have been pretty grim too. The report I read documented how the bodies were placed in coffins and transferred, via the Royal Fleet Auxiliary vessel Sir Bedivere, to designated burial grounds. I know this is what relatives had wished for, but when I read of this repatriation I thought if the spirits of the dead could have talked, they might have liked to stay in the peaceful resting place we had found for them at Teal Inlet. This matter was to prove more profound and troubling than I ever imagined possible however, as first became apparent 38 years later, as I set out here.

On the weekend of Saturday 1 August 2020, having sent the first draft of my written account to Falkland Islander Neil Rowlands, who had been at Teal Inlet in 1982 throughout the period One Troop Medical Squadron were in situ, Neil initially disputed the existence of the burial site we utilized. He described another site, well removed and remote from the Bunk House site, and showing a dedication of names, long displayed on a memorial at the remote site he described, reflecting mostly, but not exclusively, burials of most of 3 Para's fatalities from the battle of Mount Longdon. The memorial also marked the passing of SBS Sgt Ian 'Kiwi' Hunt and other Royal Marine Commandos.

Neil went on to explain he had attended the funeral service at the memorial site, which a fellow farmhand had dug with a local tractor. He recollected the fatalities were mainly Paratroopers, but he recalled Sgt Kiwi Hunt's body bag was already in place, and apart from these he believed there were no more than two others whom he believed to be Royal Marines. He also explained how he and other farmhands had, after our departure, levelled all trenches that had been back-filled around Teal Inlet, believing these were either former defensive positions or rubbish tips.

It was immediately clear to me however, when I viewed images of the memorial site on the internet, that this was not the resting place where One Troop Medical Squadron had interred the fatalities that had been flown back to our facility at Teal Inlet, nor of the two who had died in our care, one Argentine and One British. It dawned on me that the exhumations I had read about, may not have referred to the Medical Squadron location, but solely to what I now refer to as the memorial site. Neil Rowlands had also been present at the exhumations in October 1982, and he confirmed to me that only the memorial burial site had been exhumed. He was absolutely clear about this and checked with others who were also with him at Teal Inlet to verify his recollections were correct.

I therefore immediately alerted the Governor of the Falkland Islands that it appeared the Medical Squadron burial site at Teal Inlet may not have been exhumed, and if this is so, this would suggest there were anomalies in what had previously been understood to be a fully resolved account of the last resting places of British and Argentine fatalities. Indeed, it seemed increasingly likely that some individuals whose names are remembered on the remote memorial site at Teal Inlet, were individuals whom we buried at our location in the centre of the settlement adjacent to the Bunk House. It began to look as if at least some of the names of fatalities we had reported back to the Field Records Office at Ajax Bay through their JNCO Corporal Bowes who deployed with us to Teal Inlet, had simply been incorporated on the memorial dedication. At this stage, 38 years after we had left Teal Inlet, I did not have a list of names of those that we had interred by the Bunk House, but it was clear there were too few names on the memorial dedication, to account for all the fatalities One Troop Medical Squadron interred. The unidentified British fatality who had been blown to pieces was not mentioned on the memorial, and just one Argentine was listed, but not named.

Having alerted the Governor of the Falkland Islands, matters initially progressed quite quickly, involving the RAF Special Investigation Branch (SIB) who interviewed me personally for around six hours, just 3 weeks after raising the initial concern. I was able to point out within a matter of a few yards, where I believed the site of our burials at Teal Inlet took place, namely behind what was a single row of conifer trees in 1982; but despite this there was then a lapse of several weeks before I was advised that the matter had been referred to the civil Police as they should have had jurisdiction from the outset. I was invited to attend a second interview, this time with a representative of the Royal Falkland Island Police (RFIP) at a local UK Police Station on 27 October 2020. This second interview actually took place in 'a safe house' about a mile from Shrewsbury Police Station, and fully equipped to facilitate a video recording of the interview. The interview lasted a further 3 hours and following this it was suggested to me that ground radar would likely be utilized to expedite a search of the site, and this would show the complete history of what had occurred at the site, including if, for example, it had been exhumed.

Shortly after this I agreed to fly to the Falkland Islands, at the invitation of the Royal Falkland Island Police. I felt the matter needed to be resolved and this was the surest way of doing so. I made it quite clear that this was why I agreed to submit myself to a 20 hour flight from RAF Brize Norton aboard an A330 Air Tanker, whilst wearing a mask, and subsequently spending 15 nights in isolation as it was the height of the Covid 19 worldwide epidemic. A fellow passenger tested positive for Covid 19 following our arrival on the Islands, but fortunately no one else tested positive during the rigorous tests that were conducted three times on every passenger before being allowed to leave isolation on Tuesday 24 November 2020.

Whilst in isolation, I watched on the local TV station what is hopefully the last mine to be found and destroyed on the Islands. The final task of clearing the Islands of mines had been managed by John Hare, who had been the 5th casualty at Ajax Bay in 1982 when he was one of the most seriously wounded victims of the 3 Para 'blue on blue' friendly fire incident, which I have referred to in this account, and which occurred in the hinterland of Port San Carlos, on D+1 22 May 1982. Once out of Covid isolation I was later able to meet John and a member of his mine disposal team and showed them a copy of John's admission entry in the Ajax Bay Admission & Discharge Log, and we discussed many of the details that follow herein.

I accompanied the Falkland Police at 1000 on the morning of 24 November 2020, bound for Teal Inlet in two 4x4 vehicles. As we headed over the East side of Mount Kent, despite this being Spring in the Southern Hemisphere, the customary Falkland wind rapidly became a gale and rain lashed down with such ferocity that I could only wonder how any of the Units on the ground in the Falkland winter of 1982 had survived the elements. Little wonder so many had Trench Foot! The storm passed as quickly as it had started fortunately and 10 minutes later Teal Inlet was coming into view. I had enjoyed the 30 or so miles drive out from Stanley, and the new gravel road, which was still being improved upon, had reduced the journey time to about an hour, compared to 1982 when the faint trail between Stanley and Teal Inlet would take several hours to navigate, and require a great deal of driver focus and skill not to get stuck or damage a Land Rover. The Chief of Police, Superintendent Jeff McMahon, and his accompanying Sergeant, Glen Smith, were welcome company after my 15 night isolation.

Arriving through a farm gateway into the settlement, I was immediately struck with how run-down Teal Inlet looked compared to 1982 when it was owned and managed by a large corporate Falkland Island company. Now several buildings had fallen into disrepair, and others that in 1982 had housed equipment and personnel from the 3 Brigade Air Squadron for example, and provided shelter for troops transiting through, and dry storage for supplies being moved forward, had long since been demolished. Some of the remaining dwellings were in a sorry state. I was readily able to identify the Bunk House that had been the nucleus for our forward light field hospital, albeit the building had been reduced to a single storey and was in an abandoned and dilapidated state. I found it hard to comprehend that a site that had played such a prominent role in the war, where we had been able to treat so many young men from both sides of the conflict, had been allowed to fall into such a state of decay – I felt it could have been preserved as a National museum to the medical effort ashore in 1982, but there was no evidence whatsoever of what we had achieved there all those years ago. The outhouse we had used as a mortuary had been demolished and only its concrete floor remained.

The treeline behind which we had interred the fallen, had clearly thrived though, and unusually for the Falklands, where the wind prevents self-germination of trees, it had grown into quite a dense copse of trees. This tree growth confused me that morning after 15 nights in isolation, and I simply pointed out the far side of the tree growth as the burial site. Regardless of this however, we were standing within a few yards of the exact burial site, and I had expected a search to ensue, ideally with ground penetrating radar, as had been indicated during my interview with the Falkland Island Police Officer in the UK. There was also a large concrete slab, about 2 metres by 2 metres square, set level into the ground at the bay end of this copse, which had definitely not been present in 1982, and its purpose was a mystery.

Instead of conducting any search whatsoever, it was announced that we would return to the Police Station in Stanley for a sandwich lunch, and then try to identify, on paper, the names of any individual fatalities. I had hoped I would be able to at least suggest names of some of the Royal Marines whom we had interred. Also, at this point, I assumed a search to locate and investigate the exact site would still take place over the remaining two days of my visit. Just before we all left Teal Inlet, the other 'memorial' burial site was pointed out to me, but despite it now being a very clear day it was only just visible and seemed to be at least several hundred yards from the Bunk House, and certainly not where we in One Troop Medical Squadron had interred anyone; indeed, that would have required transport!

A small islet in the bay adjacent to the memorial site was also pointed out, as apparently one of the Argentine forward observation officers had been found there in 1982. Perhaps his radio had failed to function, otherwise we surely would have been subjected to relentless air attacks, just as we had experienced at Ajax Bay.

We had a pleasant return trip back to Stanley, without another storm, and passed the wreckage of Argentine helicopters that still litter the ground where they were brought down. At the Police Station I was most conscious that this building had lost its roof as a result of the attack by a Wessex Helicopter launched from Teal Inlet. It was my first ever visit inside the Station, and certainly it had not had money lavished on it over the years. We had barely sat down to enjoy some sandwiches, and I was asked to suggest any individuals whom we may have interred.

I had, from the outset, made it clear that our Admission and Discharge Book for Teal Inlet had subsequently been used in Stanley Hospital and was passed to 2 Field Hospital who relieved us in 1982, so I was not, at that stage, in possession of any definitive names apart from Sgt Ian 'Kiwi' Hunt SBS RM whose whereabouts was not in question, but my post operation report had included a tabulated numerical list of UK casualties and fatalities, and the sole Argentine who had died in our care, and a record of the number of Argentine wounded casualties whom we had treated. I had no exact number however, for the multiple Argentine fatalities whom we had received Dead on Arrival for burial in our trench. I had written my Post Operation report in late June 1982 whilst returning to the UK on the Canberra after the conflict, and I believe the numerical tabulated list was probably constructed from the duplicate copies of Field Medical Cards (FMed 28's).

I suggested four fatalities from the 45 Commando blue on blue incident, because I knew these had not been evacuated to Ajax Bay, but I was advised that these were interred at the grounds around Estancia House and, according to the records of the exhumations co-ordinated by Major John Robb in October 1982, these were, uniquely, exhumed at Estancia. I was unable to suggest any other names. The Chief Police Officer, Chief Superintendent Jeff McMahon, then asked what I had against Surgeon Commander Rick Jolly? I was shocked by this question, particularly as I couldn't recall even mentioning Rick Jolly (our former Squadron Commander), but I did answer honestly that I felt he was a self-publicist. That aside I actually got on very well with Rick however, and I was dismayed that such a question had clearly been posed to suggest or probe if I had an ulterior motive behind my concerns regarding the fatalities we had laid to rest at Teal Inlet.

The meeting ended at about 1530. I was totally deflated and overwhelmed with a deep, deep sense of indescribable despair as it became clear that no search was going to take place during my visit, nor any time soon. I felt that a search would expedite matters to identify the bodies, but instead I was merely advised that the RFIP would 'continue their enquiries'. This was the most deeply anxious and grim I have ever felt in my life, despite operations in Northern Ireland, the 1990/91 Gulf war, and subsequent operations in Northern Iraq in 1991. The handling of so many of fatalities by One Troop Medical Squadron during the Falkland war had been by far the most traumatic ghastly undertaking for us, and this apparent reliance now on a formal pursuit of an evidence trail instead of a simply conducting an exploratory survey with ground penetrating radar, that could have confirmed the presence of bodies and enabled their identities to be determined, was inexplicable. Subsequently I concluded that this inactivity at least indicated that the Police must have at least thought it possible that the fatalities were still at the site, otherwise it would have been a very simple task to conduct a ground radar search to disprove it.

It was difficult for me to get out of my mind the very downtrodden state of Teal Inlet, and its abandoned Bunk House, and our forgotten burial site, where bodies from both sides of the conflict possibly still remain, with no vestige of recognition or maintenance, and horse and sheep dung covering the site.

I was told that Major Robb's exhumation report had clearly shown that four bodies had been recovered from Estancia, which lies between Stanley and Teal Inlet, but it was also clear that only the Memorial burial site at Teal Inlet had been exhumed, and Neil Rowlands and his friends who were at Teal Inlet in 1982, had been absolutely correct about this.

I endured a totally sleepless night, as I could only focus on what is now a wooded copse at Teal Inlet, and the burials we undertook in 1982 kept going round and round in my head, like having a nightmare whilst being wide awake. I recalled at about 0200 in the night that, as I had already advised the RAF Special Investigations Branch several weeks earlier, the burials had been just behind a single treeline at Teal Inlet, and I realised that what had grown into a considerable wooded copse had either been planted or (despite the wind) self-seeded after we had left in the middle of June 1982. So the following morning I headed back to the Station and met with one of the Detective Constables and told him that it was apparent to me that the treeline behind which the burial site existed, must have grown beyond the first line of trees, and the actual site of the burial was just beyond this first line of trees, as I had detailed to the SIB in August 2020, not on the far side of what is now a copse. Moreover, the much smaller size of the trees in the centre of the copse fully supported this. I signed a statement to this effect, and he advised me they had a record that showed that a search team had been sent back to Teal Inlet in 1982 because some bodies were unaccounted for. This revelation was enough to make me weep, as to this juncture, whilst I had been treated politely and cordially by everyone, it was clear there was a large dose of scepticism, and I had found myself on more than one occasion since this situation had arisen, having to demonstrate not just the fact of the burial site, but actually the fact of what we did and what we achieved throughout our deployment at Teal Inlet, and elsewhere on the Islands. In 1982 our role was the most physically, mentally, and clinically demanding period imaginable, and only achievable because of the calibre of everyone concerned. I signed a statement to record the change of the site, which was actually the only signed statement I was asked to make about this whole situation. I still had no idea what the large concrete slab was for, at the Bay end of the copse, and at this point it was largely forgotten.

Overall, the RFIP officers' treated me very well indeed with the utmost professionalism, and the following day, Thursday 26 November, I accompanied two officers back to Teal Inlet, where my recollection of the position of the burial site was then marked out. However, when I enquired when this matter might be brought to a conclusion, the response was that the evidence would continue to be gathered until a consolidated report could be submitted to the Island's Governor, with recommendations from the RFIP and Coroner on how to proceed beyond that. Nobody at any stage offered an explanation as to why a brief exploration of the site was not being undertaken except I was told that ground penetrating radar would not work properly with tree roots surrounding the site. Given that we had buried multiple fatalities this seemed somewhat over egged. Certainly, members of the mine clearance team, whom I met with later that day, including John Hare, were clear that ground radar survey ought to have been viable.

That was the sum of my 18 nights in the Falkland Islands. 15 nights spent in isolation and around 10 subsequent hours spent with the RFIP. Aside from that I had the opportunity to visit old friends from my days with Naval Party 8901 between 1977 and 1978. Without such friends I think I could have sunk into a despondent abyss.

Four months after I first raised my concerns, I subsequently sent another email to the Falkland Island Governor expressing unease that little had happened, despite a number of One Troop Medical

Squadron members having already verified the fact of the fatalities we had received, and of the casualties that we did our utmost to ensure had the best possible survival rates and outcomes. I received a brief reply from the Governor, via his personal secretary, that was not particularly empathetic and demonstrated a lack of understanding of the anxiety this matter was causing.

I subsequently expressed my concerns in writing to our former 3 Brigade Commander, General Julian Thompson, stating that someone, ideally in the Royal Marines at the highest possible level, ought to be maintaining oversight of this matter and acting in liaison with those of us who had been Teal Inlet, with the aim of helping to ensure our well-being and wider interests were being properly guarded whilst this investigation was underway, and hopefully expediting matters. The short reply I received, which according to General Thompson was constructed with the help of Colonel Ivar Hellberg, the former CO of the Commando Logistic Regiment, basically ignored my plea that someone to be responsible for the oversight and wellbeing, and simply said he could not offer any help.

Months passed with no further word. The Governor had undertaken to update me every few weeks but never did. Indeed, it was 24 February 2021 before I heard from the Police Chief, Superintendent Jeff McMahon again, when I got a surprise telephone call and, with my wife also in the living room, and the phone on speaker, he said he was phoning to say that having questioned other members of the team he believed what I had told him, and he would be taking the necessary steps to instigate a search. He said he would phone me every six weeks or so to keep me updated. My wife wept with relief, and I was greatly relieved and felt that the months of persistence had been worth it.

Three weeks before this, during yet another sleepless night, I had recalled the very large concrete slab at the Bay end of the wood, and it dawned on me that this slab was possibly a marker that had been set in the ground to formally note the position of the burial site. Indeed, with the trees that had been planted over the burial site, it seemed probable that the site had been intentionally covered up. I discussed this with former colleagues and was placed under pressure not to report this, but after due consideration I felt I had no alternative but to pass my concerns to the RFIP Police, and I notified the duty RFIP Sergeant.

Any sense of relief that I had following my telephone conversation with Superintendent Jeff McMahon on 24 February was soon tempered. He phoned again on 6 May 2021, and on this occasion my adult daughter was in the room. He said he had reason to believe that the UK fatalities had been exhumed (which by implication would have required them to have been transferred to the memorial burial site, prior to exhumation in October 1982). He said he had obtained a photo of our burial site from one of the doctors who had served at Teal with me, and his team estimated the trench to be 15 metres long by 3 metres wide. He also said that Colonel Ivar Hellberg had finally acknowledged the presence of our burial site – which was the first time I realised Ivar Hellberg had actually denied the existence of our site. I followed up the call with an email to the RFIP detailing my concerns that a partial exhumation that excluded all but one of the Argentine fatalities made no sense, indeed it contravened the spirit of the Geneva Convention. I also passed on information I had received a few weeks earlier from a key member of my team, indicating that several of the Argentine fatalities had been mutilated. The Police Chief responded in a reassuringly professional manner to this.

I was contacted again around 26 July 2021 and finally advised that a ground radar team would be deployed from the UK in August. I was greatly heartened by this, but whilst a team did deploy, and their ground penetrating radar equipment had been sent to Brize Norton a week in advance, alas, the equipment never arrived on the Falkland Islands. The team, from Wessex Archaeology, left the Islands a few days after their 15 night compulsory Covid isolation, having achieved little or nothing. I received an email from the Police telling me it was due to the melting of the runway at RAF Brize Norton, which did indeed result in flights being diverted to another airfield, but it seems a very poor excuse for their equipment, which was fundamentally vital to this operation, never having been dispatched. I understand the team were re-united with the equipment after their return to Brize Norton.

Despite this, in September 2021, observers from the UK International Committee of the Red Cross (ICRC) arrived on the Islands, and I was advised by email that they had already been tasked to verify the recovery of an Argentine helicopter crew of four, whom I understand were interred at Darwin. In the event the number of fatality remains recovered was six, and on completion of that task, the ICRC observers set off with the Falkland Police, to Teal Inlet to verify that search, after which the ICRC issued a press release stating that they had undertaken a search and nothing was found. However, Falkland Islander Neil Rowlands emailed a picture of the 'search' and he expressed concern that it comprised a shallow dig confined to a single spot. This was the spot I had originally pointed out, and had realised was wrong in November 2020, and I had corrected by signed statement. Effectively it involved a shallow scrape in the wrong place, after which they returned to Stanley within about an hour. The wooded area that I had marked out with two police officers remained untouched. (A sequence of photographs reflecting this situation follows further on).

From that point on it was obvious to me that the matter had been turned from a genuine oversight and search, to a cover up, culminating with an email from the Chief Police Officer that totally disregarded the evidence that members of my team had given, in particular regarding Argentine fatalities, and the unidentified British fatality who was an assortment of body parts. The Chief Police Officer also indicated that the ICRC would need to authorise any further exploration. This prompted me to phone the ICRC in London. The individual I spoke with had no knowledge of the evidence that indicated several of the Argentine fatalities had been mutilated, and stressed that the role of the ICRC was that of observers, and they would attend any such exploration authorised by the UK Government, but they had no investigative powers and could not instigate a site exploration.

Unfortunately, all the ICRC seemed to do with the information I had passed to them, in particular about some of the Argentine fatalities having been mutilated, was to pass my concerns straight back to the FI Governor, as the following day on 24 September 2021 I received another email from the Islands' Chief Police Officer, Superintendent Jeff Mc Mahon, stating that the Governor had briefed him about my conversation with the ICRC. The Chief Police Officer pointed out that the details of mutilations had been 'passed to me in confidence' by one of my senior men. Was he implying some wrong doing on my part, despite having a moral and legal obligation to strive to ensure such matters are properly reported and acted upon? He went on to state that a previous allegation of mutilations was thoroughly investigated in 1994 and passed to the Director of Public Prosecutions who had deemed that there were insufficient grounds to prosecute individuals due to a lack of evidence (i.e., there were no bodies). This, he stated, demonstrated there was no point pursuing the current concerns I had been alerted to and subsequently reported. I was intrigued by this as the email inferred by implication that the 1994 case is somehow linked to this situation, and I wondered how such an association had been arrived at.

The Chief Police Officer also advised me that he had a document that indicated the Argentine who had died in our care was Ramon Quintana. Up to this point I had no information regarding Quintana's identity, but it was subsequently also confirmed by individuals who had been working in our Reception tent at Teal Inlet when Ramon Quintana died. Was the document Superintendent Mc Mahon referred to, our Teal Inlet and Stanley Hospital Admission and Discharge book I wondered, or the Field Medical Card (FMed 28) i.e., patient notes for Quintana? He stated that the document does not mention any other Argentine dead at Teal Inlet – which of course neither an individual Field Medical

Card nor the Admission and Discharge Book would, because, as I have been clear from the outset, Argentine fatalities who were not admitted to our facility, but brought to us for burial, were not entered into the admission and discharge book, but instead reported to the Field Records Office as Dead on Arrival.

Jeff McMahon said he had 'more work to do on the source of the document that has recently come into his possession'. This sounded positive, but I subsequently was to note that he had briefed a UK newspaper, Wigan Today, (I believe Wigan is his home town) on 6 July 2021 with an account of the situation at Teal Inlet in 1982, and had named Quintana in the article, some 12 weeks before notifying me and whilst I and those of the team that had been contacted were being extolled to speak to nobody about the matter, such was its sensitivity. Further, the article stated *'that the fallen soldiers were interred near to a site where medical waste – including severed combatants' limbs – was buried'*. To which I would say possibly so; but the Wigan Today article then stated that I *'claim a military digger arrived on site, dug a trench, and this was used to dispose of body parts removed during surgery…the trench was also reportedly used for burials'*.

The above latter sentence is a gross abhorrent distortion of the purpose of the burial trench, which was dug in full consultation with the Command Post at Ajax Bay and with the sole purpose of interring the dead. To put matters of 'amputated limbs' into context, during my ten days at Ajax Bay, a single limb was disposed of by burning, (as referred to much earlier herein), and it produced such a smell and acrid smoke, that we never resorted to that again, and as such at Teal Inlet if any limbs were amputated they would have been buried, but I can say that no 'medical waste' was disposed of in our burial trench. The only amputated limbs I can recall at Teal Inlet were the result of traumatic amputation from blast injuries caused by Argentine anti-personnel mines blowing feet and ankles off above the top of victims' boots. I can only recall one such injury that was still partially attached, and I believe that was prior to the surgical team being deployed forward to our facility.

As such the unfortunate victim was casevaced back to the Hospital Ship Uganda by support helicopter, with his partially amputated limb just taped back to the shin, to stop it moving around whilst the victim was being transferred by the helicopter and carried into Uganda from its makeshift flight-deck.

Perhaps the origin to this abhorrent 'clinical waste' fiction can be traced back to Colonel Ivar Hellberg, as the Chief Police Officer's email of 24 September 2021 also states:

'The other line of enquiry we are following relates to Ivor Hellberg; who rather ironically does confirm the presence of another trench and he too states it was used for dead coming from the bunkhouse as well as amputated limbs. The trench being dug for convenience. The counter-point to that of course is the documents detailing the work done to ensure identifications were accurate during Major Robb's exhumation exercise. I have read this a number of times and it is does offer reassurance that all British dead were properly identified'.

With regard to the above issue of reassurance that the documentation was correct when Major Robb oversaw the exhumations some four months later in October 1982, this ignores that we interred 10 British fatalities, one of whom was unknown and is not mentioned on the memorial at Teal Inlet, and we interred multiple Argentine fatalities, but only one, apparently Ramon Quintana, whom we admitted to our Reception tent and died shortly afterwards, was exhumed from the memorial site. The Argentine fatalities at the Darwin Cemetery, where Quintana would have been transferred to in October 1982, were much later, from 2017 onwards, identified by DNA testing. I wonder if Quintana was tested or whether his identity was taken as read? There remains no explanation how the British we interred were miraculously, supposedly, transferred to the memorial site, only to be exhumed again in October 1982.

The Wigan Today article did however state that the fact of the Bunk House burial site and fatalities had been corroborated in full by some and in part by others, who had been interviewed.

The article does not appear to have been picked up by other UK newspapers, but it was published in an English language South American newspaper the following day.

I subsequently received an email on 22 October 2021, from Colonel Ivar Hellberg:

'The Falklands Islands Police have just rung me up about the bodies at Teal and other related matters. They confirmed that under Op Quartz, they had dug up the area that you had indicated witnessed by ICRC oversight and found nothing. In their view and that of the Governor, the matter was now closed and the Argentinean authorities had been advised. I asked about another area that had initially been nearby, indicated which was a possible site of burial, they said they were not going to dig it up, but that the local farmer might do so in the next week or so to lay his mind at rest...and ours'.

Unfortunately, the photograph (shown further on) of the so-called search, which had been forwarded to me by Falkland Islander Neil Rowlands, revealed they had not searched the site I had assisted two police officers to mark out within what is now a wood. Ironically, Ivar Hellberg even named the overall Operation. It would seem that neither the Police nor Ivar Hellberg knew I was in possession of the photograph.

It was abundantly clear that a lid had been placed over this entire matter and sealed. I was appalled by this, and the fact that a search with ground penetrating radar could have simply been conducted right back in August 2020 and would have acted to definitively resolve any concerns. Instead, a game of obfuscation has played out that has more in common with the 1982 Argentine Junta, than the Mother of Democracy.

I sent a full and detailed account by letter, with all relevant email correspondence and photographs, appealing to General Lord Dannatt that a search by ground penetrating radar should be deployed. It was dispatched by next day tracked and signed for post, and was delivered to Westminster the following day. I received no reply despite sending another email to politely ask if it could have some sort of acknowledgement. I then sent the same by email to the parliamentary offices of Liz Truss (zero reply); and Dominic Rabb (told to forward it to my local MP, who was Owen Patterson, as this 'was the correct protocol'. When I pointed out Owen Patterson had resigned, I was advised to send it to a neighbouring MP, so I sent it to the Shrewsbury MP Daniel Kawczynski, who also failed to reply). I also sent it to Ben Wallace, whose office obligingly simply sent it the MOD, and none of the concerns was addressed. Finally, I sent letters to my newly elected LibDem MP (via Westminster as I could find no local constituency office) and to the leader of the opposition Sir Keir Starmer (via his local constituency office in Kings Cross as his Westminster email address would not accept the delivery) but neither replied. So not a great advert for our open democracy! The aim of this correspondence had been purely to encourage a proper search to be conducted of the burial site, using ground penetrating radar.

In January 2022 I then received an unsigned anonymous reply from someone whom I presume is a civil servant in the MOD, basically parking the matter in a cul-de-sac with a blanket thrown over it, as one of our team described.

I then contacted more of the team who were with me at Teal Inlet in 1982, and it was only then that I gleaned incontrovertible evidence that the Argentine who died in our care had also been mutilated. He had multiple gunshot wounds, which was rare but need not in itself appear suspicious, but an ear had also been cut off. I have a written account of this from the doctor who was in our Reception tent when Ramon Quintana died within an hour or so of arrival.

Subsequently, a member of the Reception team at Teal Inlet also provided me with the names and dates of arrival of several of the British fatalities, and this enabled me to refer to them by name and relevant date in the account of our time at Teal Inlet. Leading

Medical Assistant Rod Cain had written to his wife in June 1982 and named these fatalities. The letters still exist, and include the name of the Argentine who died following admission to our Reception, as his wounded comrades had identified him, so he was not anonymous and his name was recorded in our Admission and Discharge Book that went on to be passed to 2 Field Hospital RAMC when we were relieved in Stanley. It is regrettable that we do not have this Admission & Discharge Book, but as previously explained, just as we had left our first Admission & Discharge Book at Ajax Bay for continuity use by 3 Troop Medical Squadron who relieved us, so the new log we initiated at Teal and later took with us to Stanley, was subsequently handed over to 2 Field Hospital RAMC. I was fortunately able to obtain a duplicate of our Ajax Bay log relating to our time there, but we have never again seen the log we used at Teal and Stanley Hospital after it was passed to 2 Field Hospital RAMC unfortunately. I do however have reason to believe that the Falkland Police may have subsequently secured the Teal Inlet Admission and Discharge Book, because, as I have already alluded to, Superintendent Jeff McMahon refers to Quintana in his email to me in October 2021 and I note he had first informed Falkland Islanders of this in an earlier press release in the early UK summer of 2021, prior to his Wigan press release in July 2021.

This prompted me to rummage out my own letters to my wife that she has similarly kept since 1982. I was a lot more circumspect, but a few days after I arrived at Teal I commented on how draining it was to receive so many dead and wounded from both sides of the conflict. We had already managed more than 250 casualties and multiple dead at Ajax Bay, alongside our counterparts in the Parachute Clearing Troop with whom we worked 12 hour alternating shifts; all hands turning to work when the pressures dictated, and regardless of relentless bombing that culminated in the facility at Ajax Bay turning into a raging inferno of explosions prior to the assault on Goose Green. At Teal we went on to deal with similar numbers of casualties and fatalities, but with a fraction of the total team at Ajax Bay. Thankfully at Teal we were never again subjected to bombing, but we have no reason on earth to lie about the casualties and fatalities that we managed. Our letters home provide an invaluable insight into what was going on. I have several, from D Day on 20 May leading to a telegram I sent from Stanley and my wife Bev received on 20 June 1982 in Plymouth.

I have also obtained a photo of Argentine fatalities who were brought back to Ajax Bay immediately before my team left to join me at Teal, when they had dealt with the Argentine casualties (of which I have rare video footage) and buried the fatalities, from the Top Malo encounter and possibly elsewhere, which the M&AW Cadre and SBS were buoyantly discussing soon after I had arrived at the Bunk House in Teal, shortly before calling my team forward. Interestingly, like at Teal Inlet, these Argentine fatalities were not entered on the Ajax Bay Admission & Discharge log, because they were clearly dead and did not enter the facility but were quickly checked outside and forwarded on for burial preparation. I have a photocopy of the Ajax Bay log up to the departure of my team and these Argentine fatalities are not recorded.

With regard to the last email I received from the Falkland Police Chief, when he remarked that I alerted the ICRC to the 'allegation' that one of my team had advised me that several of the Argentine fatalities we 'allegedly received' had been mutilated, I should emphasise that I am far from alone in reporting the fact that we received multiple Argentine dead at our location at Teal Inlet. Aircrew must also know this, indeed in one sortie a Wessex flew several dead Argentines to our location, and the Aircrewman could barely bring himself to lift them, they were in such a dreadful state. Others must also know. Frankly it is deeply insulting to be told by someone 40 years later that this is an unsubstantiated allegation, whilst those responsible for conducting a proper search have failed in their duty to deploy a ground penetrating radar team to a site that potentially holds both UK and Argentine remains and has been wooded over.

In his last email to me, the Falkland Police Chief, Superintendent Jeff McMahon, goes on to quote the case when in 1994 Detective

Superintendent Alec Edwards filed a full and detailed case alleging mutilations committed by Paratroopers, to the DPP Dame Barbara Mills who declined to prosecute on the basis of insufficient evidence. How he is able to directly connect this case with Teal Inlet is not clear. I first alerted the Governor about what I thought might be an oversight. My fear now is that our discrete burial site may have been utilized to effectively hide these poor victims and may even have subsequently been used to hide yet more, after we had departed for Stanley. Equally disturbingly however, is that nobody has identified how our British fatalities were supposedly moved from the Bunk House burial site to the Memorial burial site, only to be exhumed again in October 1982. Worse still therefore, I cannot rule out that the Argentine dead that were interred at Ajax Bay could have been inadvertently repatriated in place of dead British fatalities.

As this situation has unravelled I feel that if the Falkland Island Governor and Police had been empowered to authorise a ground penetrating radar search of the wooded area that was marked out when I visited Teal Inlet for the first time in over 38 years in November 2020, they could have found any bodies that may or may not still lay there, and have declared it an oversight. None of us would have been any the wiser. I am certain that is what the Police would have done if they had a free rein. That option is in danger of being missed altogether, as the fiasco of the ICRC monitored search, and the email I subsequently received from Col Ivar Hellberg suggests this situation is being covered up, and in so doing actually draws the spotlight on incidents that definitely should have been dealt with in 1982, when one or more rogue psychopathic individuals who acted in a wholly unacceptable manner should have been properly dealt with. I note however that one such alleged perpetrator was himself killed in combat, and as such it would seem a line can be drawn under any such horrors he perpetrated. This however reinforces my very real concerns that some UK fatalities may still remain buried alongside Argentine conscripts at Teal Inlet. Many Argentine conscripts are still missing and their families have no information about their loved ones. As for the British fatalities, if I were a relative visiting my loved one's grave now in the UK,

I would at the very least want assurance the grave has the correct remains, and not some other body conveniently available to make up the numbers. Argentine and British fatalities had arrived at Teal Inlet from forward areas, when our medical team was constantly being run ragged saving the lives of casualties, which was our primary focus. With the failure of three Ministers, Liz Truss, Dominic Raab, and Ben Wallace; and General Lord Dannatt; Sir Keir Starmer MP; Daniel Kawczynski,MP; and Helen Morgan MP; to even deign to reply to these concerns, the situation is elevated to one that is now being covered up by the silence of the State.

Concluding Summary

In reality there are three scenarios that may explain the situation at the Teal Inlet Bunk House Burial site:

Scenario One. The site was partially exhumed, including all of the British fatalities and the one Argentine, Ramon Quintana, who died in our Reception tent.

Whilst it is just barely conceivable that the British fatalities we interred were quietly transferred to the Memorial site prior to finally being exhumed by Major Robb's Pioneer team in October 1982, nobody has come forward to verify such a transfer took place. Indeed, the window of opportunity to conduct any transfer of bodies was very short after our team left Teal Inlet and set off to Stanley. It would have required plant, men, and transport to do so, and it is hard to believe nobody at Teal Inlet would have noticed such an undertaking. The body bags would have to needed to be opened to identify individuals, and this would have taken some time, and would have smelt a great deal. It then would have necessitated ferrying bodies hundreds of metres from the Bunk House site to the memorial site, after the settlement had ceased to be the military hub that was largely responsible for ensuring the success of the build-up, and final assaults that led to the surrender of the Argentine forces on the Islands. Were they really moved and then supposedly reburied in the trench which had been dug by a Falkland farm hand, where the Memorial now stands, only to be exhumed yet again in October 1982 by Major Robb? And what of the unidentified British fatality we laid to rest who had been blown to pieces? Who was he, and who occupies his grave, given all the British are said to be properly accounted for?

What of the remaining Argentines who were flown back to us, Dead on Arrival? Why conduct only a partial exhumation? If it was because some or all of them were feared to have been mutilated, it turns what probably was an individual act of gross violation into a wider cover-up that also represents a highly inappropriate use of a medical team who were already working at full stretch coping with the flow of casualties from both sides of the conflict, mainly as a result of the weather conditions prohibiting helicopters from flying to either Ajax Bay or, to a similar facility established by 16 Field Ambulance RAMC at Fitzroy from 8 June 1982.

Scenario Two. The site was simply forgotten, and all the fatalities remain in situ, after One Troop Medical Squadron were moved to Stanley at very short notice.

The problem with this scenario is that the site was dug in full consultation with the Logistic Command Post at Ajax Bay. Indeed, the military digger had driven not just to the Bunk House, but having driven past the tree line, East to West towards the bay, it then turned up the other side of the tree line, going almost to the top, where it turned around, and stopped at a gap in the trees, through which the fatalities were carried on stretchers from our makeshift mortuary. In other words, the driver knew exactly where he was supposed to go, before I liaised with him, and he commenced his task.

This scenario also would have necessitated other bodies to have been interred at the Memorial burial site, in place of those we laid to rest at the Bunk House. Unfortunately, there were unmarked Argentine fatalities at Ajax Bay that could have enabled such an event, whether by intention or accident. The Field Records Office at Ajax Bay had at least one dog tag for every British fatality who had worn them. Only two British fatalities at Teal Inlet had no dog tags, namely the unidentified soldier blown to pieces, and Corporal I.F Spencer of 45 Commando, who Leading Medical Assistant Paul Youngman, also serving with 45 Commando, had identified and attached a Field Medical Card (FMed 28).

Scenario Three. This is the same as scenario one, but the Bunk House site could, if British fatalities and a single Argentine fatality had been removed to the Memorial burial site, have then be used to bury yet more Argentine fatalities that relate to the 1994 Metropolitan Police investigation, that the Director of Public Prosecutions would not progress due to the lack of physical evidence i.e., there were no mutilated Argentine bodies found.

Is this why the MOD and Foreign Office seem to have jointly gone to extreme lengths to declare that the faux search found nothing? 8,000 miles from the UK, it seems the authorities are confident in their ability to keep a tight lid on the Teal Inlet Bunk House burial site, but in so doing they have ignored the testimony and statements of myself and of the several others of the team whom they have questioned. Indeed, at one stage a private detective, Steve Crimmins, formerly of the same UK Police Force as Superintendent Jeff McMahon, (Greater Manchester), was going to interview more of the team, but he was quietly stood down without explanation, thus limiting the number who had given corroborating evidence.

The above scenarios are so unconscionable that the authorities seem to have opted to portray that we never received any fatalities who were Dead on Arrival. This is their **Fictitious Fourth Scenario.** This treats the fatalities and their families, from both sides of the conflict, as if the bodies are just statistics whose numbers have been moulded to fit. But these fatalities still have families and loved ones, and this denial also treats those of us who had to repeatedly carry out the ghastly task of caring for these pour dead souls, whilst showing them all due reverence, treating us as an inconvenience, or worse, dismissing us all as charlatans.

We did not and do not seek thanks or limelight, but we did not expect denial, which is despicable beyond words. It has caused us much pain and anguish

Closing comments. This is a totally unacceptable quagmire of a mess. The tactic seems increasingly to resort to denial or silence, and to disregard the evidence I and other former members of the One Troop Medical Squadron team have given, whilst accepting the 'administrative' evidence of others who were never at Teal Inlet in June 1982. The lack of an independent survey using ground penetrating radar is damning, and unless a proper search is undertaken I do not believe relatives in the UK have assurance that their loved ones are actually in their assigned resting place. Moreover, some of the missing Argentine conscripts are probably also beneath the copse alongside the Bunk House at Teal Inlet.

Forty years after this brutal war ended, the UK authorities have a moral and legal obligation to ensure the site One Troop Medical Squadron utilised at Teal Inlet Bunk House is properly investigated by deploying an independent team equipped with ground penetrating radar. I have done my best to highlight the situation but have reached the conclusion that nothing will happen without wider publicity and pressure. The dead have no voice, and they did not get up and walk from the Bunk House burial site to the Memorial burial site. So, those of us who are still alive and able to do so, need to speak up for them and for their families, because the dead did not walk!

The Bunk House 1982(facing the Bay), showing the 24 x 18 feet tents that formed the Reception and Evacuation wards under canvas, and the main radio aerial secured from the upper centre window.

The Bunk House now, (facing the Bay) with its upper floor and apex roof totally removed.

The Bunkhouse from the gap in the trees, through which fatalities were stretchered for burial - the now demolished temporary mortuary building was just to the right of the single hut still standing to the front right side of the Bunkhouse.

The Bunk House burial site being marked out in November 2020, amongst the trees, which, beyond the outer single row, were not present in 1982. These more recent trees are in rows, so they have clearly been planted. A large concrete slab is at the top (Bay end) of this copse, beyond where one of the Falkland Police Officer's secures a marker.

The line of trees from where the makeshift mortuary had stood, looking towards the gap that fatalities were carried through for burial.

The September 2021 'search', on the South side of the Bunk House, beyond the copse. This was the total extent of the exploratory dig, after which the London office of the International Committee of the Red Cross issued a statement, (with no qualification i.e. that no ground penetrating radar had been utilized and the dig was limited to a single spot),

that no bodies had been found during their search at Teal Inlet.

*Argentine medics bring their fatalities to Ajax
Bay, escorted by British Military Police.*

Annex A

The Commando Casualty Chain – Forward Units

The following Royal Navy Commando Medical Service Personnel formed the backbone of 3 Command Brigade's casualty evacuation chain during the Falkland Conflict:

40 Commando RM

MA's B.M Mc Garry (HQ); Dave Semple (B Company); B.M Mc Carty; (Note: A South Atlantic Medal was also awarded to MA D.M Wilson, but he did not deploy to the South Atlantic because he was withdrawn with a knee injury).

LMA's George Black (Mentioned in Despatches); Ron Kenny (C Company); Billy Meechan.

POMA Paul Watts (HQ RAP) Surg Lt (Dentist) Andy Prosser (HQ RAP); Surg Lt JM Hayward (HQ RAP).

Chaplain Godfrey Hillard

42 Commando RM

MA T J Morris (M Company + S. Georgia); LMA Dave Woodgate (M Company + S. Georgia); POMA Colin Jones (M Company + S. Georgia/HQ RAP); POMA Alan 'knocker' White (M Company +S. Georgia/HQ RAP); Surg Lt Crispin Swinhoe (HQ RAP and attached M Coy S. Georgia).

LMA's Terry Bradford (J Company/NP 8901); LMA 'Jumper' Collins (L Company); LMA William 'Jock' Innes (K Company); LMA Steve Hayward; LMA Sean O'Callaghan (K Company);

POMA Graham 'Taff' Evans (HQ RAP); Surg Lt Ross Adley (HQ RAP)

Chaplain J. Albert Hempenstall

45 Commando RM

MA Mike Nicely (Mentioned in Dispatches; X Company); MA Chris Penny; LMA F.W Jacques (HQ RAP); LMA Mark Hooper (X Company); LMA B.A White (Y Company); LMA Paul Youngman (Mentioned in Dispatches; Support Company);

POMA Colin Jefferson-Jones (HQ RAP); Surg Lt (Dentist) Nigel Sturgeon (HQ RAP); Surg Lt David Griffiths (HQ RAP)

Chaplain F. Wynne Jones

Brigade HQ & Signals Squadron

LMA Pat Parsons.

Parachute Battalions

The following are lists of Paratroopers and RAMC personnel of all ranks known to have played a part in 2 and 3 Para's casualty evacuations, whilst operating within 3 Commando Brigade. Four are recorded as Killed in Action:

3rd Parachute Battalion

Derek Allen; Stephen Bradley; Private Mark Doddsworth (6 Platoon; KIA) Brian Faulkner (DCM; RAP); Andrew Gow (C Company); Stephen Harding-Derr (C Company);Lance Corporal Peter Higgs (D Company; KIA); John Kennedy (RAP) Philip Proberts (B Company);Lance Corporal Christopher Lovett (A Company, KIA); John Sibley (Mentioned in Despatches; B Company); Paul Stott (C Company WIA); Ashley Wright (A Company).

2nd Parachute Battalion

L/Cpl Bill Bentley (HQ RAP); Sgt Glynn Bradshaw (HQ RAP); Pte Davies (A Company Aid Post after Goose Green, WIA); Pte P Hall (Signaller HQ RAP); Capt Steve Hughes* RAMC(Mentioned in Despatches, HQ RAP), Pte Paul Shorrock (A Company Aid Post, KIA Goose Green 28/5/1982) Capt Rory Wagon RAMC (HQ RAP).

Chaplain David Cooper

*Doctor Steve Hughes had his 25th birthday on 12 June 1982. He was 24 during the Battle of Goose Green, and this serves to reflect the very limited practical experience of young frontline doctors in the Falkland War, and how difficult it must have been for them to cope with the casualties they treated. Doctor Hughes died aged 60 in August 2018, just over six months after Rick Jolly passed away. His Falkland War personal account can be read on the website *www.paradata.org.uk*

Annex B

Medical Squadron – Reception and Treatment of Casualties from Forward Units/Battalions

The following personnel deployed with 3 Commando Brigades Medical Squadron, which was established within the command structure of the Commando Logistic Regiment Royal Marines, and remains so to this day, alongside Workshop, Transport, and Ordnance Squadrons, co-ordinated by a Headquarters Squadron. All the Medical Squadron personnel were Commando trained RN Medical Service and Royal Marines. Some of the RN Surgical Support Team personnel were Commando trained, others received military familiarisation training with the Squadron.

HQ Medical Squadron (SS Canberra then Ajax Bay from D+1 throughout the conflict):

Officer Commanding: Surg Cdr Rick Jolly OBE

Lt Fred Cook RM; Surg Lt's Graham Briars and Martyn Ward; Fleet Chief MA (WO1) Bryn Dobbs; Sgt Maj (WO2) Terry Moran; CPOMA 'Scouse' Davies; POMA Eddie Middleton; Cpl's 'Gigs' Worthington; Adam 'sigs' Rennie; L/Cpl Billy Nobble; Mne's Charlie Cork; John Norton; Matt 'Radar' Shields; Mark Cridland; Pete Pearson.

One Troop Medical Squadron (LSL Sir Lancelot to Ascension and LSL Sir Galahad to D Day; Ajax Bay to 1 June; then Teal Inlet to 16 June and Stanley until departure.

Officer Commanding: Sub Lt Malcolm Hazell RN (Commando Medical Service)

Surg Lt Howard Oakley; CPOMA's Graham Edwards; John Smith; Sgt John Simmonds; POMA John 'Jacko' Jackson; LMA's Jock Winton; Andy Ellis; Rod Cain; Dave Cook; Cpl's Paul 'Cy' Worrall; Jon Clare; Tom Robinson; MA's Taff Barlow; Nick Vrettos; Mick 'Porky' Greaves; Derek Whitfield; Mne's Jock Ewing; Jim Giles; Taff Price; Robby Robinson; Chris Thornton; Tojo Hughes; Kev Frankland; Taff Evans; John Thurlow; Neil Blain; Steve Gosling; Terry 'Wally' Wallace. *In addition the following Mne's from One Troop remained at Ajax Bay: Fraz Coats; Gene Jago; Scouse Currall; Dave Gowland; John Nelson; Ray Whittaker.

The following additional personnel were attached to One Troop at Teal Inlet and Stanley from Ajax Bay: Surg Lt Cdr Tim Douglas Riley, CPO Med Tech 1's Tony Byrne; Steve Davies; and Trevor Firth. Plus 5 RAMC members of 5 Field Surgical Team, Parachute Clearing Troop, including Major Charles Batty RAMC (Surgeon) and WO2 Fritz Sterba. The full nine member team is listed within the Parachute Clearing Troop immediately below.

Parachute Clearing Troop (PCT) RAMC (MV Norland then Ajax Bay D+1 to 4 June then elements of 5 FST to Teal Inlet and the remainder to Fitzroy by 8 June with their parent Unit 16 Field Ambulance RAMC that arrived with 5 Brigade)

5 Field Surgical Team PCT: Maj's Charles Batty and Dick Night; Capt Rory Waggon; WO2 Fritz Sterba; Staff Sgt Webby Webster;

Cpl's Jim Pearson and Gary Seabrook; L/Cpl's Rick Saunders and Roy Haley.

6 Field Surgical Team PCT: Lt Col Bill McGregor; Maj Malcolm Jowitt; Capt Mike Von Bertele; WO2 'Phred' Newbound; Sgt Russ Rusell; Cpl's Caddy Cadwell and Colin May; L/Cpl's Rick Saunders and Roy Haley.

Dressing Station PCT: Maj Peter Lansley; Capt Terry McCabe; WO2 Brian Apperley; Staff Sgt Jed Newton; Sgt's Tich Davies and Chris Fowler; Cpl's Stan Wight, Roly Young, Colin Hudson, and Neil Parkin; L/Cpl's Sweeney Lea-cox, Dave Donkin, Mick Jennings, and Mac Macleod; Pte's Tam Craine, Jock Wilson, Fozzy Foster, and Ally Alich.

No. 2 RN Surgical Support Team (SS Canberra then Ajax Bay D+1 to 19 June)

The SST 2 were RN Hospital Plymouth based, and formed the only complete entity of Medical Squadron's additional war establishment that deployed ashore:

Team Leader: Surg Lt Cdr Phil Shouler

Surg Cdr George Rudge; Surg Lt Cdr's Andy Yates and Tim Douglas Riley; Surg Lt Nick Morgan; Fleet Chief Med Tech (MT) Dave Price; CPO MT1's John Davis, Stuart McKinley; and Steve Davies* Trevor Firth* and Tony Byrne* (* at Teal Inlet from 4 June);PO MT2 Bob Griffin; POMA Chris Lloyd; LMA's John Billingham, Phil Evans, Ken Parkin, Dave Poole, Kev Dooley, Alec Pickthall; MA's Geoff Evans, Tom Boyd, Simon Judge, Kevin Shore, and Al Wallace; MT4 Steve Garth.

Elements of No 1 RN Surgical Support Team (HMS Hermes to 30 May then Ajax Bay to 19 June)

SST 1 were RN Hospital Haslar (Gosport) based and were similarly part of medical Squadron's additional war establishment. The entire 27 members of SST 1 deployed ashore at Ajax Bay on 30 May, but only the five members listed below were utilized at Ajax Bay, as the balance were transferred to the Hospital Ship Uganda.

Surg Lt Cdr Ian Geraghty; CPO MT1 Murray Bowden; POMA Bob Johnson; LMA's Steve Moutrey and Carl Rich.

No. 3 RN Surgical Support Team (SS Canberra)

In addition to those from SST 2, Surg Cdr John Williams was landed ashore at Ajax Bay from the SS Canberra on 3 June and also utilized until 19 June

RN South Georgia Task Group Surgical Team

The following had provided Surgical Support to the RN Task Group and RM Assault Group that recaptured South Georgia, and were subsequently deployed ashore and utilized at Ajax Bay from 7 June until 19 June:

Surg Lt Cdr's Tony Mugridge and Sean Tighe; CPO MT1 Malcolm Wooton; LMA Steve Walsh.

No. Three Troop Medical Squadron (SS Canberra until 2 June then Ajax Bay until 19 June.

Last but not least, 3 Troop Med Sqn had deployed South on the SS Canberra from the UK and remained aboard the Canberra to provide medical support to the recapture of South Georgia. Once this was achieved they relieved One Troop Med Sqn who had already gone forward from Ajax Bay to Teal Inlet.

OC Lt Erich Bootland RN (Commando Medical Service)

CPOMA Jethro Young; Sgt Paul Demery; POMA's Roger Beck and Jack Sibbald; Cpl's Andy Christy and Pusser Hill; LMA's Terry Andrews and Phil King; L/Cpl's Jan Mills and Jock Inglis; MA's Dave Burdett, Derek Taylor, Chris Penney, Colin Glover and Andy Blocke; Mne's Mark Bunyan, Jock Cordiner, Gavin Flemming; Roy Finbow; Dave Gooding; Colin Hewitson, Spud Murphy, Spud Hudd, Gerry O'Donovan, Bumble Hollis, Tim O'Keefe, Dave Needham, Jeff Phillips, Smudge Smith, Garry Treacher, Timber Woods, and Bungy Williams;

Elements of 16 Field Ambulance RAMC (5 Brigade)

No. 2 Field Surgical Team (FST) were deployed at Ajax Bay from 9 to 20 June:

Lt Col Jim Anderson RAMC, Maj's Jim Ryan and Jim Aitken; Sgt Cleverly-Parker; Cpl Wright; L/Cpls Robson, Lawrence, and Elsey.

Annex C

Dear Mr Hazell,

Please see the attached response from the Government regarding your correspondence.

I apologise but, as I said in my previous email, unfortunately this is not something I am able to personally get involved with at this time. Should anyone else contact me about this situation I will let you know as clearly you are an expert on the matter.

Kind regards,

Helen Morgan

Member of Parliament for North Shropshire
House of Commons, London, SW1A 0AA

**Ministry
of Defence**

MINISTRY OF DEFENCE
FLOOR 5, ZONE B, MAIN BUILDING
WHITEHALL LONDON SW1A 2HB

Telephone 020 7218 9000 (Switchboard)

JAMES HEAPPEY MP
MINISTER FOR THE ARMED FORCES

Our ref: D/Min(AF)/JH MC2022/05744e
Your ref: HM430

26ᵗʰ May 2022

Dear Helen,

Thank you for your email of 10 May 2022, on behalf of your constituent Malcom Hazell
of ███████████████████████████ regarding his concerns as to
anomalies with war graves in the Falkland Islands.

We are grateful to Mr Hazell for the information he has provided to the Ministry of
Defence. The MOD, together with the Foreign, Commonwealth and Development Office
(FCDO), Royal Falkland Islands Police (RFIP) and the International Committee of the
Red Cross (ICRC), take investigations and concerns like this extremely seriously. We
have worked closely with the RFIP and ICRC in the years since the Conflict to identify
Argentine fatalities – including in coordination with the Government of Argentina and
Argentine Families' Commission.

The investigation into unmarked graves at Teal Inlet, based on the information provided
by Mr Hazell, is led by the RFIP, with independent support provided by the ICRC. The
ICRC and RFIP conducted an investigation of the site in July 2021 and concluded that
there was no evidence of remains at that location. The UK Government has no reason
to doubt these findings at this time.

Yours ever,

JAMES HEAPPEY MP

Helen Morgan MP
House of Commons
London
SW1A 0AA